I0415665

February 2013

HIGH-RISK SERIES

An Update

To access this report electronically, scan this QR Code.
Don't have a QR code reader? Several are available for free online.

G A O

Accountability * Integrity * Reliability

GAO-13-283

February 2013

Highlights of GAO-13-283, a report to congressional committees

HIGH-RISK SERIES
An Update

Why GAO Did This Study

The federal government is the world's largest and most complex entity, with about $3.5 trillion in outlays in fiscal year 2012 funding a broad array of programs and operations. GAO maintains a program to focus attention on government operations that it identifies as high risk due to their greater vulnerabilities to fraud, waste, abuse, and mismanagement or the need for transformation to address economy, efficiency, or effectiveness challenges. Since 1990, more than one-third of the areas previously designated as high risk have been removed from the list because sufficient progress was made to address the problems identified.

This biennial update describes the status of high-risk areas listed in 2011 and identifies any new high-risk area needing attention by Congress and the executive branch. Solutions to high-risk problems offer the potential to save billions of dollars, improve service to the public, and strengthen the performance and accountability of the U.S. government.

What GAO Recommends

This report contains GAO's views on progress made and what remains to be done to bring about lasting solutions for each high-risk area. Perseverance by the executive branch in implementing GAO's recommended solutions and continued oversight and action by Congress are essential to achieving progress. GAO is dedicated to continue working with Congress and the executive branch to help ensure additional progress is made.

View GAO-13-283. For more information, contact J. Christopher Mihm at (202) 512-6806 or mihmj@gao.gov

What GAO Found

In February 2011, GAO detailed 30 high-risk areas. Sufficient progress has been made to remove the high-risk designation from two areas.

- *Management of Interagency Contracting.* Improvements include (1) continued progress made by agencies in addressing identified deficiencies, (2) establishment of additional management controls, (3) creation of a policy framework for establishing new interagency contracts, and (4) steps taken to address the need for better data on these contracts.

- *Internal Revenue Service Business Systems Modernization.* The Internal Revenue Service (IRS) made progress in addressing significant weaknesses in information technology and financial management capabilities. IRS delivered the initial phase of its cornerstone tax processing project and began the daily processing and posting of individual taxpayer accounts in January 2012. This enhanced tax administration and improved service by enabling faster refunds for more taxpayers, allowing more timely account updates, and faster issuance of taxpayer notices. In addition, IRS has put in place close to 80 percent of the practices needed for an effective investment management process, including all of the processes needed for effective project oversight.

While these two areas have been removed from the High Risk List, GAO will continue to monitor them.

This year, GAO has added two areas.

- *Limiting the Federal Government's Fiscal Exposure by Better Managing Climate Change Risks.* Climate change creates significant financial risks for the federal government, which owns extensive infrastructure, such as defense installations; insures property through the National Flood Insurance Program; and provides emergency aid in response to natural disasters. The federal government is not well positioned to address the fiscal exposure presented by climate change, and needs a government wide strategic approach with strong leadership to manage related risks.

- *Mitigating Gaps in Weather Satellite Data.* Potential gaps in environmental satellite data beginning as early as 2014 and lasting as long as 53 months have led to concerns that future weather forecasts and warnings—including warnings of extreme events such as hurricanes, storm surges, and floods—will be less accurate and timely. A number of decisions are needed to ensure contingency and continuity plans can be implemented effectively.

In the past 2 years notable progress has been made in the vast majority of areas that remain on GAO's High Risk List. This progress is due to the combined efforts of the Congress through oversight and legislation, the Office of Management and Budget through its leadership and coordination, and the agencies through their efforts to take corrective actions to address longstanding problems and implement related GAO recommendations.

GAO's 2013 High Risk List

Strengthening the Foundation for Efficiency and Effectiveness

- Limiting the Federal Government's Fiscal Exposure by Better Managing Climate Change Risks (new)
- Management of Federal Oil and Gas Resources
- Modernizing the U.S. Financial Regulatory System and Federal Role in Housing Finance
- Restructuring the U.S. Postal Service to Achieve Sustainable Financial Viability
- Funding the Nation's Surface Transportation System
- Strategic Human Capital Management
- Managing Federal Real Property

Transforming DOD Program Management

- DOD Approach to Business Transformation
- DOD Business Systems Modernization
- DOD Support Infrastructure Management
- DOD Financial Management
- DOD Supply Chain Management
- DOD Weapon Systems Acquisition

Ensuring Public Safety and Security

- Mitigating Gaps in Weather Satellite Data (new)
- Strengthening Department of Homeland Security Management Functions
- Establishing Effective Mechanisms for Sharing and Managing Terrorism-Related Information to Protect the Homeland
- Protecting the Federal Government's Information Systems and the Nation's Cyber Critical Infrastructures
- Ensuring the Effective Protection of Technologies Critical to U.S. National Security Interests
- Revamping Federal Oversight of Food Safety
- Protecting Public Health through Enhanced Oversight of Medical Products
- Transforming EPA's Processes for Assessing and Controlling Toxic Chemicals

Managing Federal Contracting More Effectively

- DOD Contract Management
- DOE's Contract Management for the National Nuclear Security Administration and Office of Environmental Management
- NASA Acquisition Management

Assessing the Efficiency and Effectiveness of Tax Law Administration

- Enforcement of Tax Laws

Modernizing and Safeguarding Insurance and Benefit Programs

- Improving and Modernizing Federal Disability Programs
- Pension Benefit Guaranty Corporation Insurance Programs
- Medicare Program
- Medicaid Program
- National Flood Insurance Program

Source: GAO.

Contents

Tables

Figures

G A O
Accountability * Integrity * Reliability

United States Government Accountability Office
Washington, DC 20548

Comptroller General
of the United States

February 2013

The Honorable Thomas R. Carper
Chairman
The Honorable Tom Coburn, M.D.
Ranking Member
Committee on Homeland Security and Governmental Affairs
United States Senate

The Honorable Darrel E. Issa
Chairman
The Honorable Elijah E. Cummings
Ranking Member
Committee on Oversight and Government Reform
House of Representatives

GAO regularly reports on government operations that it identifies as high risk. This effort, supported by the Senate Committee on Homeland Security and Governmental Affairs and the House of Representatives Committee on Oversight and Government Reform, has brought much-needed focus to problems impeding effective government and costing billions of dollars each year. To help improve these high-risk operations, GAO has made hundreds of recommendations, and the administration and agencies have addressed, or are addressing, many of them. Congress also continues to take actions that are important to helping resolve high-risk issues.

This year GAO is removing the high-risk designation from two areas—*Management of Interagency Contracting* and *IRS Business Systems Modernization*—and designating two new high-risk areas— *Limiting the Federal Government's Fiscal Exposure by Better Managing Climate Change Risks* and *Mitigating Gaps in Weather Satellite Data*. These changes bring GAO's 2013 High Risk List to a total of 30 areas.

Throughout the past two decades, attention to high-risk areas has brought results. More than one-third of the areas previously designated as high risk have been removed from the list because sufficient progress was made to address the problems identified.[1] Further, progress has

---

[1] For more information on the history of the high risk program, see appendix I.

Page 1   GAO-13-283 High-Risk Series

been made in nearly all of the areas that remain on GAO's High Risk List as a result of congressional oversight and action, high-level administration attention, efforts of the responsible agencies, and support from GAO through its many recommendations and consistent follow-up on the implementation of recommended actions. In three areas—*Management of Federal Oil and Gas Resources, Strengthening Department of Homeland Security Management Functions,* and *DOE's Contract Management for the National Nuclear Security Administration and Office of Environmental Management*—progress has been sufficient for GAO to narrow the scope of the high-risk issue.

Additional progress is both possible and needed in all 30 high-risk areas. Continued perseverance will ultimately yield significant benefits. Lasting solutions to high-risk problems offer the potential to save billions of dollars, dramatically improve service to the American public, strengthen public confidence and trust in the performance and accountability of the federal government, and ensure the ability of government to deliver on its promises.

The high risk effort continues to be a top priority and GAO will maintain its emphasis on identifying high-risk issues across government and providing insights and sustained attention to help address them, working collaboratively with Congress, agency leaders, and the Office of Management and Budget. As part of this effort, GAO continues to participate in regular meetings with the Office of Management of Budget's Deputy Director for Management and top agency officials to discuss plans for addressing high-risk areas. Such efforts are critical for progress to continue.

This high risk update is intended to help inform the oversight agenda for the 113th Congress and guide efforts of the administration and agencies to improve government performance and reduce waste and risks. GAO is providing this update to the President and Vice President, congressional leadership, other Members of Congress, the Office of Management and Budget, and the heads of major departments and agencies.

Gene L. Dodaro
Comptroller General
of the United States

High-Risk Designation Removed

When legislative, administration, and agency actions, including those in response to our recommendations, result in significant progress toward resolving a high-risk area, we remove the high-risk designation. Key to determining if the high-risk designation can be removed are the following five elements: (1) a demonstrated strong commitment to, and top leadership support for, addressing problems; (2) the capacity to address problems; (3) a corrective action plan; (4) a program to monitor corrective measures; and (5) demonstrated progress in implementing corrective measures.

For our 2013 high risk update, we determined that two areas warranted removal from the High Risk List: *Management of Interagency Contracting* and *IRS Business Systems Modernization*. As we have with areas previously removed from the High Risk List, we will continue to monitor these areas, as appropriate, to ensure that the improvements we have noted are sustained. If significant problems again arise, we will consider reapplying the high-risk designation.

Management of Interagency Contracting

We are removing the management of interagency contracting from the High Risk List based on (1) continued progress made by agencies in addressing previously identified deficiencies, (2) establishment of additional management controls, (3) creation of a policy framework for establishing new interagency contracts, and (4) steps taken to address the need for better data on these contracts. Congressional oversight and the leadership of the Office of Management and Budget's (OMB) Office of Federal Procurement Policy (OFPP)—which provides direction on government-wide procurement policies—have been vital in addressing the issues that led this area to be designated high risk.

Interagency contracting—where one agency either places an order using another agency's contract or obtains contracting support services from another agency—can help streamline the procurement process, take advantage of unique expertise in a particular type of procurement, and achieve savings. Interagency contracts are designed to leverage the government's buying power and allow for agencies to meet the demands for goods and services at a time when the federal government is focused on achieving efficiencies in the acquisition process. While this method of contracting can save the government money and effort when properly managed, it also poses a variety of risks.

In 2005, we designated the management of interagency contracting as high risk due in part to unclear lines of accountability between customer and assisting agencies and the potential for improper use, including out-of-scope work and noncompliance with competition requirements.[2] In our 2007 high risk update, we identified the continuing need for (1) additional management controls and guidance and (2) clearer definitions of roles and responsibilities as the keys to addressing these issues.[3] In our 2011 high risk update, we highlighted additional challenges agencies faced in fully realizing the benefits of interagency contracts, including the lack of data and the risk of potential duplication when new contracting vehicles are created.[4] Duplication among interagency contracts can result in missed opportunities to leverage the government's buying power and may adversely affect the administrative efficiencies and cost savings expected with their use. To address these issues, our prior work identified the need for (1) a policy framework and business case analysis requirements to support the creation of certain new contracts and (2) improved data on existing interagency contracts.

The federal government has made significant progress in reducing the interagency contracting risks that led to our high-risk designation. In our 2009 and 2011 high risk updates we noted improvements in procedures used in making purchases on behalf of the Department of Defense (DOD)—the largest user of interagency contracts. These included better defined roles and responsibilities and enhanced controls over funding procedures. Additionally, the DOD Inspector General has reported a significant decrease in problems with DOD procurements through other federal agencies in congressionally mandated reviews of interagency acquisitions. We also noted that the General Services Administration (GSA) and OMB have established corrective action plans to implement our prior recommendations. Since our last update, as discussed in the following sections, federal agencies have continued to address weaknesses related to the use, creation, and oversight of interagency contracting vehicles.

---

[2]GAO, *High-Risk Series: An Update,* GAO-05-207 (Washington, D.C.: January 2005).

[3]GAO, *High-Risk Series: An Update,* GAO-07-310 (Washington, D.C.: January 2007).

[4]GAO, *High-Risk Series: An Update,* GAO-11-278 (Washington, D.C.: February 2011).

Strengthened management controls for the use of interagency contracts. Most agencies have taken steps to implement and reinforce interagency contracting policies to address prior concerns about the improper use of these contracts. In response to congressional direction,[5] Federal Acquisition Regulation (FAR) provisions on interagency acquisitions were revised to require that agencies make a best procurement approach determination to justify the use of an interagency contract and prepare written interagency agreements outlining the roles and responsibilities of customer and assisting organizations.[6] The best procurement approach determination ensures that the requesting agency considers factors such as the suitability of the contract vehicle and compliance with laws and policies. Congress also strengthened requirements for interagency acquisitions performed on behalf of DOD as well as the competition rules for placing orders on multiple-award contracts, which are commonly used in interagency acquisitions.[7] As we recently reported, OMB's October 2012 analysis of reports from the 24 agencies that account for almost all contract spending government-wide found that most had implemented management controls to reinforce the new FAR requirements and strengthen the management of interagency acquisitions. All 24 agencies also reported having oversight mechanisms to ensure their internal controls were operating properly.[8]

---

[5]Pub. L. No. 110-417, § 865 (2008).

[6]FAR § 17.502-1. The interim FAR rule was issued in December 2010; the final rule was issued in February 2012.

[7]Pub. L. No. 110-181, § 801(b) (2008) and Pub. L. No. 110-417, § 863 (2008).

[8]GAO, *Interagency Contracting: Agency Actions Address Key Management Challenges, but Additional Steps Needed to Ensure Consistent Implementation of Policy Changes,* GAO-13-133R (Washington, D.C.: January 2013). We also reported on DOD's implementation of the new FAR requirements and found that for almost all of the selected orders, DOD effectively delineated roles and responsibilities by completing interagency agreements as required.

New controls over creation of new interagency contract vehicles. In response to congressional direction[9] and our prior recommendation, OMB established a policy framework in September 2011 to govern the creation of new interagency contract vehicles.[10] The framework addresses concerns about potential duplication by requiring agencies to develop a thorough business case prior to establishing certain contract vehicles. The guidance further requires senior agency officials to approve the business cases and post them on an OMB website to provide interested federal stakeholders an opportunity to offer feedback. OMB then is able to conduct follow-up with sponsoring agencies if significant questions, including ones related to duplication, are raised during the vetting process. OMB also has established a new strategic sourcing governance council, which is expected to examine how to use existing interagency contract vehicles to support government-wide strategic sourcing efforts.

Improved data on interagency contracts. In response to our recommendations, OMB and GSA have taken a number of steps to address the need for better data on interagency contract vehicles. These efforts should enhance both government-wide efforts to manage interagency contracts and agency efforts to conduct market research and negotiate better prices. To promote better and easier access to data on existing contracts, OMB has made improvements to its Interagency Contract Directory, a searchable online database of indefinite-delivery vehicles available for interagency use. It has also posted information on government-wide acquisition contracts and blanket purchase agreements available for use under the Federal Strategic Sourcing Initiative on an OMB website, accessible by federal agencies.[11] Improving the availability of data is also a key facet of GSA's Schedules Modernization initiative, launched in June 2012. GSA has several pilot projects underway to collect and share data on its Multiple Award Schedules program, with the goal of improving pricing. GSA also has assembled a data team to improve access to comprehensive and reliable data across GSA contracting programs.

---

[9]Pub. L. No. 110-417, § 865 (2008).

[10]OMB, OFPP, *Development, Review, and Approval of Business Cases for Certain Interagency and Agency-Specific Acquisitions* (Washington, D.C.: Sept. 29, 2011).

[11]The Federal Strategic Sourcing Initiative was established in 2005 to address government-wide opportunities to strategically source commonly purchased products and services.

Removing the management of interagency contracting from the High Risk List does not mean that the federal government's use of these contracts is without challenges. For example, we and the DOD Inspector General have found instances in which DOD did not complete best procurement approach determinations as required.[12] Continued management attention is necessary. But, we believe there are mechanisms in place that OMB and federal agencies can use to identify and address interagency contracting issues before they put the government at significant risk for waste, fraud, or abuse. For example, the revised FAR rules on interagency acquisitions require senior procurement executives to submit an annual report on interagency acquisitions to OMB, which can use these to identify issues and risks at the agency level as well as government-wide trends. In addition, many agencies have reported building interagency contracting into internal reviews. Finally, we plan to continue to monitor the management of interagency contracts in our reviews of federal contracting.

IRS Business Systems Modernization

We are removing the Internal Revenue Service's (IRS) Business Systems Modernization (BSM) program from the High Risk List because of IRS's progress in addressing the significant weaknesses in information technology (IT) and financial management capabilities that led to the high-risk designation, and its commitment to sustaining progress in the future. As we have with other areas we have removed, we will continue to monitor this area, as appropriate, to ensure that the improvements we have noted are sustained.

BSM is a multi-billion dollar, highly-complex effort that involves the development and delivery of a number of modernized tax administration and internal management systems as well as core infrastructure projects that are intended to replace the agency's aging business and tax processing systems. It is critical to providing improved and expanded service to taxpayers and internal business efficiencies for IRS and providing the reliable and timely financial management information needed to better enable the agency to justify its resource allocation decisions and funding requests. IRS began modernizing its timeworn, paper-intensive approach to tax returns processing in the mid-1980s.

---

[12]GAO-13-133R and Department of Defense, Inspector General, *Contracting Improvements Still Needed in DOD's FY 2011Purchases Made Through the Department of Veterans Affairs*, DODIG-2013-028 (Alexandria, VA.: Dec. 7, 2012).

In 1995, we identified serious management and technical weaknesses in the modernization program that jeopardized its successful completion. We recommended many actions to fix the problems, and added IRS's modernization to our High Risk List. In 1995, we also added the agency's financial management to our High Risk List due to long-standing and pervasive problems which hampered the effective collection of revenues and precluded the preparation of auditable financial statements.[13] We combined the two issues into one high-risk area in 2005 since resolution of the most serious financial management problems depended largely on the success of the business systems modernization program.

In 2007 and 2009, we reported that IRS had made progress in establishing management capabilities and addressing financial management weaknesses.[14] For example, in 2007, the agency developed a high-level modernization vision and strategy to address program changes and provide a modernization road map. In addition, it developed policies, procedures, and tools for developing and managing project requirements. IRS also implemented the initial phase of several key automated financial management systems, including a cost accounting module that it populated with data; developed a methodology to allocate costs to its business units; improved the reliability of its property and equipment records; and made significant progress in addressing long-standing deficiencies in controls over tax revenue collections, tax refund disbursements, and hard-copy tax receipts and related data. In addition, IRS completed several pilot projects to demonstrate its ability to determine the full cost of its programs and activities.

However, we kept BSM on the High Risk List because many challenges remained, including (1) improving processes for delivering modernized IT systems within cost and schedule estimates, (2) developing the cost and revenue information needed to support day-to-day decision making, and (3) addressing outstanding weaknesses in information security.[15] Throughout those years, Congress conducted oversight of the BSM program by, among other things, requiring that IRS submit annual

---

[13]GAO, *High-Risk Series: An Overview*, HR-95-1 (Washington, D.C.: Feb. 1, 1995).

[14]GAO, *High-Risk Series: An Update*, GAO-09-271 (Washington, D.C.: Jan. 22, 2009), and GAO-07-310.

[15]GAO-09-271.

expenditure plans that needed to meet certain conditions, including a review by GAO.

In our 2011 high risk update,[16] we reported that IRS had continued to make progress in addressing weaknesses in response to our recommendations but needed to leverage its capabilities to successfully deliver its BSM projects. Specifically, we noted that IRS needed to successfully deliver the initial phase of the Customer Account Data Engine 2 (CADE 2)—its cornerstone tax processing project—by moving the processing of individual taxpayer accounts from a weekly processing cycle to a daily processing cycle and delivering a modernized individual taxpayer account database by 2012. We also noted that IRS needed to continue its efforts to achieve expected benefits, including faster refunds, improved customer service, and faster resolution of taxpayer account issues (phase 2 of CADE 2). For financial management issues, in addition to addressing outstanding recommendations, including those associated with information security controls affecting the reliability of financial data, we noted that IRS needed to (1) ensure corrective action plans address all issues and define root causes and (2) strengthen its program for monitoring the effectiveness of corrective actions taken in response to our information security recommendations.

Since 2011, IRS has worked to address these issues. For example, the agency delivered the initial phase of CADE 2 and began the daily processing and posting of individual taxpayer accounts in January 2012, enhancing tax administration and improving service by enabling faster refunds for more taxpayers, allowing more timely account updates, and faster issuance of taxpayer notices.[17] Also, in March 2012, IRS established the database housing all individual taxpayer account data and has plans underway to gradually increase its use for customer service and compliance purposes. Further, in May 2012, IRS initiated plans for phase 2 of CADE 2, which is in large part intended to address the unpaid assessment financial material weakness we have reported on in the past. As IRS progresses with this planning effort, it will be important for the

---

[16]GAO-11-278.

[17]According to IRS, during Filing Season 2012, CADE 2 allowed more timely account updates (taxpayer account updates are viewable by IRS customer service representatives within 48 hours versus an average of 9 days in Filing Season 2011), and faster issuance of taxpayer notices (2.7 million notices sent to taxpayers with accounts processed daily versus 284,000 in Filing Season 2011).

agency to identify functionality it can deliver early on so it can begin reaping benefits for its employees and taxpayers and making progress towards retiring the legacy Individual Master File.

IRS also made important progress in addressing information systems-related internal control deficiencies, particularly those involving its networks and systems that had reduced the overall effectiveness of its information security controls and therefore the reliability of its financial data.[18] Notable among these efforts were the (1) formation of cross functional working groups tasked with the identification and remediation of specific at-risk control areas, (2) improvement in controls over the encryption of data transferred between accounting systems, and (3) upgrades to critical network devices on the agency's internal network system. In addition, during fiscal year 2012, IRS continued to devote significant attention and resources to addressing information security controls, and resolved a significant number of the information system-related internal control deficiencies that we previously reported. For example, IRS (1) addressed its outdated operating system and application software so that the versions in use are now supported by vendors, (2) improved the auditing and monitoring capabilities of a general support system, and (3) tested its general ledger system for tax transactions in its current operating environment. Further, IRS funded critical software upgrades for some of its key financial reporting systems, including its administrative accounting system and its procurement system, which was an important step toward addressing its information system issues. These improvements led us to conclude that IRS's remaining deficiencies in internal controls over information security no longer constitute a material weakness for financial reporting as of September 30, 2012. However, IRS still needs to strengthen its program for monitoring the effectiveness of corrective actions taken in response to our information security recommendations.

IRS also took additional steps to strengthen its IT management capabilities. For example, in July 2011, we noted that IRS had in place close to 80 percent of the practices needed for an effective investment management process, including all of the practices needed for effective

---

[18]GAO, *Financial Audit: IRS's Fiscal Years 2012 and 2011 Financial Statements,* GAO-13-120 (Washington, D.C.: Nov. 9, 2012).

project oversight.[19] In October 2011, we also reported that IRS had embarked on an effort to improve its software development practices using the Carnegie Mellon University Software Engineering Institute's Capability Maturity Model Integration (CMMI), which calls for disciplined software development and acquisition practices which are considered industry best practices. In September 2012, IRS's application development organization reached CMMI maturity level 3, a high achievement by industry standards.[20]

Finally, in October 2011, we highlighted CADE 2 as one of seven successful acquisitions in the federal government because, up to that point, it had achieved cost, schedule, scope, and performance goals through the use of critical success factors, including program staff actively engaged with stakeholders, program staff having the right knowledge and skills, agency executives engaged in the program, and streamlined and targeted governance.[21, 22] IRS officials are also applying these critical success factors to other programs at IRS. Because of the significant progress made in addressing this high-risk area over the years, starting in fiscal year 2012, Congress did not require the submission of an annual expenditure plan.

While we are removing IRS's BSM program from the High Risk List, we will nonetheless continue to closely monitor the agency's efforts because the modernization program is complex and critical to administering and

---

[19]GAO, *Investment Management: IRS Has a Strong Oversight Process But Needs to Improve How It Continues Funding Ongoing Investments*, GAO-11-587 (Washington, D.C.: July 20, 2011).

[20]The CMMI ranks organizational maturity according to five levels. Maturity levels 2 through 5 require verifiable existence and use of certain key process areas. At maturity level 3, known as the "defined" level, processes are well characterized and understood, and are descr bed in standards, procedures, tools, and methods. The organization's set of standard processes, which is the basis for maturity level 3, is established and improved over time. A defined process clearly states the purpose, inputs, entry criteria, activities, roles, measures, verification steps, outputs, and exit criteria. In addition, processes are managed more proactively using an understanding of the interrelationships of process activities and detailed measures of the process, its work products, and its services.

[21]GAO, *Information Technology: Critical Factors Underlying Successful Major Acquisitions*, GAO-12-7 (Washington, D.C.: Oct. 21, 2011).

[22]In quarterly status briefings to us and the Senate and House of Representatives Appropriations Committees, IRS has been reporting that the first phase of the CADE 2 program is still generally on track.

enforcing tax laws. In addition, the remaining recurring deficiencies in information security, along with new deficiencies we identified during our audit of IRS's fiscal year 2012 financial statements, merit continued and consistent commitment and attention from IRS management. Specifically, IRS will need to continue to take steps to (1) improve its testing and monitoring capabilities, (2) ensure that policies and procedures are updated, and (3) address unresolved and newly identified control deficiencies, to sustain progress in improving its information system controls and have greater assurance that financial and taxpayer data will not remain vulnerable to inappropriate use, modification, or disclosure, possibly without being detected. We currently have a mandate to perform annual reviews of IRS's major information technology programs and also perform the annual audit of IRS's annual financial statements including the effectiveness of internal controls over financial reporting systems. We plan to continue to monitor IRS's BSM program through these reviews.

New High-Risk Areas

To determine which federal government programs and functions should be designated high risk, we use our guidance document *Determining Performance and Accountability Challenges and High Risks.*[23] In making this determination, we consider whether the program or function is of national significance or is key to performance and accountability.

Further, we consider qualitative factors, such as whether the risk

- involves public health or safety, service delivery, national security, national defense, economic growth, or privacy or citizens' rights, or

- could result in significantly impaired service, program failure, injury or loss of life, or significantly reduced economy, efficiency, or effectiveness.

In addition, we also consider the exposure to loss in monetary or other quantitative terms. At a minimum, $1 billion must be at risk in areas such as the value of major assets being impaired; revenue sources not being realized; major agency assets being lost, stolen, damaged, wasted, or underutilized; improper payments; and contingencies or potential liabilities.

Before making a high-risk designation, we also consider corrective measures planned or under way to resolve a material control weakness and the status and effectiveness of these actions.

For 2013, we are designating two new high-risk areas—*Limiting the Federal Government's Fiscal Exposure by Better Managing Climate Change Risks* and *Mitigating Gaps in Weather Satellite Data.*

---

[23]GAO, *Determining Performance and Accountability Challenges and High Risks,* GAO-01-159SP (Washington, D.C.: November 2000).

Limiting the Federal Government's Fiscal Exposure by Better Managing Climate Change Risks

Climate change poses risks to many environmental and economic systems—including agriculture, infrastructure, ecosystems, and human health—and presents a significant financial risk to the federal government. The United States Global Change Research Program (USGCRP) has observed that the impacts and costliness of weather disasters will increase in significance as what are considered "rare" events become more common and intense due to climate change.[24] Among other impacts, climate change could threaten coastal areas with rising sea levels, alter agricultural productivity, and increase the intensity and frequency of severe weather events such as floods, drought, and hurricanes. Weather-related events have cost the nation tens of billions of dollars in damages over the past decade. For example, in 2012, the administration requested $60.4 billion for Superstorm Sandy recovery efforts. These impacts pose significant financial risks for the federal government, which owns extensive infrastructure, insures property through federal flood and crop insurance programs, provides technical assistance to state and local governments, and provides emergency aid in response to natural disasters. However, the federal government is not well positioned to address this fiscal exposure, partly because of the complex, cross-cutting nature of the issue. Given these challenges and the nation's precarious fiscal condition, we have added *Limiting the Federal Government's Fiscal Exposure to Climate Change* to our 2013 list of high-risk areas.[25]

Climate change adaptation—defined as adjustments to natural or human systems in response to actual or expected climate change—is a risk-management strategy to help protect vulnerable sectors and communities that might be affected by changes in the climate. For example, adaptation measures may include raising river or coastal dikes to protect

---

[24]Thomas R. Karl, Jerry M. Melillo, and Thomas C. Peterson, eds. *Global Climate Change Impacts in the United States* (Cambridge University Press: 2009). USGCRP coordinates and integrates the activities of 13 federal agencies that conduct research on changes in the global environment and their implications for society. USGCRP began as a presidential initiative in 1989 and was codified in the Global Change Research Act of 1990 [Pub. L. No. 101-606, § 103 (1990)]. USGCRP-participating agencies are the Departments of Agriculture, Commerce, Defense, Energy, Interior, Health and Human Services, State, and Transportation; U.S. Agency for International Development; Environmental Protection Agency; National Aeronautics and Space Administration; the National Science Foundation; and the Smithsonian Institution.

[25]The focus of this high-risk area may evolve over time to the extent that federal climate change programs and policies change.

infrastructure from sea level rise, building higher bridges, and increasing the capacity of storm water systems. Policymakers increasingly view climate change adaptation as a risk-management strategy to protect vulnerable sectors and communities that might be affected by changes in the climate, but, as we reported in 2009, the federal government's emerging adaptation activities were carried out in an ad hoc manner and were not well coordinated across federal agencies, let alone with state and local governments.[26]

The federal government has a number of efforts underway to decrease domestic greenhouse gas emissions, but decreasing global emissions depends in large part on cooperative international efforts. Further, according to the National Research Council (NRC) and USGCRP, greenhouse gases already in the atmosphere will continue altering the climate system for many decades. As such, the impacts of climate change can be expected to increase fiscal exposure for the federal government in many areas:

- *Federal government as property owner.* The federal government owns and operates hundreds of thousands of buildings and facilities that could be affected by a changing climate. In addition, the federal government manages about 650 million acres—29 percent of the 2.27 billion acres of U.S. land—for a wide variety of purposes, such as recreation, grazing, timber, and fish and wildlife. In 2007, we recommended that that the Secretaries of Agriculture, Commerce, and the Interior develop guidance for resource managers that explains how they are expected to address the effects of climate changes, and the three departments generally agreed with the recommendation. We have ongoing work related to adapting infrastructure and the management of federal lands to a changing climate.

- *Federal insurance programs.* Two important federal insurance efforts— the National Flood Insurance Program (NFIP) and the Federal Crop Insurance Corporation—are based on conditions, priorities, and approaches that were established decades ago and do not account for climate change. NFIP has been on our High Risk List since March 2006 because of concerns about its long-term financial solvency and related

---

[26]GAO, *Climate Change Adaptation: Strategic Federal Planning Could Help Government Officials Make More Informed Decisions*, GAO-10-113 (Washington, D.C.: Oct. 7, 2009).

operational issues.[27] In March 2007, we reported that both of these insurance programs' exposure to weather-related losses had grown substantially, and that the agencies responsible for them had done little to develop the information necessary to understand their long-term exposure to climate change.[28] We recommended that the responsible agencies analyze the potential long-term fiscal implications of climate change and report their findings to Congress. The agencies agreed with the recommendation and contracted with experts to study their programs' long-term exposure to climate change, but the results of the work have not yet been reported to Congress. In addition, in June 2011, we reported that external factors continue to complicate the administration of NFIP and affect its financial stability.[29] In particular, the Federal Emergency Management Agency (FEMA), which administers NFIP, has not been authorized to account for long-term erosion when updating flood maps used to set premium rates for NFIP, increasing the likelihood that premiums would not cover future losses. We suggested that Congress consider authorizing NFIP to account for long-term flood erosion in its flood maps, and the Biggert-Waters Flood Insurance Reform Act of 2012 requires FEMA to use information on topography, coastal erosion areas, changing lake levels, future changes in sea levels, and intensity of hurricanes in updating its flood maps. While these provisions respond to our suggestion to Congress, their ultimate effectiveness will depend on their implementation by FEMA. It is too early to evaluate such efforts, but we plan to examine NFIP in the near future.

- *Technical assistance to state and local governments.* The federal government invests billions of dollars annually in infrastructure projects that state and local governments prioritize and supervise. These projects have large up front capital investments and long lead times that require decisions about how to address climate change to be made well before its potential effects are discernable. We reported in October 2009 that

---

[27]The potential losses generated by NFIP have created substantial financial exposure for the federal government and U.S. taxpayers. While Congress and Federal Emergency Management Agency (FEMA) intended that NFIP be funded with premiums collected from policyholders and not with tax dollars, the program was, by design, not actuarially sound. As of November 2012, FEMA owes the Treasury approximately $20 billion—up from $17.8 billion pre-Sandy—and had not repaid any principal on the loan since 2010.

[28]GAO, *Climate Change: Financial Risks to Federal and Private Insurers in Coming Decades Are Potentially Significant*, GAO-07-285 (Washington, D.C.: Mar. 16, 2007).

[29]GAO, *FEMA: Action Needed to Improve Administration of the National Flood Insurance Program*, GAO-11-297 (Washington, D.C.: June 9, 2011).

insufficient site-specific data—such as local temperature and precipitation projections—make it hard for state and local officials to justify the current costs of adaptation efforts for potentially less certain future benefits.[30] We recommended that the appropriate entities within the Executive Office of the President develop a strategic plan for adaptation that, among other things, identifies mechanisms to increase the capacity of federal, state, and local agencies to incorporate information about current and potential climate change impacts into government decision making. USGCRP's 2012-2021 strategic plan for climate change science, released in April 2012, recognizes this need by identifying enhanced information management and sharing as a key objective, and USGCRP is undertaking several actions designed to better coordinate that use and application of federal climate science. We have ongoing work related to these issues. In addition, gaps in satellite coverage, which could occur as soon as 2014, are expected to affect the continuity of climate and space weather measurements important to developing the information needed by state and local officials.[31] According to National Oceanic and Atmospheric Administration program officials, a satellite data gap would result in less accurate and timely weather forecasts and warnings of extreme events—such as hurricanes, storm surges, and floods. We have concluded that the potential gap in weather satellite data is a high-risk area and added it to the High Risk List this year.

- *Disaster aid.* In the event of a major disaster, federal funding for response and recovery comes from the Disaster Relief Fund managed by FEMA and disaster aid programs of other participating federal agencies. The federal government does not budget for these costs and runs the risk of facing a large fiscal exposure at any time. We reported in September 2012 that disaster declarations have increased over recent decades to a record of 98 in fiscal year 2011 compared with 65 in 2004. Over that period, FEMA obligated over $80 billion in federal assistance for disasters.[32] We found that FEMA has had difficulty implementing

---

[30]GAO-10-113.

[31]See, for example, GAO, *Environmental Satellites: Focused Attention Needed to Mitigate Program Risks*, GAO-12-841T (Washington, D.C.: June 27, 2012), and *Environmental Satellites: Strategy Needed to Sustain Critical Climate and Space Weather Measurements*, GAO-10-456 (Washington, D.C.: Apr. 27, 2010).

[32]GAO, *Federal Disaster Assistance: Improved Criteria Needed to Assess a Jurisdiction's Capability to Respond and Recover on Its Own*, GAO-12-838 (Washington, D.C.: Sept. 12, 2012).

longstanding plans to assess national preparedness capabilities and that FEMA's indicator for determining whether to recommend that a jurisdiction receive disaster assistance does not accurately reflect the ability of state and local governments to respond to disasters.[33] In September 2012, we recommended, among other things, that FEMA develop a methodology to more accurately assess a jurisdiction's capability to respond to and recover from a disaster without federal assistance. FEMA concurred with this recommendation.

The federal government would be better positioned to respond to the risks posed by climate change if federal efforts were more coordinated and directed toward common goals. In 2009, we recommended that the appropriate entities within the Executive Office of the President develop a strategic plan to guide the nation's efforts to adapt to climate change, including the establishment of clear roles, responsibilities, and working relationships among federal, state, and local governments.[34] Some actions have subsequently been taken, including the development of an interagency climate change adaptation task force.[35] However, a 2012 NRC report states that while the task force has convened representatives of relevant agencies and programs, it has no mechanisms for making or enforcing important decisions and priorities.[36]

In May 2011, we found no coherent strategic government-wide approach to climate change funding and that federal officials do not have a shared

---

[33]GAO, *Managing Preparedness Grants and Assessing National Capabilities*, GAO-12-526T (Washington, D.C.: Mar. 20, 2012). See also GAO, *Disaster Response: Criteria for Developing and Validating Effective Response Plans*, GAO-10-969T (Washington, D.C.: Sept. 22, 2010).

[34]GAO-10-113.

[35]Executive Order 13514 on Federal Leadership in Environmental, Energy, and Economic Performance calls for federal agencies to participate actively in the already existing Interagency Climate Change Adaptation Task Force. The task force, which began meeting in Spring 2009, is co-chaired by the Council on Environmental Quality, the National Oceanic and Atmospheric Administration, and the Office of Science and Technology Policy, and includes representatives from more than 20 federal agencies and executive branch offices. The task force was formed to assess key steps needed to help the federal government understand and adapt to climate change.

[36]NRC, Committee on a National Strategy for Advancing Climate Modeling, Board on Atmospheric Studies and Climate, Division on Earth and Life Sciences, *A National Strategy for Advancing Climate Modeling* (Washington, D.C.: 2012).

understanding of strategic government-wide priorities.[37] At that time, we recommended that the appropriate entities within the Executive Office of the President clearly establish federal strategic climate change priorities, including the roles and responsibilities of the key federal entities, taking into consideration the full range of climate-related activities within the federal government. The relevant federal entities have not directly addressed this recommendation.

Federal agencies have made some progress toward better organizing across agencies, within agencies, and among different levels of government; however, the increasing fiscal exposure for the federal government calls for more comprehensive and systematic strategic planning including, but not limited to, the following:

- A government-wide strategic approach with strong leadership and the authority to manage climate change risks that encompasses the entire range of related federal activities and addresses all key elements of strategic planning.

- More information to understand and manage federal insurance programs' long-term exposure to climate change and analyze the potential impacts of an increase in the frequency or severity of weather-related events on their operations.

- A government-wide approach for providing (1) the best available climate-related data for making decisions at the state and local level and (2) assistance for translating available climate-related data into information that officials need to make decisions.

- Actions to address potential gaps in satellite data.

- Improved criteria for assessing a jurisdiction's capability to respond and recover from a disaster without federal assistance, and to better apply lessons from past experience when developing disaster cost estimates.

Additional information on *Limiting the Federal Government's Fiscal*

---

[37]GAO, *Climate Change: Improvements Needed to Clarify National Priorities and Better Align Them with Federal Funding Decisions*, GAO-11-317 (Washington, D.C.: May 20, 2010).

Exposure by Better Managing Climate Change Risks is provided on page 61 of this report.

Mitigating Gaps in Weather Satellite Data

For 2013, we are designating a new high-risk area—*Mitigating Gaps in Weather Satellite Data*. We and others—including an independent review team reporting to the Department of Commerce and the department's Inspector General—have raised concerns that problems and delays on environmental satellite acquisition programs will result in gaps in the continuity of critical satellite data used in weather forecasts and warnings. The importance of such data was recently highlighted by the advance warnings of the path, timing, and intensity of Superstorm Sandy.

Since the 1960s, the United States has used both polar-orbiting and geostationary satellites to observe the Earth and its land, oceans, atmosphere, and space environments. Polar-orbiting satellites constantly circle the Earth in an almost north-south orbit providing global coverage of environmental conditions that affect the weather and climate. As the Earth rotates beneath it, each polar-orbiting satellite views the entire Earth's surface twice a day. In contrast, geostationary satellites maintain a fixed position relative to the Earth from a high-level orbit of about 22,300 miles in space. Used in combination with ground, sea, and airborne observing systems, both types of satellites have become an indispensable part of monitoring and forecasting weather and climate. For example, polar-orbiting satellites provide the data that go into numerical weather prediction models, which are a primary tool for forecasting weather days in advance, including forecasting the path and intensity of hurricanes and tropical storms. Geostationary satellites provide frequently-updated graphical images that are used to identify current weather patterns and provide short-term warnings.

Polar-orbiting Satellites

For more than 40 years, the United States has operated two separate operational polar-orbiting meteorological satellites systems: the Polar-orbiting Operational Environmental Satellite series, which is managed by National Oceanic and Atmospheric Administration (NOAA)—a component of the Department of Commerce; and the Defense Meteorological Satellite Program (DMSP), which is managed by the Air Force. The government also relies on data from a European satellite program, called the Meteorological Operational (MetOp) satellite series. These satellites are positioned so that they cross the Equator in the early morning, midmorning, and early afternoon in order to obtain regular updates throughout the day.

With the expectation that combining the two separate U.S. polar satellite programs would result in sizable cost savings, a May 1994 Presidential Decision Directive required NOAA and DOD to converge the two programs into a single new satellite acquisition, which became the National Polar-orbiting Operational Environmental Satellite System (NPOESS). However, in the years that followed, NPOESS encountered significant technical challenges in sensor development and experienced program cost growth and schedule delays, in part due to problems in the program's management structure. After several restructurings and recurring challenges, in February 2010, the Executive Office of the President's Office of Science and Technology Policy announced that NOAA and DOD would no longer jointly procure NPOESS; instead, each agency would plan and acquire its own satellite system. Specifically, NOAA, with support from the National Aeronautics and Space Administration (NASA), would be responsible for the afternoon orbit, and DOD would be responsible for the early morning orbit. The U.S. partnership with the European satellite agency for data from the midmorning orbit would continue as planned.

Subsequently, NOAA initiated its replacement program, the Joint Polar Satellite System (JPSS). JPSS consists of a demonstration satellite—called the Suomi National Polar-orbiting Partnership (NPP)—launched in October 2011; two satellites, with at least five instruments planned for each, to be launched by March 2017 and December 2022, respectively; two stand-alone satellites to accommodate three additional instruments; and ground systems for the entire program. The program is currently estimated to cost $12.9 billion. In June 2012, we reported that NOAA and NASA made progress in establishing the JPSS program and in launching and operating the demonstration satellite, but noted that program officials expect there to be a gap in satellite observations before the first JPSS satellite is launched.

Specifically, NOAA officials anticipate a gap in the afternoon orbit from 18 to 24 months between the time that NPP reaches the end of its lifespan and when the first JPSS satellite is fully ready for operational use. We identified other scenarios where the gap could last from 17 to 53 months. For example, the gap would be 17 months if NPP lasts 5 years until October 2016 and JPSS is launched as planned in March 2017 and undergoes a 12-month on-orbit checkout before it is fully operational. Alternatively, if NPP lasts only 3 years—which NASA engineers consider possible due to poor workmanship in the fabrication of the instruments—and JPSS launches 1 year later than currently planned, the gap in satellite observations could reach 53 months. Figure 1 depicts a potential gap in the afternoon orbit.

Figure 1: A Potential Gap in the Afternoon Orbit

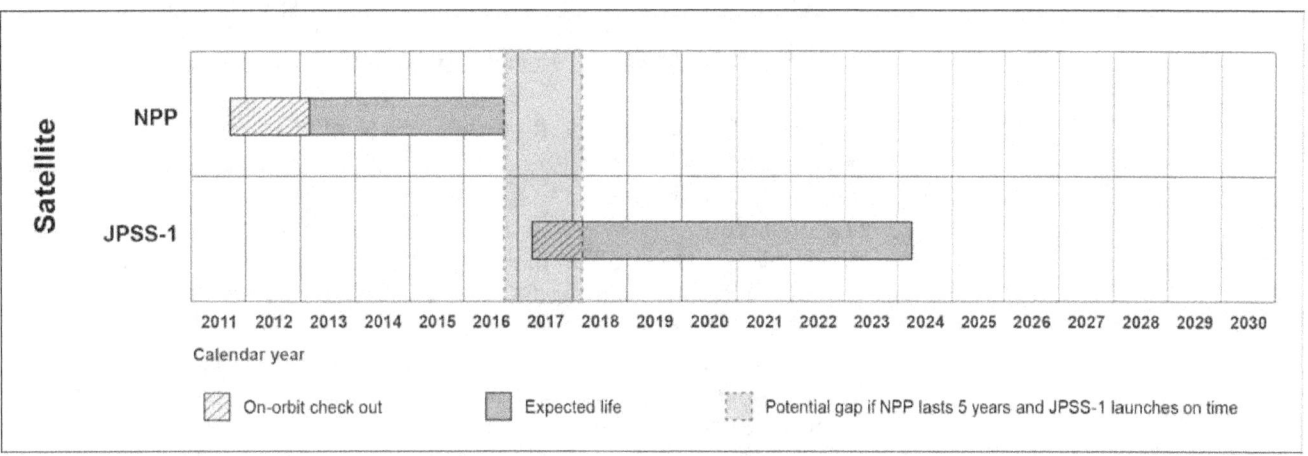

Source: GAO analysis of NOAA data.

After NPOESS was disbanded, DOD also began planning its own follow-on polar satellite program. However, it halted work in early 2012 because it still has two legacy DMSP satellites in storage that will be launched as needed to maintain observations in the early morning orbit. The agency currently plans to launch its two remaining satellites in 2014 and 2020. Moreover, DOD is working to identify alternatives to meet its future environmental satellite requirements. However, in June 2012, we reported that there is a possibility of satellite data gaps in DOD's early morning orbit. The two remaining DMSP satellites may not work as intended because they were built in the late 1990s and will be quite old by the time they are launched. If the satellites do not perform as expected, a data gap in the early morning orbit could occur as early as 2014.

Satellite data gaps in the morning or afternoon polar orbits would lead to less accurate and timely weather forecasting; as a result, advanced warning of extreme events would be affected. Such extreme events could include hurricanes, storm surges, and floods. For example, the National Weather Service performed case studies to demonstrate how its forecasts would have been affected if there were no polar satellite data in the afternoon orbit, and noted that its forecasts for the "Snowmaggedon" winter storm that hit the Mid-Atlantic coast in February 2010 would have predicted a less intense storm further east, with about half of the precipitation at 3, 4, and 5 days before the event. Specifically, the models would have under-forecasted the amount of snow by at least 10 inches. Similarly, a European weather organization[38] recently reported that NOAA's forecasts of Superstorm Sandy's track could have been hundreds of miles off without polar-orbiting satellites—rather than identifying the New Jersey landfall within 30 miles 4 days before landfall, the models would have shown the storm remaining at sea.

In June 2012, we reported that while NOAA officials communicated publicly and often about the risk of a polar satellite data gap, the agency had not established plans to mitigate the gap. At the time, NOAA officials stated that the agency would continue to use existing satellites as long as they provide data and that there were no viable alternatives to the JPSS program. However, our report noted that a more comprehensive mitigation plan was essential since it is possible that other governmental, commercial, or foreign satellites could supplement the polar satellite data. For example, other nations continue to launch polar-orbiting weather satellites to acquire data such as sea surface temperatures, sea surface winds, and water vapor. Also, over the next few years, NASA plans to launch satellites that will collect information on precipitation and soil moisture. Because it could take time to adapt ground systems to receive, process, and disseminate an alternative satellite's data, we noted that any delays in establishing mitigation plans could leave the agency little time to leverage its alternatives. We recommended that NOAA establish mitigation plans for pending satellite gaps in the afternoon orbit as well as potential gaps in the early morning orbit.

In September 2012, the Under Secretary of Commerce for Oceans and Atmosphere (who is also the NOAA Administrator) reported that NOAA had several actions under way to address polar satellite data gaps, including (1) an investigation on how to maximize the life of the demonstration satellite, (2) an investigation on how to accelerate the development of the second JPSS satellite, and (3) the development of a mitigation plan to address potential data gaps until the first JPSS satellite becomes operational. The Under Secretary also directed NOAA's Assistant Secretary to, by mid-October 2012, establish a contract to conduct an enterprise-wide examination of contingency options and to

---

[38]The European Centre for Medium Range Weather Forecasts is an independent, intergovernmental organization supported by 34 European nations, providing global medium-to-extended range forecasts.

develop a written, descriptive, end-to-end plan that considers the entire flow of data from possible alternative sensors through data assimilation and on to forecast model performance. In October 2012, NOAA issued a mitigation plan for a potential 14 to 18 month gap in the afternoon orbit, between the current polar satellite and the first JPSS satellite. The plan identifies and prioritizes options for obtaining critical observations, including alternative satellite data sources and improvements to data assimilation in models. It also lists technical, programmatic, and management steps needed to implement these options.

However, these plans are only the beginning. The agency must make difficult decisions on which steps it will implement to ensure that its mitigation plans are viable when needed. For example, NOAA must make decisions about (1) whether and how to extend support for legacy satellite systems so that their data might be available if needed, (2) how much time and resources to invest in improving satellite models so that they assimilate data from alternative sources, (3) whether to pursue international agreements for access to additional satellite systems and how best to resolve any security issues with the foreign data, (4) when and how to test the value and integration of alternative data sources, and (5) how these preliminary mitigation plans will be integrated with the agency's broader end-to-end plans for sustaining weather forecasting capabilities. NOAA must also identify time frames for when these decisions will be made. We have ongoing work assessing NOAA's efforts to limit and mitigate potential polar satellite data gaps.

Geostationary Satellites

Geostationary environmental satellites transmit frequently updated images of the weather currently affecting the United States to every national weather forecast office in the country. These are the satellite images that the public often sees on television news programs. NOAA plans to have its $10.9 billion Geostationary Operational Environmental Satellite-R (GOES-R) series replace the current fleet of geostationary satellites, which will begin to reach the end of their useful lives in 2015. The GOES-R program has undergone a series of changes since 2006 and now consists of four geostationary satellites and a ground system. However, problems with instrument and ground system development caused a 19-month delay in completing the program's preliminary design review, which occurred in February 2012. In June 2012, we reported that GOES-R schedules were not fully reliable and that they could contribute to delays in satellite launch dates. Program officials acknowledged that the likelihood of meeting the October 2015 launch date was 48 percent.

While NOAA's policy is to have two operational satellites and one backup satellite in orbit at all times, continued delays in the launch of the first GOES-R satellite could lead to a gap in satellite coverage. This policy proved useful in December 2008 and again in September 2012 when the agency experienced problems with one of its operational satellites, but was able to move its backup satellite into place until the problems were resolved. However, beginning in April 2015, NOAA expects to have only two operational satellites and no backup satellite in orbit until GOES-R is launched and completes an estimated 6-month post-launch test period. As a result, there could be a year or more gap during which time a backup satellite would not be available. If NOAA were to experience a problem with either of its operational satellites before GOES-R is in orbit and operational, it would need to rely on older satellites that are beyond their expected operational lives and may not be fully functional. Any further delays in the launch of the first satellite in the GOES-R program would likely increase the risk of a gap in satellite coverage.

In September 2010, we reported that NOAA had not established adequate continuity plans for its geostationary satellites. Specifically, in the event of a satellite failure, with no backup available, NOAA planned to reduce its operations to a single satellite and if available, rely on a satellite from a foreign nation. However, the agency did not have plans that included processes, procedures, and resources needed to transition to a single or foreign satellite. Without such plans, there would be an increased risk that users would lose access to critical data. We recommended that NOAA develop and document continuity plans for the operation of geostationary satellites that included implementation procedures, resources, staff roles, and timetables needed to transition to a single satellite, foreign satellite, or other solution. In September 2011, NOAA developed an initial continuity plan that generally includes these elements. Specifically, NOAA's plan identified steps it would take in transitioning to a single or foreign satellite; the amount of time this transition would take; roles of product area leads; and resources such as imaging product schedules, disk imagery frequency, and staff to execute the changes. In December 2012, NOAA issued an updated plan that provides additional contingency scenarios.

However, it is not evident that critical steps have been implemented, including simulating continuity situations and working with the user community to account for differences in various continuity scenarios. These steps are critical for NOAA to move forward in documenting the processes it will take to implement its contingency plans. Once these activities are completed, NOAA should update its contingency plan to provide more details on its contingency scenarios, associated time frames, and any preventative actions it is taking to minimize the possibility of a gap. We have ongoing work assessing NOAA's actions to ensure that its plans are viable and that continuity procedures are in place and have been tested. Additional information on *Mitigating Gaps in Weather Satellite Data* is provided on page 155 of this report.

Evolving High-Risk Areas

In the 2 years since the last high risk update, three areas have narrowed in scope—*Management of Federal Oil and Gas Resources*, *Strengthening Department of Homeland Security Management Functions*, and *DOE's Contract Management for the National Nuclear Security Administration and Office of Environmental Management*. For the remaining areas, there has been important but varying progress. In addition, one area—*Modernizing the U.S. Financial Regulatory System and Federal Role in Housing Finance*—has been modified due to changing circumstances to include the Federal Housing Authority (FHA).

Our experience with the high-risk series over the past 23 years has shown that the key elements needed to make progress in high-risk areas are congressional action, high-level administration initiatives, and agencies' efforts grounded in the five criteria we established for removal from the High Risk List (see table 1).

Table 1: Criteria for Removal from High Risk List and Examples of Actions by Congress, the Administration, and Agencies Leading to Progress

1. **Demonstrated top leadership commitment**
   - Congressional oversight and, if necessary, legislation
   - OMB leadership
   - Top leadership in individual agencies
2. **Capacity**
   - People and other resources to reduce risks
   - Processes for reporting and accountability
3. **Corrective action plan**
   - Analysis identifying root causes of problems
   - Plans targeted to address root causes
   - Implementation of solutions to root causes
4. **Monitoring**
   - Established performance measures
   - Data collection and analysis
5. **Demonstrated progress**
   - Evidence of implemented corrective actions
   - Appropriate adjustments to action plans based on data

Source: GAO.

Note: These five criteria can form a road map for efforts to improve and ultimately address high-risk issues. Addressing some of the criteria leads to progress, while satisfying all of the criteria is central to removal from the list. See GAO-01-159SP.

Narrowing High-Risk Areas

Because of the progress that has been made, the scope has been narrowed for three areas that remain on our 2013 High Risk List— *Management of Federal Oil and Gas Resources, Strengthening Department of Homeland Security Management Functions*, and *DOE's Contract Management for the National Nuclear Security Administration and Office of Environmental Management.*

Management of Federal Oil and Gas Resources. Progress has been made in one of the three areas we identified in our 2011 High Risk List— the Department of the Interior's (Interior) reorganization of its oversight of offshore oil and gas activities.

- *Reorganization.* In October 2011, following the transfer of the Minerals Management Service's oil and gas revenue collection functions to the newly created Office of Natural Resources Revenue, Interior established two new bureaus to provide oversight of offshore resources and operational compliance with environmental and safety requirements. The new Bureau of Ocean Energy Management (BOEM) is responsible for leasing and approval of offshore development plans while the new Bureau of Safety and Environmental Enforcement (BSEE) is responsible for lease operations, safety, and enforcement. Because the responsibilities of these two bureaus are closely interconnected and depend on effective coordination, Interior developed memoranda and standard operating procedures to define roles and responsibilities and facilitate and formalize coordination. Interior also enacted numerous policy changes intended to improve its oversight of offshore oil and gas activities, such as new requirements and policies designed to mitigate the risk of a subsea well blowout or spill. In July 2012, we concluded that Interior has fundamentally completed its reorganization of its oversight of offshore oil and gas activities.

  In ongoing and future reviews, our primary focus will be to assess Interior's remaining challenges to managing oil and gas resources— revenue collection and human capital. In so doing, we will also continue to consider Interior's reorganization and its effect on the agency's ability to oversee federal lands and waters.

- *Revenue collection.* In 2008, we reported that Interior collected lower levels of revenues for oil and gas production than all but 11 of 104 oil and gas resource owners whose revenue collection systems were evaluated in a comprehensive industry study—these resource owners included many other countries as well as some states. We recommended that Interior (1) undertake a comprehensive reassessment of its revenue collection policies and processes and (2) establish a balance between collecting revenues and ensuring that public lands and waters remain an attractive option for oil and gas development. In response to our recommendation, Interior contracted for a study called "Comparative Assessment of the Federal Oil and Gas Fiscal System" with the goal to inform decisions about federal lease terms, such as royalties, by consistently comparing the federal oil and gas fiscal systems with those of other countries and identifying ways to increase revenues and improve diligent development. Interior completed this study in October 2011 but Interior is still in the process of deciding if and how to use the results of the study to alter its lease terms. In addition, Interior continues to work to implement a number of our recommendations directed at improving Interior's ability to conduct oil and gas production verification inspections. Finally, Interior is working to implement our recommendations to correct numerous problems with it's efforts to collect data on oil and gas produced on federal lands, including missing data, errors in company-reported data on oil and gas production, sales data that did not reflect prevailing market prices for oil and gas, and a lack of controls over changes to the data that companies reported. We are currently engaged in a review of Interior's revenue collection practices that will evaluate, among other things, Interior's progress in addressing our recommendations.

- *Human capital.* We have reported that the bureaus responsible for oversight and management of federal oil and gas resources on federal lands and in federal waters—Bureau of Land Management (BLM) and the Minerals Management Service (the predecessor to BOEM and BSEE)—have encountered persistent problems in hiring, training, and retaining staff. For example, in 2010, we found that both BLM and the Minerals Management Service experienced high turnover rates in key oil and gas inspection and engineering positions, potentially affecting their oversight of oil and gas development on federal leases. For fiscal years 2012 and 2013, Congress provided funds to BOEM and BSEE in the Gulf of Mexico to establish higher minimum rates of pay for key positions—chiefly geophysicists, geologists, and petroleum engineers—for up to 25 percent of the usual minimum rate of pay. BOEM and BSEE officials in the Gulf of Mexico told us that the pay increase reduced attrition rates for these positions. However, it is uncertain how Interior will address staffing shortfalls to oversee offshore resources in the long term. In July 2012, we reported that Interior was creating a new training program for its inspection staff (such as BSEE's National Offshore Training Program to train inspectors and engineers), but that it may take up to 2 years before new inspection staff are fully trained. Further, human capital issues also exist at BLM and the management of onshore oil and gas. For example,

BLM faces similar challenges in hiring, training, and retaining staff for key positions but Interior has not received congressional approval or funds to establish higher minimum rates of pay for these positions as did BOEM and BSEE. We are currently engaged in a review of Interior's efforts to meet its human capital challenges. As part of this effort, we will focus on the causes of Interior's human capital challenges, actions taken, and how Interior plans to measure the effectiveness of corrective actions. Additional information on *Management of Federal Oil and Gas Resources* is provided on page 76 of this report.

Strengthening Department of Homeland Security Management Functions. In 2003, we designated implementing and transforming the Department of Homeland Security (DHS) as high risk because DHS had to transform 22 agencies—several with major management challenges—into one department. Further, failure to effectively address DHS's management and mission risks could have serious consequences for U.S. national and economic security. Given the significant effort required to build and integrate a department as large and complex as DHS, our initial high-risk designation addressed the department's initial transformation and subsequent implementation efforts, to include associated management and programmatic challenges. At that time, we reported that the creation of DHS was an enormous undertaking that would take time to achieve, and that the successful transformation of large organizations, even those undertaking less strenuous reorganizations, could take years to implement.

Over the past 10 years, the focus of this high-risk area has evolved in tandem with DHS's maturation and evolution. The overriding tenet has consistently remained the department's ability to build a single, cohesive and effective department that is greater than the sum of its parts—a goal that requires effective collaboration and integration of its various components and management functions. In 2007, in reporting on DHS's progress since its creation, as well as in our 2009 high risk update, we reported that DHS had made more progress in implementing its range of missions rather than its management functions, and that continued work was needed to address an array of programmatic and management challenges. DHS's initial focus on mission implementation was understandable given the critical homeland security needs facing the nation after the department's establishment, and the challenges posed by its creation, integration, and transformation.

As DHS continued to mature, and as we reported in our assessment of DHS's progress and challenges 10 years after 9/11, we found that the department implemented key homeland security operations and achieved important goals in many areas to create and strengthen a foundation to reach its potential.[39] For example, DHS developed strategic and operational plans to guide its efforts, such as the National Response Framework that outlines disaster response guiding principles; successfully hired, trained, and deployed workforces, including the federal screening workforce to assume screening responsibilities at airports nationwide; and established new, or expanded existing, offices and programs to implement its homeland security responsibilities, such as the National Cybersecurity and Communications Integration Center to help coordinate efforts to address cybersecurity threats. However, we also identified that more work remained for DHS to address weaknesses in its operational and implementation efforts, and to strengthen the efficiency and effectiveness of those efforts. We further reported that continuing weaknesses in DHS's management functions had been a key theme impacting the department's implementation efforts. Recognizing DHS's progress in transformation and mission implementation, our 2011 high risk update focused on the continued need to strengthen DHS's management functions and integrate those functions within and across the department, as well as the impact of these challenges on the department's ability to effectively and efficiently carry out its missions.

While challenges remain for DHS to address across its range of missions, the department has made considerable progress in transforming its original component agencies into a single cabinet-level department and positioning itself to achieve its full potential. Important strides have also been made in strengthening the department's management functions and in integrating those functions across the department, particularly in recent years. However, continued progress is needed in order to mitigate the risks that management weaknesses pose to mission accomplishment and the efficient and effective use of the department's resources. In particular, the department needs to demonstrate continued progress in

---

[39]GAO, *Department of Homeland Security: Progress Made and Work Remaining in Implementing Homeland Security Missions 10 Years after 9/11*, GAO-11-881 (Washington, D.C.: Sept. 7, 2011). This report addressed DHS's progress in implementing its homeland security missions since it began operations, work remaining, and issues affecting implementation efforts. Drawing from over 1,000 GAO reports and congressional testimony related to DHS programs and operations, and approximately 1,500 recommendations made to strengthen mission and management implementation, this report addressed progress and remaining challenges in such areas as border security and immigration, transportation security, and emergency management, among others.

implementing and strengthening key management initiatives and addressing corrective actions and outcomes. Therefore, we are narrowing the scope of the high-risk area and changing the name from *Implementing and Transforming the Department of Homeland Security* to *Strengthening the Department of Homeland Security Management Functions* to reflect this focus.

Although considerable work remains, DHS has made important progress that should be commended. Specifically, DHS has made progress in strengthening and integrating its acquisition, information technology, financial, and human capital management functions. Senior leaders at the department have also continued to demonstrate strong commitment to addressing the department's management challenges across the management functions. For example, in January 2011, DHS developed its *Integrated Strategy for High Risk Management.* The strategy included key management initiatives and corrective actions to address this high-risk area and the 31 actions and outcomes that we identified as needed to address the high-risk designation, to which DHS agreed, and designated senior DHS officials to be responsible for implementing the actions. Since then, DHS has generally made improvements to the strategy with each update based on feedback we provided. For example, in the June 2012 update to the strategy, DHS included, for the first time, performance measures and progress ratings for all of the management initiatives. The June 2012 update also identified the resources needed to implement most (154 of 173) of its corrective actions, although DHS needs to further identify its resource needs and communicate and mitigate critical gaps. The strategy, if implemented and sustained, provides a path for DHS to be removed from our High Risk List.

DHS also implemented a number of actions outlined in the strategy, demonstrating the department's progress in achieving the long-term goal of enhancing its management capabilities and building a more integrated department. For example, DHS chartered eight Centers of Excellence to bring together program managers, senior leadership staff, and subject matter experts, with the goal of enhancing component acquisition capabilities and improving insight into program management challenges before they become major problems. DHS has also defined and begun to implement a vision for a tiered governance structure intended to improve its information technology (IT) program and portfolio management. Within financial management, DHS obtained a qualified audit opinion on its fiscal year 2012 financial statements. DHS also issued a workforce strategy and a revised *Workforce Planning Guide* to help the department address its human capital challenges and plan for its workforce needs. Further,

DHS has taken action to integrate its management functions by, for example, drafting a policy in September 2012 for managing investments across the department's components and management functions.

However, to fully address our high-risk designation, DHS needs to continue to implement its initiatives for strengthening its management functions and demonstrate measurable and sustainable results. For example, most of DHS's major acquisition programs continue to cost more than expected, take longer to deploy than planned, or deliver less capability than promised; and DHS leadership has authorized and continued to invest in major acquisition programs even though the vast majority of those programs lack foundational documents demonstrating the knowledge needed to help manage risks and measure performance. Further, while DHS has defined and begun to implement a vision for a tiered governance structure to improve IT management, we reported in July 2012 that the governance structure covers less than 20 percent (about 16 of 80) of DHS's major IT investments and 3 of its 13 portfolios, and the department has not yet finalized the policies and procedures associated with this structure. With respect to financial management, DHS has been unable to obtain an audit opinion on its internal controls over financial reporting, and needs to obtain and sustain unqualified audit opinions for at least two consecutive years on the department-wide financial statements. In the area of human capital management, DHS has not yet implemented an effective oversight approach for monitoring and evaluating components' progress in implementing strategic workforce planning, and federal surveys have consistently found that DHS employees are less satisfied with their jobs than the government-wide average.

Key to addressing the department's management challenges and this high-risk area is DHS demonstrating continued progress implementing its high-risk plan and the ability to achieve sustained progress across the 31 actions and outcomes we identified. DHS has made important progress across all of its management functions and significant progress in the area of management integration. However, DHS still has considerable work ahead in many areas. Specifically, we believe DHS has fully addressed 6, mostly addressed 2, partially addressed 16, and initiated 7 of the 31 key actions and outcomes (see table 2). A full assessment of DHS's progress and work remaining in addressing these actions and outcomes is provided beginning on page 161 of this report. We will continue to monitor DHS's efforts in this high-risk area to determine if the actions and outcomes are achieved and sustained.

Table 2: GAO's Assessment of DHS's Progress in Addressing Key Actions and Outcomes

Key Outcomes	Fully addressed[a]	Mostly addressed[b]	Partially addressed[c]	Initiated[d]	Total
Acquisition management			2	3	5
IT management	1	1	4		6
Financial management	2		3	4	9
Human capital management		1	6		7
Management integration	3		1		4
Total	**6**	**2**	**16**	**7**	**31**

Source: GAO analysis of DHS documents, interviews, and prior GAO reports.

[a]"Fully addressed": outcome is fully addressed.

[b]"Mostly addressed": progress is significant and a small amount of work remains.

[c]"Partially addressed": progress is measurable, but significant work remains.

[d]"Initiated": activities have been initiated to address outcome, but it is too early to report progress.

In recognition of the evolution of this high-risk area, we are narrowing its scope and changing the name from *Implementing and Transforming the Department of Homeland Security* to *Strengthening the Department of Homeland Security Management Functions* to reflect a focus on the department's remaining management challenges.

Going forward, to more fully address our high-risk designation, DHS needs to continue implementing its *Integrated Strategy for High Risk Management* and show measurable, sustainable progress in implementing its key management initiatives and corrective actions and achieving outcomes. Specifically, DHS needs to

- make continued progress in addressing the 31 actions and outcomes and demonstrate that systems, personnel, and policies are in place to ensure that progress can be sustained over time;

- maintain its current level of top leadership support and sustained commitment to ensure continued progress in executing its corrective actions through completion;

- continue to implement its plan for addressing this high-risk area and periodically report its progress to Congress and GAO;

- closely track and independently validate the effectiveness and sustainability of its corrective actions and make midcourse adjustments, as needed; and

- monitor the effectiveness of its efforts to establish reliable resource estimates at the department and component levels, address and work to mitigate any resource gaps, and prioritize initiatives as needed to ensure it has the capacity to implement and sustain its corrective actions.

Additional information on *Strengthening Department of Homeland Security Management Functions* is provided on page 161 of this report.

DOE's Contract Management for the National Nuclear Security Administration and Office of Environmental Management. To recognize progress at the Department of Energy (DOE) on the National Nuclear Security Administration's (NNSA) and Office of Environmental Management's (EM) execution of nonmajor projects—projects with values of less than $750 million—we are shifting the focus of its high-risk designation to major contracts and projects executed by NNSA and EM, those contracts and projects with values of $750 million or greater. Two of our reviews completed in 2012 focused on nonmajor projects found that these projects were being completed in large part, although additional and sustained attention by DOE is needed to adequately set and document performance baselines and further demonstrate that these actions result in improved performance. These reports included recommendations to DOE to clearly define, document, and track the scope, cost, and completion date targets for each of its projects, as required by DOE's project management order. DOE agreed with these recommendations and plans to apply lessons learned from successful EM projects to its broader portfolio of projects and activities. With further monitoring of this area to ensure that progress is sustained, coupled with continued efforts and commitment by top leadership to address contract and project management weaknesses, nonmajor project performance issues will have been sufficiently addressed.

DOE continues to demonstrate strong commitment and top leadership support for improving contract and project management in EM and NNSA, building on its corrective action plan developed in 2008. In December 2010, the Deputy Secretary convened a DOE Contract and Project Management Summit to discuss strategies for additional improvement in contract and project management. The participants identified six barriers to improved performance and reported in April 2012 on the status of initiatives to address these barriers. In addition, DOE has continued to release guides for implementing its revised order for Program and Project Management for the Acquisition of Capital Assets (DOE O 413.3B), such as for cost estimating, using earned value management, and for forming project teams. Further, DOE has taken steps to enhance project management and oversight by requiring peer reviews and independent cost estimates for projects with values over $100 million and by improving the accuracy and consistency of data in DOE's central repository for project data.

Challenges remain for the successful execution of major projects. NNSA and EM are currently managing 10 major projects with combined estimated costs totaling as much as $65.7 billion. We have continued to document significant cost increases and schedule delays as well as technical challenges impacting project design. NNSA is tasked with modernizing the nation's aging nuclear weapons production facilities, a challenging effort that will take years and cost billions of dollars. EM faces ongoing complex and long-term challenges in removing radioactive and hazardous chemical contaminants—left over from decades of weapons production—from soil, groundwater, and facilities. Billions of dollars have already been spent, and will continue to be spent over the coming decades to treat and dispose of this waste. In recognition of the significance of these challenges, particularly in a time of fiscal constraint, in 2012, multiple committees of the Senate and House of Representatives held oversight hearings focused on needed improvements to DOE contract management and project performance. Further, the *National Defense Authorization Act for Fiscal Year 2013* includes provisions significant to considerations about NNSA contract and project management, such as cost containment provisions for two of NNSA's largest construction projects, both of which have experienced cost and schedule delays; a requirement that NNSA submit to Congress reports including expected cost savings associated with the award of contracts to manage and operate NNSA facilities; and creation of an advisory panel to make recommendations on revising the governance of the nuclear security enterprise. Until DOE can consistently demonstrate that recent changes to policies and processes are resulting in improved performance on major projects, NNSA and EM will remain on the High Risk List. Additional information on *DOE's Contract Management for the National Nuclear Security Administration and Office of Environmental Management* is provided on page 218 of this report.

Progress Being Made in Remaining High-Risk Areas

Several high-risk areas also received congressional oversight and legislation needed to make progress in addressing risks. Congress will continue to play an important role through its oversight and, where appropriate, through legislative action targeting both specific problems and the high-risk areas overall.

Top administration officials have continued to show their commitment to ensuring that high-risk areas receive attention and oversight. OMB regularly convenes meetings for agencies to provide progress updates on high-risk issues. When a high-risk issue area ranges across agencies, OMB coordinates with representatives from multiple agencies to participate. These meetings typically include OMB's Deputy Director for Management, the Comptroller General, participating agencies' representatives to the President's Management Council, and other administration and agency staff members responsible for addressing the high-risk issue.

The meetings provide an opportunity for discussion on agency initiatives, updates, and plans, as well as progress and challenges to resolving high-risk issues. As described by an OMB official, these discussions have served to keep the lines of communication open and continue to build the deeper connections needed to find solutions to these high-risk problems. These meetings are useful and have produced tangible results by opening and sustaining conversations among leaders responsible for addressing the high-risk areas. The OMB meetings have been sustained from prior administrations and continue to serve as a tool for accountability for sustaining progress on issues. Continued attention by OMB, concerted effort by GAO and other agencies, as well as sustained congressional oversight are critical to making more progress; our experience has shown that perseverance is required to fully resolve high-risk areas.

We have continued to focus on high-risk issues. Related to our high-risk work in fiscal years 2012 and 2011, we issued 374 reports, delivered 112 testimonies to Congress, and prepared numerous other products, such as briefings and presentations. For these 2 years, we documented more than $57 billion in financial benefits and over 1,000 other improvements related to high-risk areas. These results are based on reviews spanning a wide range of issues on the High Risk List. All of our recommendations are described in our reports and on our website at www.gao.gov.

Table 3 provides examples of congressional actions and high-level administration initiatives—discussed in more detail throughout this report—that have led to progress in addressing high-risk areas.

Table 3: Examples of Congressional Actions and Administration Initiatives Leading to Progress on High-Risk Areas

High-risk area	Actions and initiatives
Protecting Public Health through Enhanced Oversight of Medical Products	The **Food and Drug Administration Safety and Innovation Act** (Pub. L. No. 112-144), enacted in 2012, included several provisions that enhance the Food and Drug Administration's (FDA) ability to protect the public health. Among other things, it directed FDA to take a more risk-based approach in selecting foreign drug establishments for inspections, as we recommended in September 2008. It also required FDA to take actions consistent with all of our June 2011 recommendations to improve oversight of medical device recalls. Further, it required drug manufacturers to advise the agency of potential drug shortages as we suggested in a November 2011 report. In addition, the President issued an executive order in October 2011 that instructs FDA to take steps that are intended to enhance the agency's response to drug shortages and directs FDA to expand its efforts to expedite review of applications to market drugs that would help to prevent or resolve shortages.
DOD Supply Chain Management	In fiscal year 2010, the Department of Defense (DOD) began implementing a congressionally mandated plan to reduce its excess inventory and improve inventory management. As of January 2012, implementation was largely on-schedule and DOD reported reductions in excess inventory. For example, between fiscal years 2009 and 2011, DOD reduced on-order excess inventory, those items already purchased but likely to be excess due to changes in requirements, by $632 million. Additionally, DOD has achieved some positive results reducing materiel distribution costs and improving distribution service to the warfighter.
Pension Benefit Guaranty Corporation Insurance Programs	In July 2012, the **Moving Ahead for Progress in the 21st Century Act** (Pub. L. No. 112-141) was enacted that included provisions to stabilize sponsors' pension contribution requirements, adjust premium rates, and improve the Pension Benefit Guaranty Corporation's (PBGC) governance. In addition, PBGC has taken steps to address several areas of weakness noted in our previous reports, including adopting a new investment policy statement in May 2011, modeling more risk-based premium options to enhance understanding of the administration's September 2011 proposal to reform PBGC's premium structure, and implementing several new practices to strengthen the accountability of contract management.
Funding the Nation's Surface Transportation System	In July 2012, Congress passed the **Moving Ahead for Progress in the 21st Century Act** (Pub. L. No. 112-141), which included provisions to move toward a more performance-based highway and transit program and to establish a framework to address key challenges in the area of freight movement.
Strategic Human Capital Management	In 2011, the Office of Personnel Management, in concert with the Office of Management and Budget and agencies' Chief Human Capital Officers, established an interagency working group tasked with identifying skills gaps and developing strategies for closing them. In July 2012, the final rule went into effect for implementing a new program for the hiring of students and recent college graduates. Congress continued its oversight as well including a hearing on the state of the federal workforce in September 2012.
Enforcement of Tax Laws	Since 2011, various legislative provisions requiring financial institutions to report to the Internal Revenue Service (IRS) information on taxpayers' financial accounts and transactions began to take effect. IRS data show that tax compliance is very high when substantial information reporting exists. Also, IRS has collected billions of dollars through its initiatives to encourage taxpayers to voluntarily report their previously undisclosed foreign accounts and assets.
Medicaid Program	In 2012, committees in Congress held hearings on reducing Medicaid improper payments and on improving oversight of the program. Also, in May 2011, the Centers for Medicare & Medicaid Services issued guidance to states on removing providers from their programs that have been terminated for committing fraud in other state Medicaid programs or Medicare as required by the **Patient Protection and Affordable Care Act** (Pub. L. No. 111-148).
Medicare Program	Congressional committees provided extensive oversight of Medicare program integrity and payment issues through at least 25 hearings—including discussions on Centers for Medicare & Medicaid Services implementation of key legislation, such as the **Patient Protection and Affordable Care Act** (Pub. L. No. 111-148), which contained provisions intended to strengthen integrity efforts, and the **Small Business Jobs Act of 2010** (Pub. L. No. 111-240), which provided funding and contained requirements to implement predictive analytic technologies to prevent and detect fraud, waste, and abuse.
Improving and Modernizing Federal Disability Programs	The Office of Management and Budget—the focal point for management in the executive branch—reported that the Domestic Policy Council has begun an internal review of ways to improve the effectiveness of disability programs through better coordination and alignment of priorities and strategies.

Source: GAO.

Several additional examples of solid progress made to address high-risk issues underscore the importance of high-level attention by the executive branch and coordinated action by Congress and efforts by agencies to implement our recommendations and targeted corrective actions to address high-risk areas within the context of our criteria.

Establishing Effective Mechanisms for Sharing and Managing Terrorism-Related Information to Protect the Homeland. We found that the federal government's commitment to establishing effective mechanisms for sharing and managing terrorism-related information has improved because the federal government has made significant progress defining a governance structure to implement the Information Sharing Environment (Environment). The Environment is an approach to facilitate the sharing of terrorism and homeland security information established pursuant to the Intelligence Reform and Terrorism Prevention Act of 2004, as amended.[40] The Office of the Program Manager for the Environment is situated within and funded through amounts appropriated to the Office of the Director of National Intelligence (ODNI). The Program Manager, designated by the President to lead this effort, as well as key departments critical to implementing the Environment—the Departments of Homeland Security (DHS), Justice, State, and Defense, as well as ODNI—have taken actions to enhance sharing. The Program Manager and key departments have established and sustained an Information Sharing and Access Interagency Policy Committee (Policy Committee), co-chaired by the Program Manager and the National Security Staff Senior Director for Information Sharing and Security and composed of senior department officials. The members have defined the overall vision of what the Environment is to include and developed an implementation roadmap and guidance for the Environment, as we recommended. These actions have laid out the critical steps agencies are to take over the next 3 years to further develop and implement the Environment.

In addition, OMB, in conjunction with the Program Manager, issues higher-level programmatic guidance that sets annual Environment priorities for agencies to address in their budgets. The Program Manager issues more detailed annual guidance—developed in collaboration with the five key departments—that provides specific actions, time frames, and

---

[40]See Pub. L. No. 108-458, § 1016 Stat. 3638, 3664-70 (2004) (codified as amended at 6 U.S.C. § 485). See also 6 U.S.C. § 482 (requiring the establishment of procedures for the sharing of homeland security information).

milestones to implement the priorities. These include, for example, efforts to develop an automated means to determine who is authorized to access data and establish a method for verifying user identities; identify data holdings that agencies possess that are critical to counterterrorism efforts; define how the federal government will support state and major urban area fusion centers, which were created to fill gaps in sharing that the government could not address; and promote the adoption of standards to improve interoperability among systems and networks. The Program Manager also established a performance framework that is evolving from an assessment of departments' participation in key information sharing initiatives to a measurement of the information sharing, and ultimately the homeland security benefits realized. Finally, the Office of the Program Manager is publicly accounting for progress in its Information Sharing Environment Annual Report to Congress.[41]

While progress has been made establishing a governance structure to implement the Environment, the Program Manager and key departments need to take additional action to mitigate the potential risks from gaps in sharing terrorism-related information. Such action includes demonstrating that the Program Manager and key departments have a process for defining the incremental costs needed to complete corrective actions and developing strategies to mitigate potential funding constraints; issuing an enterprise architecture management plan, expected in 2013, to guide the identification of technological capabilities and services to share information across the Environment; ensuring that they are leveraging individual agency initiatives to benefit all partners; continuing work to develop metrics that evolve from counting the number of agencies participating in an activity to measuring the improved sharing of homeland security results achieved; and using the National Strategy of Information Sharing and Safeguarding and related implementation plans to develop an integrated way to publicly account for and measure the progress of individual initiatives, as well as the overall Environment, against established baselines, time frames, and milestones. Additional information on *Establishing Effective Mechanisms for Sharing and Managing Terrorism-Related Information to Protect the Homeland* is provided on page 173 of this report.

---

[41]See 6 U.S.C. § 485(h).

**Protecting Public Health through Enhanced Oversight of Medical
Products.** The Food and Drug Administration (FDA) has taken steps to
strengthen its oversight of medical products—drugs, biologics, and
medical devices. In response to recommendations we made in 2009, the
agency took steps to improve the management of its medical product
resources. FDA conducted a comprehensive assessment of its staffing
resources, gathered data on the work it conducts to fulfill its
responsibilities, assessed the extent to which it was meeting its
responsibilities, and developed an evidence-based estimate of its
resource needs. FDA also implemented other recommendations we made
in 2009 to protect patients participating in clinical trials and to preserve
the integrity of clinical trial data. FDA amended regulations related to the
disqualification of clinical investigators engaged in serious misconduct.
This action should help ensure that those who have engaged in such
misconduct involving one medical product are unable to continue serving
as clinical investigators for any other FDA-regulated medical products.
FDA also established related procedural requirements, developed
tracking systems, issued guidance, and monitored the timeliness of
debarment and disqualification proceedings.

FDA also improved the quality of some of the data it uses to manage its
foreign drug inspection program, as we suggested in 2008. FDA
developed a new database to generate consistent and reliable
information about foreign inspections, replacing an older system that
contained inaccurate information regarding the seriousness of some
inspection results. Its new database will also allow the agency to generate
a variety of reports, such as analyses of the number of inspections and
outcomes of inspections in other countries. FDA also formed a new office,
the Office of Global Regulatory Operations and Policy, affirming the
agency's commitment to confronting the challenges of globalization. And,
recognizing the need to focus greater attention on the recent public health
crisis related to shortages of life-saving and life-sustaining drugs, FDA
recently increased the size of its staff working on this critical issue, as we
recommended in 2011.

The Food and Drug Administration Safety and Innovation Act (FDASIA)
(Public Law 112-144), enacted in July 2012, included several provisions
that enhance FDA's ability to protect the public health and also reflected
our recommendations to enhance postmarket safety of drugs and medical
devices. FDASIA directed FDA to take a risk-based approach to
inspecting both foreign and domestic drug manufacturing establishments,
consistent with a recommendation we made in 2008. This provision will
help protect public health by improving FDA's ability to respond to

globalization and oversee the growing number of drugs coming into the U.S. market from overseas. In June 2011, we reported on weaknesses in FDA's oversight of medical device recalls and recommended that FDA routinely assess information on device recalls, clarify procedures for conducting recalls, develop criteria for assessing the effectiveness of recalls, and document the agency's basis for terminating individual recalls. FDASIA requires FDA to take actions consistent with all of these recommendations. FDA is now beginning to implement these recommendations, which should enable it to better protect public health.

Shortages of critically important drugs have been dramatically increasing in recent years. These shortages directly threaten public health by preventing patients from accessing medications that are essential to their care. In the wake of these nationwide shortages, we reported in November 2011, that FDA was constrained in its ability to respond. We specifically highlighted FDA's lack of authority to require manufacturers to report actual or potential shortages to the agency. As a result, the agency's approach to managing drug shortages was predominately reactive. We suggested that Congress consider establishing a requirement for manufacturers to report to FDA any changes that could affect the supply of their drugs. FDASIA contains such a provision, requiring manufacturers of drugs that are life-supporting, life-sustaining, or used to prevent or treat debilitating diseases or conditions to notify FDA at least 6 months in advance if they either plan to discontinue manufacturing the drug or anticipate an interruption in manufacturing that is likely to lead to a meaningful disruption in the drug's supply.

In addition to the enactment of FDASIA, the President issued an executive order on drug shortages in October 2011. This order directs FDA to take steps that are intended to support, enhance, and amplify the agency's response to drug shortages. It directed FDA to expand its efforts to expedite review of applications that would help to prevent or resolve shortages. FDA also issued a report summarizing its response to drug shortages which includes a list of actions the agency should take to strengthen its response to drug shortages. In addition, the Department of Health and Human Services also issued a report summarizing the economic factors that cause drug shortages.

Despite making progress, some things remain to be done before the high-risk designation can be removed. Among other things, to effectively implement needed changes, FDA must act on FDASIA's requirement to take a risk-based approach in selecting foreign establishments for inspections, correct weaknesses in its medical device recall process, and continue to strengthen its Drug Shortage Program. Additional information on *Protecting Public Health through Enhanced Oversight of Medical Products* is provided on page 202 of this report.

NASA Acquisition Management. NASA has made progress in meeting cost and schedule goals for some of its more recent projects. For example, in 2011, two of NASA's spacecraft projects—Juno and the Gravity Recovery and Interior Laboratory—launched within their cost and schedule baselines. In addition, we reported in 2012 that many of the newer projects in the portfolio have not reported significant cost and schedule growth from established baselines. NASA has also taken steps to improve its acquisition management and continues to work to address systemic weaknesses by adopting practices that focus on closing gaps in knowledge about requirements, technology, funding, time, and other resources before commitments are made to a new project. For example, NASA has enhanced its cost-estimating methodologies to ensure that independent analyses are used to provide decision makers with an objective representation of likely project cost and schedule results before projects are baselined. In addition, the agency has modified its acquisition policy to strengthen requirements for earned value management—a key tool to help project managers to manage risk. Finally, NASA has taken steps to improve its ability to monitor project progress throughout a project's development by modifying its systems engineering policy to require projects to report on three technical indicators of design maturity—the percentage of actual mass margin versus planned mass margin, the percentage of actual power margin versus planned power margin, and the percentage of overdue project requests for action.[42]

All of these steps are important to NASA's continued progress in addressing past issues with acquisition management; key to assessing whether NASA's efforts are effective will be continued and sustained progress in meeting cost and schedule goals on its major projects and consistent application and further refinement of its strengthened policies. For example, cost and schedule growth on one of NASA's most

---

[42]Mass is a measurement of how much matter is in an object. It is related to an object's weight, which is mathematically equal to mass multiplied by acceleration due to gravity. Margin is the spare amount of mass or power allowed or given for contingencies or special situations. A request for action is a formal written request sponsored by the review panel asking for additional information or action by the project team. It is generally developed as a result of insufficient safety, technical, or programmatic information being available at the time of the review.

expensive and complex science projects—the James Webb Space Telescope—has had a significant impact on NASA's overall performance. The James Webb Space Telescope was rebaselined in 2011 with a $3.7 billion increase in lifecycle costs and a 52 month launch delay. Such a significant increase impacted NASA's ability to fund other important missions going forward. Significant effort to ensure that other large, complex, and expensive projects—such as the Space Launch System and Orion Multi-Purpose Crew Vehicle, which are in early stages of development—are planned and executed appropriately will be key to ensuring continued agency progress in meeting cost and schedule goals. Furthermore, it may take several years to assess the effectiveness of NASA's enhanced cost estimating practices, including earned value management and its indicators to assess design maturity. We reported in 2012 that earned value management has not been fully and consistently implemented by NASA's major projects and as a result many projects lack reliable data for monitoring contractor performance. We have also reported that NASA needs to consistently implement early indicators for design maturity and evaluate their effectiveness in assessing design progress. Additional information on *NASA Acquisition Management* is provided on page 225 of this report.

DOD Supply Chain Management. DOD has made moderate progress in addressing weaknesses in supply chain management, particularly in the management of supply inventories. DOD is implementing a statutorily mandated corrective action plan to reduce excess inventory and improve inventory management practices. DOD established overarching goals in its plan to reduce on-order excess inventory, those items already purchased but likely to be excess due to changes in requirements, and on-hand excess inventory, those items categorized for potential reuse or disposal. We reported in 2012 that DOD had made progress in implementing its inventory improvement plan and was tracking reductions to its excess inventory. DOD reported that from fiscal years 2009 to 2011, it had reduced on-order excess inventory by approximately $632 million— a reduction that achieved its initial target 4 years early. With respect to on-hand excess inventory, since fiscal year 2009, DOD had met its fiscal year 2012 target of having no more than 10 percent of its inventory categorized as on-hand excess. DOD's implementation of its corrective action plan was generally on schedule and focused on revising guidance to standardize and strengthen inventory management practices across the department. DOD also demonstrated progress in specific areas of the plan's implementation. For example, DOD completed a review of demand forecasting methods for one of three life cycle phases of a weapon system as part of an effort to improve methods and techniques for demand forecasting as well as increasing participation among the services in an in-storage visibility program that prevents unnecessary procurements of items.

DOD also has had efforts under way to improve materiel distribution and asset visibility—two areas that are associated with the delivery of needed supplies to the warfighter. An indication of progress in this area is that DOD has recently begun developing a strategy to coordinate efforts to improve asset tracking and in-transit visibility. Such a strategy, once completed and implemented, could provide a basis for DOD to integrate its corrective measures and ultimately demonstrate progress in improving asset visibility. Additionally, DOD implemented several improvement efforts—under an umbrella initiative known as Distribution Process Owner Strategic Opportunities—to reduce distribution costs and improve distribution service to the warfighter. For example, DOD reported that it had achieved cost avoidances by increasing its utilization of containers, pallets, and aircraft; shifting more cargo to larger containers; and positioning supplies closer to overseas customers.

Although progress has been made, more remains to be done to fully address the issues identified for this high-risk area. DOD's plan to improve its inventory management practices runs through fiscal year 2015 and the remaining issues to be addressed, such as improving demand forecasting, present considerable implementation challenges due to their complexity. Additionally, DOD needs to continue to monitor its progress in achieving its targets for reducing on-order and on-hand excess inventory and update these targets, as necessary, to ensure the department has targets that guide continued improvement. In the areas of materiel distribution and asset visibility, DOD needs to take a number of additional actions to address problems and challenges that affect delivery of critical items to the warfighter, and to ensure that its improvement efforts are integrated and comprehensive. DOD also needs to complete the development of enterprise-wide performance metrics and incorporate these into efforts aimed at improving the effectiveness and efficiency of supply chain management. Additional information about the actions needed to reduce risks for *DOD Supply Chain Management* is discussed on page 142 of this report.

Pension Benefit Guaranty Corporation Insurance Programs. Both Congress and the Pension Benefit Guaranty Corporation (PBGC) have taken significant steps to address many of our concerns with PBGC's overall management and governance structure, reflecting increased top-level attention to the challenges facing this agency. In July 2012, the

Moving Ahead for Progress in the 21st Century Act became law, with several provisions pertaining to PBGC, including measures to stabilize sponsors' pension contribution requirements, adjust premium rates, and strengthen PBGC's governance.[43] The provisions intended to improve PBGC's governance include such things as placing new requirements on PBGC's Board of Directors to meet more regularly; detailing its interactions with the agency's Inspector General, General Counsel, and Advisory Committee; creating new positions for a Risk Management Officer and a Participant and Plan Sponsor Advocate; requiring an independent peer review of PBGC's pension insurance modeling systems, to be conducted annually; and providing for the National Academy of Public Administration to conduct a study and, within a year, make recommendations to Congress about possible changes to PBGC's governance structure. We have long recommended that the composition of PBGC's board—currently made up of the Secretaries of the Treasury, Commerce, and Labor—be expanded to include additional members with diverse backgrounds who possess knowledge and expertise useful to PBGC's mission.

PBGC has also taken steps to address several areas of weakness noted in previous our reports. For example, in response to concerns about the agency's management of its assets, PBGC issued a new investment policy statement in May 2011 and has subsequently aligned its portfolio with these new objectives. Due to improved market conditions since adoption of this new policy, PBGC's investment income has rebounded from its sharp decline in 2008. In response to concerns about the inadequacy of PBGC's premium rates, which are set by law, in 2011 the Administration proposed legislative reforms to redesign PBGC's premium structure to better reflect the risk of future claims on PBGC. PBGC has made efforts to enhance understanding of these proposed reforms by modeling various premium options that factor in consideration of a sponsor's financial health as well as plan underfunding; however, no action has yet been taken in response to these proposed reforms.

In addition, in response to our and PBGC's Inspector General recommendations, PBGC has taken steps to strengthen the accountability of its contract management. For example, PBGC has implemented new practices requiring that service contracts of more than

---

[43]Pub. L. No.112-141, 126 Stat. 405, 846-864.

$100,000 include documentation of the decision to use contractors instead of federal employees, that contract files be reviewed annually, and that staff assigned contract monitoring duties have their performance of these duties reflected in their performance evaluations.

Once fully implemented, these changes should allow PBGC to improve its management and better protect the retirement incomes of workers in private-sector defined benefit pension plans. However, despite these actions, PBGC's financial future remains uncertain. PBGC continues to carry a large net deficit ($34 billion at the end of fiscal year 2012). Moreover, certain challenges related to PBGC's governance and funding structure remain. To improve the stability of PBGC's insurance programs, further congressional action should be considered with respect to: expanding and diversifying PBGC's board, redesigning PBGC's premium structure, strengthening pension plan funding requirements, and developing a strategy for PBGC's long-term financial solvency as the defined benefit sector continues to decline. Additional information on *Pension Benefit Guaranty Corporation Insurance Programs* is provided on page 241 of this report.

Transforming EPA's Process for Assessing and Controlling Toxic Chemicals.

- *Integrated Risk Information System (IRIS).* In December 2011, we reported that EPA's May 2009 revisions to the IRIS process restored EPA's control of the process and increased transparency, and established a 23-month time frame for its less challenging assessments. Notably, EPA has addressed concerns we raised in our March 2008 report and now makes the determination of when to move an assessment to external peer review and issuance—decisions that were made by OMB under the prior IRIS process. In addition, EPA has increased the transparency of the IRIS process by making comments provided by other federal agencies during the interagency science consultation and discussion steps of the IRIS process available to the public. Progress in other areas, however, has been limited and EPA has taken longer than the established time frames for completing steps in the revised process for most of its less challenging assessments. Continued progress will require that EPA develop and achieve productivity goals over a sustained period of time.

- *Toxic Substances Control Act (TSCA).* We have also reported that EPA has found it difficult to obtain the information needed to determine whether a chemical poses an unreasonable risk to human health or the environment and then take action to regulate such chemicals. Subsequent to our reports, the EPA Administrator has expressed support for TSCA reforms and developed principles for addressing them. In parallel with the announcement of these principles, in 2009, EPA initiated a new approach to managing chemicals within the limits of existing authorities—which, according to agency documents, will transition the agency from an approach dominated by voluntary data submissions by industry to a more proactive action-oriented approach to ensure chemical safety. Among other things, EPA must demonstrate progress toward fully utilizing its existing authorities under the act to obtain the toxicity and exposure information and take the necessary actions to regulate chemicals that pose an unreasonable risk to human health or the environment.

Additional information on *Transforming EPA's Process for Assessing and Controlling Toxic Chemicals* is provided on page 209 of this report.

Funding the Nation's Surface Transportation System. Congress has made progress in clarifying federal goals and roles and linking federal programs to performance, as we have recommended. In July 2012, Congress passed the Moving Ahead for Progress in the 21st Century Act, which included provisions to move toward a more performance-based highway and transit program. For example, for highways, the act establishes national performance goals in several areas and requires the Secretary of Transportation, in consultation with states and others, to establish performance measures for pavement and bridge conditions, injuries and fatalities, traffic congestion, and for other areas, and requires states and other grantees to report their progress in achieving these targets. The act also links funding to performance by requiring states to take corrective actions should progress in key areas be insufficient and to spend a specified portion of its funds to improve pavement and bridge conditions should conditions fall below minimum standards set by the Secretary. The act also established a framework to address key challenges in the area of freight movement, including freight rail. Specifically, the act establishes national goals and directs the Secretary to establish a national freight network, a strategic plan, and tools to support a performance-based approach to evaluate and select and fund new freight projects. Going forward, Congress and the administration need to agree on a long-term plan for funding surface transportation. Continuing to fund the Highway Trust Fund through general revenues may not be sustainable given competing demands and the federal government's fiscal challenges. A sustainable solution is based on balancing revenues to and spending from the Highway Trust Fund. New revenues from users can come only from taxes and fees, and ultimately major changes in transportation spending, revenues, or both will be needed to bring the two into balance. Additional information on *Funding the Nation's Surface Transportation System* is provided on page 92 of this report.

Strategic Human Capital Management. Since February 2011, when we narrowed the scope of the human capital high-risk area to focus on the most significant challenge remaining—closing mission critical skills gaps—the Office of Personnel Management (OPM), individual agencies, and Congress have continued to make progress on this issue. The support of agency officials combined with ongoing congressional oversight demonstrate the leadership and commitment in both the executive and legislative branches toward ensuring agencies have a high-quality workforce to carry out their vital missions.

For example, in September 2011, OPM and the Chief Human Capital Officers Council, as part of ongoing discussions between OPM, OMB, and us on the steps needed to address the federal government's human capital challenges, established a working group to identify and mitigate critical skills gaps. Underscoring the top leadership commitment to this task, the Working Group is led by OPM and DOD; agencies' Chief Human Capital Officers and their representatives were involved in forming the Working Group and are participating in its deliberations. Further, the Working Group's efforts were designated a cross-agency priority goal within the administration's fiscal year 2013 federal budget.

Although much remains to be done, using a multi-faceted approach, including a literature review and an analysis of various staffing gap indicators, the Working Group has thus far identified a list of government-wide mission critical occupations including information technology management and a family of occupations in the fields of science, technology, engineering, and mathematics. The Working Group also identified a list of government-wide mission critical competencies including data analysis and strategic thinking. At the same time, individual agencies identified agency-specific mission critical occupations such as nurses at the Department of Veterans Affairs. OPM has also taken steps to improve the federal hiring process with the aim of making it easier for people to apply for a federal job and strengthen the ability of agencies to compete with the private sector for filling entry-level positions. One such effort is the Pathways Program which created two new conduits into federal service and modified an existing program. The final rule implementing the Pathways Program took effect in July 2012.

Congress continued its oversight as well. For example, in September 2012, the Senate Subcommittee on Oversight of Government Management, the Federal Workforce, and the District of Columbia, held a hearing on the state of the federal workforce in which representatives from OPM, GAO, federal labor unions, and other stakeholders testified on the progress being made in modernizing the government's human capital policies and procedures. This hearing, along with research requests made to us and other initiatives, helped policymakers oversee and inform decision-making on OPM's and individual agencies' efforts to acquire, develop, and retain employees with the skills needed to carry out the government's vital work.

Going forward, further progress will depend on the extent to which OPM and agencies sustain their planning, implementation, and monitoring efforts using a strategic approach that (1) involves top management, employees, and other stakeholders; (2) identifies the critical skills and competencies that will be needed to achieve current and future programmatic results; (3) develops strategies that are tailored to address skills gaps; (4) builds the internal capability needed to address administrative, training and other requirements important to support workforce planning strategies; and (5) includes plans to monitor and evaluate progress toward closing skills gaps and meeting other human capital goals using a variety of appropriate metrics. Further, OPM and agencies need to implement refinements to the approaches the Working Group used to identify and address critical skills gaps to in order to enhance their effectiveness in the future. Additional information on *Strategic Human Capital Management* is provided on page 97 of this report.

Enforcement of Tax Laws. Although the tax gap—the difference between taxes owed and taxes paid on time—was recently estimated at $450 billion for tax year 2006, IRS has made progress in identifying and implementing a wide range of innovative measures that could help reduce it. For example, IRS has made its National Research Program study on the extent and causes of individual taxpayer compliance an annual program. While still in the early planning stages, IRS has met with key stakeholders to develop options for expanding compliance checks before issuing refunds to taxpayers. IRS is extending a program to encourage taxpayers to voluntarily report their previously undisclosed foreign accounts and assets, which has resulted in billions of dollars in collections. Two initiatives for corporate taxpayers could make examinations less resource-intensive. First, IRS is requiring businesses to report on their tax returns uncertain tax positions—those for which a business reported a reserve amount in its financial statements to account for the possibility that IRS does not sustain the position upon examination or that the position may be litigated. Second, IRS will work with corporations participating in its Compliance Assurance Process to identify and resolve potential tax issues before the corporations file tax returns. Although these measures all have the potential to improve compliance and reduce the tax gap, their impact is not yet known.

Several major new information reporting requirements, passed by Congress, have recently taken effect. Since 2012, brokers have been required to report their clients' basis for securities sales. Since 2011, banks and other third parties have been required to report businesses' credit card and similar receipts. Starting in 2014, U.S. financial institutions and other entities are required to withhold a portion of certain payments made to foreign financial institutions that have not entered into an agreement with IRS to report details on U.S. account holders to IRS. These requirements could help reduce tax evasion and help taxpayers comply voluntarily. However, as with the IRS's initiatives described earlier, it is too soon to tell the actual impact the requirements are having on taxpayer compliance. Additional information on *Enforcement of Tax Laws* is provided on page 230 of this report.

Medicaid Program. Both Congress and the administration have made Medicaid fiscal and program integrity a priority. Committees in Congress held multiple hearings on reducing Medicaid improper payments and on improving oversight of the program. The Department of Health and Human Services and the Centers for Medicare & Medicaid Services (CMS) have also made some progress in improving program oversight. For example, the Department of Health and Human Services continues to review and report on the rate of Medicaid improper payments, and continues to train and provide technical assistance to states on approaches to prevent improper payments, which are positive steps for improving transparency and reducing improper payments. CMS has issued guidance to states on removing providers from their Medicaid programs who have been terminated for committing fraud in other states' Medicaid programs or in Medicare as required by the Patient Protection and Affordable Care Act. In addition, CMS has begun implementing reporting and auditing requirements that have the potential to improve agency oversight of supplemental payments that state Medicaid programs make to hospitals serving a disproportionate share of uninsured and low-income individuals.

Sustained leadership and commitment to mitigating program risks and enhancing agency oversight of state efforts are important to improving the fiscal and program integrity of Medicaid. While the Department of Health and Human Services and CMS have taken positive steps, several oversight weaknesses previously identified by us have not been addressed. For example, CMS data systems do not provide complete, reliable, and timely data to support agency oversight and program integrity efforts; CMS's national Medicaid audit program—which reviews states' claims data to identify overpayments—duplicates state initiatives, and overpayments identified by CMS audits are not commensurate with the costs of the audits; and requirements to improve transparency and accountability are still lacking for one type of supplemental payment for which total payments are the largest. In addition, CMS has not improved the criteria and process it uses to review the budget neutrality of Medicaid demonstrations prior to approving them.

The overall cost to the federal government as a result of high-risk issues facing the agency is unknown; however, the estimated magnitude of Medicaid improper payments—an estimated $19.2 billion in federal funds in 2012—illustrates the challenge CMS faces in overseeing state Medicaid programs and improving state program integrity efforts. The importance of reducing the rate of improper payments is heightened by the expected increase in individuals eligible for Medicaid in the future under Patient Protection and Affordable Care Act—an estimated 7 million in 2014, growing to 11 million in 2022. Additional information on the *Medicaid Program* is provided on page 255 of this report.

Medicare Program. Both Congress and the administration have focused on the integrity of the Medicare program, including decreasing improper payments and fraud and abuse. Since February 2011, congressional committees held at least 25 hearings on the integrity of Medicare and agency progress in addressing integrity issues. The administration has made reducing improper payments a priority, and CMS has set targets for reducing improper payments in all parts of Medicare, which were estimated to be more than $44 billion in 2012. CMS has made progress measuring improper payments and now has an estimate for each part of the program. However, CMS will need to sustain progress in reducing improper payments and better addressing fraud and abuse by shifting more focus to prevention.

CMS has also implemented certain broad-based reforms to payment systems affecting providers in the traditional Medicare fee-for-service program and Medicare Advantage (MA) plans, many of which introduce financial incentives to explicitly reward quality and efficiency.

In addition to focusing on quality through the payment system, CMS also continued making efforts to improve oversight of patient care and safety in different care settings. Our work has identified challenges with these efforts and made recommendations about refinements that could help improve Medicare payment methods and oversight of patient care and safety, such as introducing additional controls and payment changes when physicians refer patients to obtain services from entities in which the physician has a financial interest and increasing oversight of poorly performing nursing homes. In regard to payments to MA plans, we found that instead of implementing the MA quality bonus payment provisions in the Patient Protection and Affordable Care Act, as amended, CMS established a demonstration to test an alternative bonus payment structure, which is estimated to cost more and precludes the evaluation of the demonstration's effectiveness due to significant design shortcomings. As a result, we recommended that this demonstration be cancelled. In regard to patient care and safety, we also found issues that hampered CMS's oversight of states' nursing home complaint investigation processes.

While CMS has shown high level management commitment to measuring and reducing improper payments and has implemented important payment reforms, much still remains to be done. This includes continuing efforts to reduce improper payments, develop payment methods to encourage efficient provision of services and better manage the program's services, and improve oversight of patient care and safety. We have made a number of recommendations for improvement that could help address these management challenges—such as fully implementing Medicare integrity provisions in recent laws, improving accuracy of payments to MA plans, and improving nursing home complaint processes. Additional information on the *Medicare Program* is provided on page 246 of this report.

Improving and Modernizing Federal Disability Programs. Although broad action is still needed to address fragmentation among numerous federal disability programs—such as the 45 programs under nine agencies that we identified as supporting employment for people with disabilities—key agencies have taken important early steps. For example, OMB officials stated that the Domestic Policy Council began an internal review of ways to improve the effectiveness of disability programs through better coordination and alignment of priorities and strategies. As a result, according to OMB officials, the Departments of Education and Labor are coordinating spending plans related to disability technical assistance and research and exploring funding flexibilities, collaboration, and common measures among related program grantees. OMB officials expect the Domestic Policy Council to continue holding strategy sessions. Further, per two executive orders, the administration reported implementing a government-wide diversity and inclusion plan and making progress toward a goal to hire 100,000 people with disabilities in the federal government. Programs that support employment can play a critical role in helping people with disabilities become more self-sufficient and reduce their reliance on federal disability benefit programs. Given the importance of these programs, OMB needs to maintain and expand its role in improving coordination across programs—such as the 45 we identified— that support employment for those with disabilities, and ultimately work with all relevant agencies to develop measurable government-wide goals to spur further coordination and improved outcomes for those who are seeking to find and maintain employment.

The Social Security Administration (SSA) and the Department of Veterans Affairs (VA) have recently taken important steps toward comprehensively updating medical and other information that underlies the eligibility criteria used in making decisions about disability benefits, thereby demonstrating a strong commitment and top leadership support. As of December 2012, SSA had completed comprehensive revisions of its medical criteria for 10 of the 14 adult body systems and initiated targeted reviews of certain conditions under these systems, as appropriate, according to SSA officials. To update its medical criteria, VA developed a multi-phase process and project plan with time frames and hired full-time staff. In addition, SSA and VA have embarked on ambitious plans to update the labor market information in their respective criteria. For example, SSA is designing a new occupational information system for use by 2016 while VA plans to conduct studies to evaluate disabled veterans' average loss of earnings in today's economy, a practice consistent with recommendations from expert panels and our prior work. However, to sustain this progress and more strategically manage the criteria updates, SSA and VA should address deficiencies we identified—especially around the agencies' planning and research efforts—for example, by completing plans to replace SSA's occupational information system and taking steps to increase VA's research capacity to determine veterans' earnings loss in a timely manner, as well as developing a longer term strategy for implementing revisions to VA's disability criteria.

Beyond updating medical and other information in their criteria, SSA and VA also have taken steps toward giving greater consideration of an individual's ability to function with medical impairments in their work or other environments. For example, as of July 2012, VA officials told us that the agency is moving forward with revisions to the mental health body system that incorporates measures of functional impairment and is considering similar changes for the other body system revisions. Similarly, SSA has incorporated into some of its medical criteria an assessment of whether a claimant's impairments result in functional limitations that can prohibit the ability to work and is sponsoring research to further consider these types of assessments in determining disability. However, the agencies still do not take into consideration the full range of assistive devices—such as a prosthetic device for walking or a device to assist with a vision impairment—or, in the case of SSA, workplace accommodations available today. SSA disagreed with our recommendation to conduct limited, focused studies on how to more fully consider such factors in its disability determinations, stating that such studies would be inconsistent with Congress' intentions. We noted, however, that Congress has not explicitly prohibited SSA from considering these factors and believe that conducting these studies would put SSA in a better position to thoughtfully weigh the costs and benefits of these various policy options before deciding on a course of action.

Over the past several years, agencies have made progress in managing growing disability claims workloads; however, workload challenges persist due, in part, to unprecedented demand for benefits. SSA, VA, and DOD have made progress by significantly increasing the number of claims processed at the initial decision and appellate levels. For example, SSA reported reducing the average hearing processing time from 532 days in August 2008 to 354 in October 2012 and reducing the number of aged cases that were the longest pending and often the most complex. Similarly, VA has ramped up case completion since 2009 by more than 6 percent—completing more than 1 million claims in fiscal year 2011. Finally, we found that VA and DOD completed expansion of the Integrated Disability Evaluation System program military-wide, processing 7,106 cases in fiscal year 2011, up from 210 in fiscal year 2008. DOD has reported improved overall processing times in 2012 compared to fiscal year 2011 levels, although the Integrated Disability Evaluation System program is still not meeting timeliness goals and has not since 2008. Although SSA, VA, and DOD's efforts are promising, workload challenges will likely persist, and even increase, amid a difficult job market, a fiscally strained environment, and hundreds of thousands of military servicemembers returning to civilian life. The agencies' success in managing their workloads will be contingent on continued management attention. Specifically, SSA requires continued attention to claims processing initiatives articulated in its strategic plan while VA needs to

develop a robust backlog reduction plan that includes performance goals
that incorporate the impact of improvement initiatives on processing
timeliness. Finally, VA and DOD need to develop time frames for the
ongoing Integrated Disability Evaluation System business process review
as well as for implementing any resulting recommendations. Additional
information on *Improving and Modernizing Federal Disability Programs* is
provided on page 235 of this report.

**Modernizing the U.S. Financial Regulatory System and Federal Role
in Housing Finance.** Since the 2007-2009 financial crisis, policymakers
have taken actions intended to reform the U.S. financial regulatory
system to address the risks associated with evolving financial firms,
markets, and products, including the passage of the Dodd-Frank Wall
Street Reform and Consumer Protection Act (Dodd-Frank Act). This act
mandates a broad range of reforms that aim to better position the
financial regulatory system in areas addressing the changes and risks
that we identified. These include the creation of new regulatory bodies.
For example, the Financial Stability Oversight Council was established to,
among other things, identify systemic threats, and it has taken steps to
carry out its responsibilities. However, we recently made a number of
recommendations to enhance the accountability and transparency of the
Financial Stability Oversight Council's decisions and activities and
improve collaboration among its members. A new Bureau of Consumer
Financial Protection created by the act has been issuing rules and begun
taking enforcement actions, including obtaining refunds for consumers
and imposing penalties on certain credit card issuers for practices that
violated the law.

Financial regulators have also taken actions to implement some key
reforms mandated by the Dodd-Frank Act. For example, key aspects of
new liquidation authorities created by the Dodd-Frank Act for resolving
troubled large financial firms have been implemented, and certain
institutions have submitted required resolution plans—"living wills"— that
would guide their rapid and orderly resolution in a bankruptcy, if needed.
However, market observers noted the effectiveness of these provisions
would not be known until the first large failure.

Regulators have also made progress in the rulemakings that are
necessary to implement the various reforms mandated by the Dodd-Frank
Act, but many remain unfinished. Overall, we identified 236 provisions of

the act for which regulators are issuing rulemakings or taking other actions across nine key areas.[44] As of December 2012, regulators had issued final rules for about 48 percent of these provisions. However, in some cases the dates by which affected entities had to comply with the rules had yet to be reached. Of the remaining provisions, regulators had proposed rules for about 29 percent, and rulemakings had not occurred for about 23 percent.

Additionally, although various proposals to resolve the role of the two housing enterprises—Fannie Mae and Freddie Mac—have been issued, no definitive actions have been taken as of yet. Actions to determine the roles of these two entities also need to consider the potential impacts on the risk exposure of the Department of Housing and Urban Development's Federal Housing Administration, especially in light of its current financial difficulties. Also, further actions could be taken to help restore the Federal Housing Administration's financial soundness. In addition, regulators have yet to fully address other sources of risk in the financial markets, including potential systemic risks posed by money market funds and those arising from institutions that represent concentrations of credit risk. Accordingly, the title and scope of this high-risk area has evolved from *Modernizing the Outdated U.S. Financial Regulatory System* to *Modernizing the U.S. Financial Regulatory System and Federal Role in Housing Finance.* Information on the modification of this area is provided on page 59 of this report. Additional information on this area is provided on page 81 of this report.

---

[44]To develop this count, we used information from a private law firm, financial regulators, and other sources. Using different sources, assumptions, and judgments in compiling the list of provisions requiring rulemaking and other key actions could result in different totals, and therefore the information we provide should not be taken as a definitive count of all actions required by the Dodd-Frank Act.

Modifying High-Risk Area

We first designated *Modernizing the Outdated U.S. Financial Regulatory System* as high-risk in 2009 due to the urgent need to reform the fragmented and outdated U.S. financial regulatory system. As discussed later, many actions are underway to implement oversight by new regulatory bodies and new requirements for market participants, although many rulemakings remain unfinished. Among the additional actions needed are resolving the role of the two housing-related government-sponsored enterprises—Fannie Mae and Freddie Mac—that continue operating under government conservatorships. However, a new challenge for the markets has also evolved as the decline in private sector participation in housing finance that began with the 2007-2009 financial crisis has resulted in much greater activity by the Federal Housing Administration (FHA), whose single-family loan insurance portfolio has grown from about $300 billion in 2007 to more than $1.1 trillion in 2012. Although required to maintain capital reserves equal to at least 2 percent of its portfolio, FHA's capital reserves have fallen below this level, due partly to increases in projected defaults on the loans it has insured. As a result, we are modifying this high-risk area to include FHA and acknowledge the need for actions beyond those already taken to help restore FHA's financial soundness and define its future role. Accordingly, the title and scope of this area has evolved to *Modernizing the U.S. Financial Regulatory System and Federal Role in Housing Finance*. One such action would be to determine the economic conditions that FHA's primary insurance fund would be expected to withstand without drawing on the Treasury. Recent events suggest that the 2-percent capital requirement may not be adequate to avoid the need for Treasury support under severe stress scenarios. Additionally, actions to reform the government-sponsored enterprises (GSE) and to implement mortgage market reforms in the Dodd-Frank Act will need to consider the potential impacts on FHA's risk exposure. Information on progress made in this area is provided on page 57 of this report. Additional information on this area is provided on page 81 of this report.

Overviews for Each High-Risk Area

Overall, the government continues to take high-risk problems seriously and is making long-needed progress toward correcting them. Congress has also acted to address several high-risk areas through hearings and legislation.

The following pages provide overviews of each of the 30 high-risk areas on our updated list. The overviews show (1) why the area is high risk, (2) the actions that have been taken and that are under way to address the problem since our last update in 2011, and (3) what remains to be done. Each of these high-risk areas is also described on our High Risk List website at www.gao.gov/highrisk.

Limiting the Federal Government's Fiscal Exposure by Better Managing Climate Change Risks

Why Area Is High Risk

Climate change is a complex, crosscutting issue that poses risks to many environmental and economic systems—including agriculture, infrastructure, ecosystems, and human health—and presents a significant financial risk to the federal government. Among other impacts, climate change could threaten coastal areas with rising sea levels, alter agricultural productivity, and increase the intensity and frequency of severe weather events. As observed by the United States Global Change Research Program (USGCRP), the impacts and costliness of weather disasters—resulting from floods, drought, and other events such as tropical cyclones—will increase in significance as what are considered "rare" events become more common and intense due to climate change.[1] In addition, less acute changes in the climate, such as sea level rise, could also result in significant long-term impacts. According to the National Research Council (NRC)—the principal operating agency of the National Academy of Sciences and the National Academy of Engineering—although the exact details cannot be predicted with certainty, there is a clear scientific understanding that climate change poses serious risks to human society and many of the physical and ecological systems upon which society depends, with the specific impacts of concern, and the relative likelihood of those impacts, varying significantly from place to place and over time.[2]

These impacts will result in increased fiscal exposure for the federal government in many areas, including, but not limited to its role as (1) the owner or operator of extensive infrastructure such as defense facilities

---

[1]Thomas R. Karl, Jerry M. Melillo, and Thomas C. Peterson, eds. *Global Climate Change Impacts in the United States*, (Cambridge University Press: 2009). This document, referred to as the 2009 National Climate Assessment, is in the process of being updated. USGCRP coordinates and integrates the activities of 13 federal agencies that conduct research on changes in the global environment and their implications for society. USGCRP began as a presidential initiative in 1989 and was codified in the Global Change Research Act of 1990 [Pub. L. No. 101-606, § 103 (1990)]. USGCRP-participating agencies are the Departments of Agriculture, Commerce, Defense, Energy, Interior, Health and Human Services, State, and Transportation; the U.S. Agency for International Development, the Environmental Protection Agency, the National Aeronautics and Space Administration, the National Science Foundation, and the Smithsonian Institution.

[2]NRC, Committee on America's Climate Choices, *America's Climate Choices* (Washington, D.C.: 2011). See also NRC, *Climate Change: Evidence, Impacts, and Choices. Answers to common questions about the science of climate change.* (Washington, D.C.: 2012). For more information about NRC's recent reports on climate change at http://www.globalchange.gov/what-we-do/assessment (last accessed Jan. 25, 2013).

and federal property vulnerable to climate impacts, (2) the insurer of property and crops vulnerable to climate impacts, (3) the provider of data and technical assistance to state and local governments responsible for managing the impacts of climate change on their activities, and (4) the provider of aid in response to disasters. For example, disaster declarations have increased over recent decades, and the Federal Emergency Management Agency (FEMA) has obligated over $80 billion in federal assistance for disasters declared during fiscal years 2004 through 2011.[3] In addition, on December 7, 2012, the Office of Management and Budget (OMB) within the Executive Office of the President requested $60.4 billion in federal resources for Superstorm Sandy recovery efforts to "build a more resilient Nation prepared to face both current and future challenges, including a changing climate." To prepare adequately in the event of such a disaster, federal agencies need to work with state and local governments and volunteer agencies to produce and evaluate information so that they can fully assess risk and make appropriate response and recovery decisions.

Climate change adaptation—defined as adjustments to natural or human systems in response to actual or expected climate change—is a risk-management strategy to help protect vulnerable sectors and communities that might be affected by changes in the climate. Adaptation measures to protect infrastructure, for example, include raising river or coastal dikes to protect infrastructure from sea level rise, building higher bridges, and increasing the capacity of storm water systems. State and local authorities are responsible for the planning and implementation of many types of infrastructure projects, and decisions at these levels of government can drive the federal government's fiscal exposure. While implementing adaptive measures may be costly, there is a growing recognition that the cost of inaction could be greater and—given the government's precarious fiscal position—increasingly difficult to manage given expected budget pressures which will constrain not just future ad hoc responses but other federal programs as well. As stated in a 2010 NRC report, increasing the nation's ability to respond to a changing

---

[3]GAO, *Federal Disaster Assistance: Improved Criteria Needed to Assess a Jurisdiction's Capability to Respond and Recover on Its Own*, GAO-12-838 (Washington, D.C.: Sept. 12, 2012). As discussed in this report, FEMA criteria for recommending that a jurisdiction receive disaster assistance play a role in the increasing number of declared disasters.

climate can be viewed as an insurance policy against climate change
risks.[4]

Furthermore, according to NRC and USGCRP the nation's vulnerability
can be reduced by limiting the magnitude of climate change through
actions to limit greenhouse gas emissions.[5] GAO recognizes that (1) the
federal government has a number of efforts underway to decrease
domestic greenhouse gas emissions and (2) the success of greenhouse
gas emissions reduction efforts depends in large part on cooperative
international efforts. However, limiting the federal government's fiscal
exposure to climate change risks will present a challenge no matter the
outcome of domestic and international efforts to reduce emissions, in part
because greenhouse gases already in the atmosphere will continue
altering the climate system for many decades, according to NRC and
USGCRP.[6]

What GAO Found

The federal government is not well organized to address the fiscal
exposure presented by climate change, partly because of the inherently
complicated, crosscutting nature of the issue. GAO reported in 2009 that
while policymakers increasingly viewed climate change adaptation as a
risk-management strategy to protect vulnerable sectors and communities
that might be affected by changes in the climate, the federal
government's emerging adaptation activities were carried out in an ad hoc
manner and were not well coordinated across federal agencies, let alone
with state and local governments.[7] Subsequently, GAO's 2011 report on

---

[4]NRC, America's Climate Choices: Panel on Adapting to the Impacts of Climate Change,
Adapting to the Impacts of Climate Change (Washington, D.C.: 2010).

[5]In the atmosphere, greenhouse gases absorb and reemit radiation within the thermal
infrared range of the electromagnetic spectrum. This is the fundamental cause of the
greenhouse effect, or the warming of Earth's atmosphere. In order of their prevalence by
volume, the primary greenhouse gases are water vapor (H_2O), CO_2, methane (CH_4),
nitrous oxide (N_2O), and ozone (O_3).

[6]The focus of this high-risk area may evolve over time to the extent that federal climate
change programs and policies change.

[7]GAO, *Climate Change Adaptation: Strategic Federal Planning Could Help Government
Officials Make More Informed Decisions*, GAO-10-113 (Washington, D.C.: Oct. 7, 2009).

climate change funding found no coherent strategic government-wide approach to climate change.[8]

The federal government would be better positioned to respond to the risks posed by climate change if federal efforts were more coordinated and directed toward common goals. With regards to providing climate-related information, NRC observed that no single government agency or centralized unit could perform all the required functions, and that coordination of agency roles and regional activities is a necessity. In 2009, GAO recommended that the appropriate entities within the Executive Office of the President, such as the Council on Environmental Quality (CEQ) and the Office of Science and Technology Policy (OSTP), in consultation with relevant federal agencies, state and local governments, and key congressional committees of jurisdiction, develop a strategic plan to guide the nation's efforts to adapt to climate change, including the establishment of clear roles, responsibilities, and working relationships among federal, state, and local governments.[9,10] In written comments, CEQ generally agreed with the recommendations of the report, noting that leadership and coordination is necessary within the federal government to ensure an effective and appropriate adaptation response and that such coordination would help to catalyze regional, state, and local activities. Some actions have subsequently been taken to improve federal adaptation efforts—including the development of an interagency climate change adaptation task force.[11] However, a 2012 NRC report describes the task force as having largely been confined to

---

[8]GAO, *Climate Change: Improvements Needed to Clarify National Priorities and Better Align Them with Federal Funding Decisions*, GAO-11-317 (Washington, D.C.: May 20, 2011).

[9]CEQ coordinates federal environmental efforts and the development of environmental policies and initiatives. The Office of Science and Technology Policy was established by statute in 1976 to serve as a source of scientific and technological analysis and judgment for the President with respect to major policies, plans, and programs of the federal government, among other things.

[10]GAO-10-113.

[11]Executive Order 13514 on Federal Leadership in Environmental, Energy, and Economic Performance calls for federal agencies to participate actively in the already existing Interagency Climate Change Adaptation Task Force. The task force, which began meeting in Spring 2009, is co-chaired by CEQ, National Oceanic and Atmospheric Administration, and OSTP, and includes representatives from more than 20 federal agencies and executive branch offices. The task force was formed to assess key steps needed to help the federal government understand and adapt to climate change.

convening representatives of relevant agencies and programs for dialogue, without mechanisms for making or enforcing important decisions and priorities.[12]

GAO's May 2011 report on climate change funding also found that federal officials do not have a shared understanding of strategic government-wide priorities.[13] Funding for climate change activities reported by OMB increased from $4.6 billion in 2003 to $8.8 billion in 2010. In addition, OMB reported $26.1 billion for climate change programs and activities provided in the American Recovery and Reinvestment Act of 2009, and $7.23 billion in tax expenditures in 2010 related to climate change, which are federal income tax provisions that grant preferential tax treatment to encourage emissions reductions by, for example, providing tax incentives to promote the use of renewable energy.[14] To improve the coordination and effectiveness of federal climate change programs and activities, GAO recommended in May 2011 that the appropriate entities within the Executive Office of the President clearly establish federal strategic climate change priorities, including the roles and responsibilities of the key federal entities, taking into consideration the full range of climate-related activities within the federal government. GAO requested comments on a draft of the May 2011 report from the Chair of CEQ, the Director of OMB, and the Director of OSTP. They did not provide official written comments to include in GAO's report and have not directly addressed this recommendation.

Federal agencies have made some progress on better organizing across agencies, within agencies, and among different levels of government; however, the need for more comprehensive and systematic strategic planning is illustrated by the increased fiscal exposure for the federal government in many areas, including, but not limited to the following:

Federal government as property owner. The federal government owns and operates hundreds of thousands of buildings and facilities that could be affected by a changing climate. For example, in its 2010 Quadrennial

---

[12]NRC, Committee on a National Strategy for Advancing Climate Modeling, Board on Atmospheric Studies and Climate, Division on Earth and Life Sciences, *A National Strategy for Advancing Climate Modeling* (Washington, D.C.: 2012).

[13]GAO-11-317.

[14]American Recovery and Reinvestment Act of 2009, Pub. L. No. 111-5 (2009).

Defense Review, the Department of Defense (DOD) recognized the risk to its defense facilities posed by climate change, noting that:

> climate change will pose challenges for civil society and DOD alike, particularly in light of the nation's extensive coastal infrastructure. In 2008, the National Intelligence Council judged that more than 30 U.S. military installations were already facing elevated levels of risk from rising sea levels. DOD's operational readiness hinges on continued access to land, air, and sea training and test space. Consequently, the Department must complete a comprehensive assessment of all installations to assess the potential impacts of climate change on its missions and adapt as required.

The federal government also manages about 650 million acres, or 29 percent of the 2.27 billion acres of U.S. land, for a wide variety of purposes, such as recreation, grazing, timber, and the conservation of fish and wildlife. In 2007, GAO recommended that that the Secretaries of Agriculture, Commerce, and the Interior develop guidance for resource managers that explains how they are expected to address the effects of climate change, identifies how managers are to obtain any site-specific information that may be necessary, and reflects best practices shared among the relevant agencies.[15] In commenting on a draft of this report, the three departments generally agreed with the recommendation. In 2009, the Secretary of the Interior issued an order, amended in 2010, to address the impacts of climate change on U.S. water, land, and other natural and cultural resources that the department manages. The order directed, among other things, Interior bureaus and agencies to further develop a network of collaborative Landscape Conservation Cooperatives, comprised of public and private agencies, working to provide the science and technical expertise needed to support conservation planning at landscape scales and to promote collaboration among their members in defining shared conservation goals. GAO has ongoing work related to adapting infrastructure and the management of federal lands to a changing climate.

Federal insurance programs. Two important federal insurance efforts—the National Flood Insurance Program and the Federal Crop Insurance Corporation—are based on conditions, priorities, and approaches that

---

[15]GAO, *Climate Change: Agencies Should Develop Guidance for Addressing the Effects on Federal Land and Water Resources*, GAO-07-863 (Washington, D.C.: Aug. 7, 2007).

were established decades ago and are not well suited to addressing emerging issues like climate change. The National Flood Insurance Program, administered by FEMA, has been on GAO's High Risk List since March 2006 because of concerns about its long-term financial solvency and related operational issues.[16] In March 2012, GAO reported on the federal crop insurance programs' important role in managing the risk of farming losses caused by natural disasters like the 2012 drought and the associated federal costs.[17]

GAO's March 2007 report assessing the financial risks to the National Flood Insurance Program and the Federal Crop Insurance Corporation found that their exposure to weather-related losses had grown substantially.[18] Among other things, the report contrasted the experience of private and public insurers. GAO found that many major private insurers proactively incorporated some elements of climate change into their risk management practices. In contrast, GAO noted that the agencies responsible for the nation's two key federal insurance programs had done little to develop the kind of information needed to understand their long-term exposure to climate change and had not analyzed the potential impacts of an increase in the frequency or severity of weather-related events on their operations. GAO recommended that the Secretaries of Agriculture and Homeland Security analyze the potential long-term fiscal implications of climate change for the Federal Crop Insurance Corporation and the National Flood Insurance Program, respectively, and report their findings to Congress. The two agencies agreed with the recommendation and contracted with experts to study

---

[16]The potential losses generated by the National Flood Insurance Program have created substantial financial exposure for the federal government and U.S. taxpayers. While Congress and FEMA intended that the National Flood Insurance Program be funded with premiums collected from policyholders and not with tax dollars, the program was, by design, not actuarially sound. As of November 2012, FEMA owes the Treasury approximately $20 billion—up from $17.8 billion pre-Superstorm Sandy—and had not repaid any principal on the loan since 2010.

[17]GAO, *Crop Insurance: Savings Would Result from Program Changes and Greater Use of Data Mining*, GAO-12-256 (Washington, D.C.: Mar. 13, 2012). The federal government's crop insurance costs have increased in recent years—rising from an average of $3.1 billion per year from fiscal years 2000 through 2006 to an average of $7.6 billion per year from fiscal years 2007 through 2012—and are projected to increase further.

[18]GAO, *Climate Change: Financial Risks to Federal and Private Insurers in Coming Decades Are Potentially Significant*, GAO-07-285 (Washington, D.C.: Mar. 16, 2007).

their programs' long-term exposure to climate change, but the results of the work have not yet been reported to Congress. Since GAO's 2007 report, the Biggert-Waters Flood Insurance Reform Act of 2012 created a technical mapping advisory council, which must produce a "Future Conditions Risk Assessment and Modeling Report" with recommendations on how to ensure (1) rate maps incorporate best available climate science, and (2) FEMA uses the best available methodology to consider the impact of rising sea levels and future development on flood risk.[19] The act requires the council to submit a risk assessment report to FEMA, which FEMA is then required to incorporate into its ongoing program to review and update rate maps.

In June 2011, GAO reported on other actions needed to improve the administration of the National Flood Insurance Program.[20] This report found that external factors continue to complicate the administration of the National Flood Insurance Program and affect its financial stability. Specifically, as it relates to climate change and sea level rise, FEMA, historically, has not been authorized to account for long-term erosion when updating flood maps used to set premium rates for the National Flood Insurance Program. Flood maps are supposed to accurately estimate the likelihood of flooding in specific areas given certain characteristics including elevation and topography, but they can quickly become inaccurate because of changes from long-term erosion, particularly in coastal areas.[21] This could prove problematic in areas susceptible to sea level rise. Not accurately reflecting the actual risk of flooding increases the likelihood that even full-risk premiums will not cover future losses and adds to concerns about the National Flood Insurance Program's financial stability. Consequently, among a range of other recommendations, GAO in June 2011 presented a matter for congressional consideration to authorize the National Flood Insurance

---

[19]Pub. L. No 112-141, tit. II, subtit. A, § 100215(d) (2012).

[20]GAO, *FEMA: Action Needed to Improve Administration of the National Flood Insurance Program*, GAO-11-297 (Washington, D.C.: June 9, 2011).

[21]For more information about FEMA's challenges related to flood maps, see GAO, *FEMA Flood Maps: Some Standards and Processes in Place to Promote Map Accuracy and Outreach, but Opportunities Exist to Address Implementation Challenges*, GAO-11-17 (Washington, D.C.: Dec. 2, 2010).

Program to account for long-term flood erosion in its flood maps.[22] The Biggert-Waters Flood Insurance Reform Act of 2012 requires FEMA to use, among other things, information on topography, coastal erosion areas, changing lake levels, future changes in sea levels, and intensity of hurricanes in updating its flood maps. While these provisions respond to GAO's suggestion to Congress, their ultimate effectiveness will depend on their implementation by FEMA. It is too early to evaluate such efforts, but GAO plans to examine the National Flood Insurance Program in the near future.

Technical assistance to state and local governments. Federal efforts are beginning to shift their focus to adaptation and to the provision of information to state and local decision makers so they can make more informed decisions about the fiscal exposure posed by potential climate impacts. As GAO reported in October 2009, challenges from insufficient site-specific data—such as local temperature and precipitation projections—make it hard for state and local officials to justify the current costs of adaptation efforts for potentially less certain future benefits.[23] For example, planning decisions involving infrastructure projects require large up front capital investments, and the long lead time and life of such projects requires adaptive decisions to be made well before potential climate change effects are discernable. The federal government annually invests billions of dollars in infrastructure projects that state and local governments prioritize and supervise. For example, state and local governments control zoning decisions and make decisions about how to build certain types of critical infrastructure that are vulnerable to climate change, such as roads and bridges. Challenges providing technical assistance to state and local decision makers generally fit into two main categories: (1) translating climate data—such as projected temperature and precipitation changes—into information that officials need to make decisions, and (2) the difficulty in justifying the current costs of adaptation with limited information about future benefits.

---

[22]GAO-11-297 also contained two other related matters for congressional consideration: (1) allowing the National Flood Insurance Program to charge full-risk premium rates to all property owners and providing assistance to some categories of owners to pay those premiums and (2) clarifying and expanding FEMA's ability to increase premiums or discontinue coverage for owners of certain repetitive loss properties.

[23]GAO-10-113.

In GAO's October 2009 recommendation that the appropriate entities within the Executive Office of the President develop a strategic plan for adaptation, GAO stated that the plan should, among other things, identify mechanisms to increase the capacity of federal, state, and local agencies to incorporate information about current and potential climate change impacts into government decision making. USGCRP's 2012-2021 strategic plan for climate change science, released in April 2012, recognizes this need by identifying enhanced information management and sharing as a key objective. USGCRP is pursing the development of a global change information system to support coordinated use and application of federal climate science. USGCRP plans to leverage existing tools, services, and portals from the USGCRP agencies to develop a "one-stop shop" for accessing global change data and information, according to the strategic plan. GAO has ongoing work related to these issues.

In addition, gaps in satellite coverage, which could occur as soon as 2014, are expected to affect the continuity of climate and space weather measurements important to developing the information needed by state and local officials.[24] According to National Oceanic and Atmospheric Administration program officials, a satellite data gap would result in less accurate and timely weather forecasts and warnings of extreme events— such as hurricanes, storm surges and floods. Such degradation in forecasts and warnings would place lives, property, and the nation's critical infrastructure in danger. Given the importance of satellite data to weather forecasts, the likelihood of significant gaps, and the potential impact of such gaps on the health and safety of the U.S. population and economy, GAO has concluded that the potential gap in weather satellite data is a high-risk area and added it to the High Risk List this year. The importance of such data was recently highlighted by the advance warnings of the path, timing, and intensity of Superstorm Sandy. GAO made several recommendations to establish mitigation plans for pending satellite gaps, and GAO has ongoing work assessing related agency efforts.

---

[24]See, for example, GAO, *Environmental Satellites: Focused Attention Needed to Mitigate Program Risks*, GAO-12-841T (Washington, D.C.: June 27, 2012). See also GAO, *Environmental Satellites: Strategy Needed to Sustain Critical Climate and Space Weather Measurements*, GAO-10-456 (Washington, D.C.: Apr. 27, 2010).

Disaster aid. Federal disaster aid functions as the insurance of last resort in certain circumstances, increasing the federal government's fiscal exposure to a changing climate. Weather-related events—some of which have been observed and are projected by NRC and USGCRP to become more frequent and intense due to climate change—have cost the nation tens of billions of dollars in damages over the past decade. In 2012, for example, Superstorm Sandy caused tens of billions of dollars in damages to buildings, utilities, transportation systems, and other infrastructure. Whatever is not covered by insurance or built to be resilient to such events increases the federal government's implicit fiscal exposure through federal disaster relief programs. Fiscal constraints will make it more difficult for the federal government to respond effectively in the future, and such expenses could affect resources available for other key government programs.

As GAO reported in September 2012, disaster declarations have increased over recent decades, and FEMA has obligated over $80 billion in federal assistance for disasters declared during fiscal years 2004 through 2011.[25] The growing number of disaster declarations—a record 98 in fiscal year 2011 compared with 65 in 2004—has contributed to increased federal disaster costs. FEMA has had difficulty implementing longstanding plans to assess national preparedness capabilities to prepare for and respond effectively to these disasters. Its efforts have been repeatedly delayed and are not yet complete.[26] In addition, FEMA's indicator for determining whether to recommend that a jurisdiction receive disaster assistance is artificially low because it does not accurately reflect the ability of state and local governments to respond to disasters. GAO's 2012 report and others have identified challenges in the determination of costs to be borne by federal, state, and local governments or the private sector in preparing for, responding to, and recovering from disasters of all

---

[25]GAO-12-838.

[26]GAO, *Managing Preparedness Grants and Assessing National Capabilities: Continuing Challenges Impede FEMA Progress*, GAO-12-526T (Washington, D.C.: Mar. 20, 2012). See also GAO, *Disaster Response: Criteria for Developing and Validating Effective Response Plans*, GAO-10-969T (Washington, D.C.: Sept. 22, 2010).

types.[27] In September 2012, GAO recommended, among other things, that FEMA develop a methodology to more accurately assess a jurisdiction's capability to respond to and recover from a disaster without federal assistance. FEMA concurred with this recommendation.

In the event of a major disaster, federal funding for response and recovery comes from the Disaster Relief Fund managed by FEMA and disaster aid programs of other participating federal agencies. These programs are provided emergency supplemental appropriations to cover the costs of damages. The federal government does not budget for these costs, and without proper budgeting and forecasting to account for these events, the federal government runs the risk of facing a large fiscal exposure at any time. Further increasing the challenge faced by the federal government in managing such fiscal exposures is that annual budget requests and appropriations for disaster relief do not include all known costs from still open disaster declarations, in particular those from catastrophic disasters.[28] This has led to requests for supplemental appropriations not only for new disasters, but also for costs related to ongoing, past disasters. As a result, decision makers may not have a comprehensive view of overall funding claims and trade-offs.

What Remains to Be Done

The federal government needs a strategic approach with strong leadership and the authority to manage climate change risks that encompasses the entire range of related federal activities and addresses all key elements of strategic planning. Such an approach includes the establishment of strategic priorities and the development of roles, responsibilities, and working relationships among federal, state, and local

---

[27]Since September 11, 2001, the federal government has provided billions of dollars to state and local governments for planning, equipment, and training to enhance the capabilities of first responders to respond to both smaller-scale natural disasters and terrorist attacks. However, the federal financial assistance provided in the last several years has not been guided by a clear risk-based strategic plan that outlines the role of federal, state, and local governments in identifying, enhancing, maintaining, and financing critical first responder capabilities for emergencies. See GAO, *21st Century Challenges: Reexamining the Base of the Federal Government*, GAO-05-325SP (Washington, D.C.: Feb. 1, 2005).

[28]GAO, *Disaster Cost Estimates: FEMA Can Improve Its Learning From Past Experience and Management of Disaster-Related Resources*, GAO-08-301 (Washington, D.C.: Feb. 22, 2008). See also GAO, *Supplemental Appropriations: Opportunities Exist to Increase Transparency and Provide Additional Controls*, GAO-08-314 (Washington, D.C.: Jan. 31, 2008).

entities. Recognizing that each department and agency operates under its own authorities and responsibilities—and can therefore be expected to address climate change in different ways relevant to its own mission—existing federal efforts have encouraged a decentralized approach, with federal agencies incorporating climate-related information into their planning, operations, policies, and programs. While individual agency actions are necessary, a centralized strategy driven by a government-wide plan is also needed to reduce the federal fiscal exposure to climate change, maximize investments, achieve efficiencies, and better position the government for success. Even then, such approaches will not be fully sufficient unless also coordinated with decisions at the state and local levels that drive much of the federal government's fiscal exposure. The challenge is to develop a cohesive approach at the federal level that also informs action at the state and local levels.

In addition to addressing these broad strategic challenges, there are specific areas among many that may require attention including:

- *Federal flood and crop insurance programs.* This entails developing the information needed to understand and manage federal insurance programs' long-term exposure to climate change and analyze the potential impacts of an increase in the frequency or severity of weather-related events on their operations. There is a need to consider climate-related factors such as sea level rise and long-term erosion when updating flood maps, for example. GAO has ongoing work related to climate change and federal insurance programs.

- *Technical assistance to state and local governments.* This involves developing a government-wide approach for providing (1) the best available climate-related data for making decisions at the state and local level and (2) assistance for translating available climate-related data into information that officials need to make decisions. GAO has ongoing work on the climate-related information needs of local infrastructure decision makers.

- *Environmental satellites.* Potential gaps in satellite data need to be effectively addressed. The National Oceanic and Atmospheric Administration must make difficult decisions on which technical, programmatic, and management steps it will implement to ensure that its preliminary plans to address potential gaps in satellite data are viable when needed. GAO has ongoing work assessing the National Oceanic and Atmospheric Administration's actions on its satellite programs to determine whether its plans are viable. GAO has concluded that the potential gap in weather satellite data is a high-risk area and added it to the High Risk List this year.

- *Disaster aid.* FEMA needs improved criteria to assess a jurisdiction's capability to respond and recover on its own, and also to better apply lessons from past experience when developing disaster cost estimates so decision makers have a comprehensive view of overall funding claims and trade-offs. GAO has ongoing work related to disaster assistance and budgeting for emergencies.

GAO Contact

For additional information about this high-risk area, contact Alfredo Gomez at 202-512-3841 or gomezj@gao.gov.

Related GAO Products

Federal Disaster Assistance: Improved Criteria Needed to Assess a Jurisdiction's Capability to Respond and Recover on Its Own. GAO-12-838. Washington, D.C.: September 12, 2012.

FEMA: Action Needed to Improve Administration of the National Flood Insurance Program. GAO-11-297. Washington, D.C.: June 9, 2011.

Climate Change: Improvements Needed to Clarify National Priorities and Better Align Them with Federal Funding Decisions. GAO-11-317. Washington, D.C.: April 27, 2010.

Environmental Satellites: Strategy Needed to Sustain Critical Climate and Space Weather Measurements. GAO-10-456. Washington, D.C.: April 27, 2010.

Climate Change Adaptation: Strategic Federal Planning Could Help Government Officials Make More Informed Decisions. GAO-10-113. Washington, D.C.: October 7, 2009.

Disaster Cost Estimates: FEMA Can Improve Its Learning From Past Experience and Management of Disaster-Related Resources. GAO-08-301. Washington, D.C.: February 22, 2008.

Supplemental Appropriations: Opportunities Exist to Increase Transparency and Provide Additional Controls. GAO-08-314. Washington, D.C.: January 31, 2008.

Climate Change: Agencies Should Develop Guidance for Addressing the Effects on Federal Land and Water Resources. GAO-07-863. Washington, D.C.: August 7, 2007.

Climate Change: Financial Risks to Federal and Private Insurers in Coming Decades Are Potentially Significant. GAO-07-285. Washington, D.C.: March 16, 2007.

Management of Federal Oil and Gas Resources

Why Area Is High Risk

GAO's work has identified challenges in the Department of the Interior's (Interior) management of oil and gas on leased federal lands and waters; specifically, Interior (1) does not have reasonable assurance that it is collecting its share of revenue from oil and gas produced on federal lands and (2) continues to experience problems in hiring, training and retaining sufficient staff to provide oversight and management of oil and gas operations on federal lands and waters. As a result, GAO concluded that management of federal oil and gas resources is a high-risk area and added it to the High Risk List in 2011.

Federal oil and gas resources provide an important source of energy for the United States; create jobs in the oil and gas industry; and generate billions of dollars annually in revenues that are shared between federal, state, and tribal governments. Revenue generated from federal oil and gas production is one of the largest nontax sources of federal government funds, accounting for about $9 billion in fiscal year 2009 and $10.1 billion in each of fiscal years 2010 and 2011. Also, the explosion onboard the Deepwater Horizon and oil spill in the Gulf of Mexico in April 2010 emphasized the importance of Interior's management of permitting and inspection processes to ensure operational and environmental safety.

Historically, Interior's Bureau of Land Management (BLM) managed onshore federal oil and gas activities while the Minerals Management Service (MMS) managed offshore activities and collected royalties for all leases. Interior recently restructured its oil and gas program, transferring offshore oversight responsibilities to two new bureaus, the Bureau of Ocean Energy Management (BOEM) and the Bureau of Safety and Environmental Enforcement (BSEE), and assigning the revenue collection function to a new Office of Natural Resources Revenue. This restructuring did not include BLM's management of onshore federal oil and gas activities.

What GAO Found

In July 2012, GAO reported that Interior had reorganized its oversight of offshore oil and gas activities when it established two new bureaus— BOEM and BSEE—to provide oversight of offshore resources and operational compliance with environmental and safety requirements. This reorganization had originally been a factor that GAO considered high risk, particularly because the reorganization was begun in the immediate aftermath of the Deepwater Horizon incident, when many of the agency's resources were engaged in the incident response. However, because Interior completed that reorganization, GAO is narrowing the federal oil and gas high-risk area to focus on the remaining issues related to revenue collection and human capital challenges. Interior continues to face ongoing challenges in these two broad areas:

- *Revenue collection.* In 2010, GAO reported that neither BLM nor MMS (the predecessor to BOEM and BSEE) had consistently met their statutory requirements or agency goals for oil and gas production verification inspections. Without such verification, Interior cannot provide reasonable assurance that the public is collecting its legal share of revenue from oil and gas development on federal lands and waters. In addition, in 2009, GAO reported on numerous problems with Interior's efforts to collect data on oil and gas produced on federal lands, including missing data, errors in company-reported data on oil and gas production, sales data that did not reflect prevailing market prices for oil and gas, and a lack of controls over changes to the data that companies reported. As a result of Interior's lack of consistent and reliable data on the production and sale of oil and gas from federal lands, Interior could not provide reasonable assurance that it was assessing and collecting the appropriate amount of royalties on this production. GAO made a number of recommendations to Interior to improve controls on the accuracy and reliability of royalty data. Interior generally agreed with GAO's recommendations and is working to implement many of them, but these efforts are not complete and it remains uncertain at this time if they will be fully successful. For example, in response to a GAO recommendation that Interior undertake a comprehensive reassessment of its revenue collection policies and processes, Interior contracted for such a study with the goal of informing decisions about lease terms, including royalties. However, while the study has been completed, Interior is still in the process of deciding if and how to use the results of the study to alter its lease terms.

- *Human capital.* GAO has reported that the bureaus responsible for oversight and management of federal oil and gas resources on federal lands and in federal waters—BLM, BOEM, and BSEE—have encountered persistent problems in hiring, training, and retaining staff. For example, in 2010, GAO found that BLM and MMS (the predecessor to BOEM and BSEE) experienced high turnover rates in key oil and gas inspection and engineering positions. As a result, Interior faces challenges meeting its responsibilities to oversee oil and gas development on federal leases, potentially placing both the environment and royalties at risk. While Interior's reorganization of its offshore management of oil and gas includes plans to hire additional staff with expertise in inspections and engineering, these plans have not been fully implemented and it remains unclear whether Interior will be fully successful in hiring, training, and retaining these staff. For fiscal years

2012 and 2013, Congress provided funds to BOEM and BSEE in the Gulf of Mexico to establish higher minimum rates of pay for key positions—chiefly geophysicists, geologists, and petroleum engineers—for up to 25 percent of the usual minimum rate of pay. However, it is uncertain how Interior will address staffing shortfalls to oversee offshore resources long term. In July 2012, GAO reported that, to improve inspector training, Interior was creating a new training program for its inspection staff (such as BSEE's National Offshore Training Program to train inspectors and engineers), but that it may take up to 2 years before new inspection staff are fully trained. Human capital issues also exist at BLM and the management of onshore oil and gas, and these issues were not been fully addressed in Interior's reorganization. For example, Interior has not received congressional approval or funds to establish higher minimum rates of pay for key positions as did BOEM and BSEE.

What Remains to Be Done

Interior must successfully address the challenges GAO has identified, implement open recommendations, and meet its responsibilities to manage federal oil and gas resources in the public interest. While Interior recently began implementing a number of GAO recommendations, including those intended to improve the reliability of data necessary for determining royalties, the agency has yet to implement a number of other recommendations, including those intended to (1) provide reasonable assurance that oil and gas produced from federal leases is accurately measured and that the public is getting an appropriate share of oil and gas revenues and (2) address its long-standing human capital issues. Interior agreed with GAO's recommendations regarding human capital, noting that BOEM pilot and evaluate a workforce planning tool to institutionalize workforce planning and guide the long-term strategic planning process. Similarly, Interior stated that BSEE will develop a comprehensive bureau-wide strategic human capital plan to address anticipated workforce changes and gaps in critical skills and competencies. The target dates for these efforts are the summer and fall of 2013, respectively.

GAO is currently engaged in a review of Interior's collection of revenues from the production of oil and gas on federal lands and waters. As part of this review, GAO will examine Interior's progress, if any, in (1) ensuring the government is getting a fair return for federal oil and gas resources, (2) meeting agency targets for conducting oil and gas production verification inspections, and (3) providing greater assurance that oil and gas production and royalty data are consistent and reliable. In addition, GAO is currently reviewing the extent to which Interior continues to face problems hiring, training, and retaining staff and how this affects Interior's ability to oversee oil and gas activities on federal lands and waters. As part of this effort, GAO will focus on the causes of Interior's human capital challenges, actions taken, and how Interior plans to measure the effectiveness of corrective actions. In addition, while GAO has narrowed the focus of its high-risk review to revenue collection and human capital issues, GAO will, in the course of ongoing work on these issues, continue to consider Interior's reorganization and its affect on the agency's ability to oversee federal lands and waters.

GAO Contact

For additional information about this high-risk area, contact Frank Rusco at (202) 512-3841 or ruscof@gao.gov.

Related GAO Products

Oil and Gas Management: Interior's Reorganization Complete, but Challenges Remain in Implementing New Requirements. GAO-12-423. Washington, D.C.: July 30, 2012.

Interior Has Strengthened Its Oversight of Subsea Well Containment, but Should Improve Its Documentation. GAO-12-244. Washington, D.C.: February 29, 2012.

Oil and Gas: Interior's Restructuring Challenges in the Aftermath of the Gulf Oil Spill. GAO-11-734T. Washington, D.C.: June 2, 2011.

Federal Oil and Gas Leases: Opportunities Exist to Capture Vented and Flared Natural Gas, Which Would Increase Royalty Payments and Reduce Greenhouse Gases. GAO-11-34. Washington, D.C.: October 29, 2010.

Oil and Gas Management: Interior's Oil and Gas Production Verification Efforts Do Not Provide Reasonable Assurance of Accurate Measurement of Production Volumes. GAO-10-313. Washington, D.C.: March 15, 2010.

Offshore Oil and Gas Development: Additional Guidance Would Help Strengthen the Minerals Management Service's Assessment of Environmental Impacts in the North Aleutian Basin. GAO-10-276. Washington, D.C.: March 8, 2010.

Energy Policy Act of 2005: Greater Clarity Needed to Address Concerns with Categorical Exclusions for Oil and Gas Development under Section 390 of the Act. GAO-09-872. Washington, D.C.: September 16, 2009.

Mineral Revenues: MMS Could Do More to Improve the Accuracy of Key Data Used to Collect and Verify Oil and Gas Royalties. GAO-09-549. Washington, D.C.: July 15, 2009.

Oil and Gas Leasing: Interior Could Do More to Encourage Diligent Development. GAO-09-74. Washington, D.C.: October 3, 2008.

Mineral Revenues: Data Management Problems and Reliance on Reported Data for Compliance Efforts Put MMS Royalty Collections at Risk. GAO-08-893R. Washington, D.C.: September 12, 2008.

Oil and Gas Royalties: The Federal System for Collecting Oil and Gas Revenues Needs Comprehensive Reassessment. GAO-08-691. Washington, D.C.: September 3, 2008.

Oil and Gas Royalties: Royalty Relief Will Cost the Government Billions of Dollars but Uncertainty Over Future Energy Prices and Production Levels Make Precise Estimates Impossible at this Time. GAO-07-590R. Washington, D.C.: April 12, 2007.

Oil and Gas Development: Increased Permitting Activity Has Lessened BLM's Ability to Meet Its Environmental Protection Responsibilities. GAO-05-418. Washington, D.C.: June 17, 2005.

Results-Oriented Cultures: Implementation Steps to Assist Mergers and Organizational Transformations. GAO-03-669. Washington, D.C.: July 2, 2003.

Modernizing the U.S. Financial Regulatory System and Federal Role in Housing Finance

Why Area Is High Risk

The United States continues to recover from the aftermath of the worst financial crisis in more than 75 years, which led to federal assistance being provided to many firms, including the two large housing-related government-sponsored enterprises (the enterprises). These events clearly demonstrated that the U.S. financial regulatory system was in need of significant reform. GAO designated reform of the financial regulatory system as a high-risk area in 2009. Since then, the Federal Housing Administration's (FHA) mortgage insurance portfolio has continued to grow, and its insurance fund has experienced major financial difficulties. Accordingly, the title and scope of this high-risk area has evolved from *Modernizing the Outdated U.S. Financial Regulatory System* to *Modernizing the U.S. Financial Regulatory System and Federal Role in Housing Finance.*

What GAO Found

During the past few decades, the U.S. financial regulatory system failed to adapt to significant changes. First, although the U.S. financial system had increasingly become dominated by large interconnected financial conglomerates, no single regulator was tasked with monitoring and assessing the risks that these firms' activities posed across the entire financial system. Second, various entities, such as nonbank mortgage lenders, hedge funds, and credit rating agencies, were not subject to sufficiently comprehensive regulation and oversight, despite their critical roles in financial markets. Third, the regulatory system was not effective at providing key information and protections for new and more complex financial products for consumers and investors. Taking steps to better position regulators to oversee firms and products that pose risks to the financial system and consumers and adapt to new products and participants as they arise could reduce the likelihood that the financial markets will experience another financial crisis similar to one in 2007-2009. Losses from risky mortgage products also resulted in two large housing-related enterprises—Fannie Mae and Freddie Mac—being placed into government conservatorship, and the distressed housing and mortgage markets have led to a growing role by the Department of Housing and Urban Development's FHA in mortgage finance.

Since the crisis, policymakers have taken significant actions intended to reform the U.S. financial regulatory system to address the risks associated with evolving financial firms, markets, and products. After considerable debate within the administration and Congress, in July 2010, the Dodd-Frank Wall Street Reform and Consumer Protection Act (Dodd-Frank Act) was enacted. The Dodd-Frank Act's reforms aim to better position the financial regulatory system in many of the areas addressing the changes and risks that GAO identified.

- A new Financial Stability Oversight Council made up of the various financial regulators was created to identify risks to U.S. financial stability, including risks posed by large, interconnected financial conglomerates. This council has begun operating, including holding numerous meetings and issuing various congressionally-mandated studies and two annual reports addressing market and regulatory developments across the financial system. The new office that is intended to collect and analyze data to assist this council—the Office of Financial Research—has also begun hiring staff and conducting activities, such as assisting with a global effort to develop a worldwide standard for uniquely identifying parties to financial transactions.

- Financial regulators are also making progress in issuing proposed rules to implement the Dodd-Frank Act's requirements that U.S. bank holding companies with total consolidated assets of $50 billion or more and U.S. nonbank financial companies supervised by the Federal Reserve be subject to enhanced prudential standards and oversight, including enhanced requirements for these firms regarding their capital, leverage, liquidity, and stress testing efforts.

- The act also creates a new resolution authority to address failing financial firms whose disorderly resolution would have serious adverse effects on U.S. financial stability by granting the Federal Deposit Insurance Corporation the authority to liquidate large financial firms, including nonbanks, outside of the bankruptcy process. After banking regulators finalized related rules, the large financial institutions first required to prepare the resolution plans—"living wills"—called for under this authority submitted their plans to regulators as expected in July 2012.

- Securities and futures regulators are also attempting to finalize many of the rules that will create a new regulatory structure and requirements for the over-the-counter derivatives known as swaps. This new regulatory framework for swaps is intended to reduce risk, increase transparency, and promote market integrity by, among other things, moving trading to exchanges and requiring trades to be centrally cleared.

- Regulators have also made progress in implementing additional requirements and oversight on advisers to hedge and private funds and credit rating agencies that were previously subject to less regulation. For example, final rules were issued specifying the information that hedge fund advisers that trade either securities or futures should provide to these regulators periodically. The Securities and Exchange Commission has also created a new internal office to oversee credit rating agency activities and additional requirements for these entities are forthcoming.

- To address concerns over consumer regulation, the new Bureau of Consumer Financial Protection—a new agency created by the Dodd-Frank Act—has begun operations. This entity now has responsibility for consumer protection laws previously overseen by different regulators. It has been issuing rules and begun taking enforcement actions, including obtaining refunds for consumers and imposing penalties on certain credit card issuers for practices that violated the law.

A variety of challenges affected regulators' progress in fully implementing the act's reforms. Regulators noted that completing rules has taken time because of the number and complexity of the issues and because many rules are interconnected. Further, regulators said that implementing the act's reforms require a great deal of coordination, at the domestic and international levels, which increased the amount of time needed to finalize rulemakings. Finally, regulators noted that they have prioritized developing responsive, appropriate rules over meeting tight statutory deadlines. As a result, some of the important rules are taking considerable time to develop.

Some actions were also taken to address the role of the two housing enterprises. Both continue to operate under the conservatorship placed on them in September 2008, but continue to support the majority of single-family mortgage loans. As of the end of fiscal year 2012, under agreements with Treasury, these enterprises had received over $187 billion, although recently both entities began earning profits that are being returned to the U.S. Treasury. In February 2011, the Department of the Treasury and the Department of Housing and Urban Development issued a plan that outlines a vision for the government's role in housing finance, including reducing the activities of the two enterprises over time until they are eventually wound down completely. In addition, in 2012, the Federal Housing Finance Agency (FHFA), which oversees the enterprises' operations, put out a strategic plan that identified three strategic goals for the next phase of Fannie Mae and Freddie Mac conservatorships, including building a new infrastructure for the secondary mortgage market, gradually contracting the enterprises' dominant presence in the marketplace while simplifying and shrinking their operations, and maintaining foreclosure prevention activities and credit availability for both new and refinanced mortgages. In August 2012, this agency took two actions affecting the enterprises. First, to encourage greater participation in housing markets by private firms, FHFA directed Fannie Mae and Freddie Mac to raise the fees they charge lenders for securitizing mortgage loans to reduce the cost difference between securitizations done by the enterprises compared to those done by private firms. Second, FHFA, in conjunction with Treasury, revised the senior preferred stock purchase agreements to have the enterprises pay dividends to the U.S. Treasury based on their net worth when positive rather than as a fixed percentage of the outstanding senior preferred stock, which, among other things, should eliminate the need for the enterprises to borrow from Treasury to pay such dividends. In October 2012, FHFA also sought public comment on a proposal for developing a new mortgage securitization platform to process payments and perform other functions that could be used by multiple issuers that would replace the enterprises' proprietary systems.

Decisions about the future role of the enterprises will need to consider impacts on other parts of the housing finance system, including the single-family mortgage insurance programs of FHA. During the recent financial crisis, FHA's insurance activity rose dramatically and provided key support to distressed housing and mortgage markets. However, FHA's financial condition deteriorated rapidly over the same period. As GAO has reported, since 2009, FHA's Mutual Mortgage Insurance (MMI) Fund has not met its statutory 2-percent capital requirement. Further, a weakening in the performance of FHA-insured mortgages has heightened the possibility that FHA will require funding from the U.S. Treasury to help cover its costs on insurance issued to date. FHA has taken a number of steps to improve its financial health and help reduce its market share, including fee increases and underwriting changes, but additional actions may be necessary. GAO previously recommended that Congress or FHA specify the economic conditions that the MMI Fund would be expected to withstand without drawing on the Treasury. Recent events suggest that the 2-percent capital requirement may not be adequate to avoid the need for Treasury support under severe stress scenarios. Implementing this recommendation would be an important step not only in addressing FHA's long-term financial viability, but also in clarifying FHA's role. Efforts to reduce the market presence of the enterprises could shift some borrowers currently served by that market segment to FHA, and the resulting impacts on FHA's risk exposure should be considered. In addition, changes in the role of the enterprises will need to consider interactions with mortgage market reforms contained in the Dodd-Frank Act. For example, regulations required by the Dodd-Frank Act will have major implications for the size and borrower composition of the private-label market for mortgage-backed securities, which, in turn, could affect the risk exposure of FHA and the enterprises.

Although mandating a broad range of reforms, the Dodd-Frank Act did not address other risks that many see as significant and worthy of regulatory attention. For example, concerns have been raised about the potential systemic risks posed by money market funds. These funds provide short-term funding to many financial institutions but lack capital buffers and other protections that could reduce the likelihood of destabilizing runs on their holdings. The Securities and Exchange Commission has taken some actions to increase these funds' resiliency and in November 2012 the Financial Stability Oversight Council approved for public comment various additional reforms for these funds. Concerns also continue about the potential systemic implications of certain concentrations of credit risk. These include the potential for serious problems to arise from the failure of one of the two institutions that provide credit to facilitate transactions in the tri-party repurchase (repo) market that provides short-term funding to many financial institutions. Similarly, concerns exist over the increased concentration of risk arising from the act's movement of swaps to clearinghouses. Although this change can reduce the market's risk, a systemic disruption could occur if financial soundness problems affected a clearinghouse. Various proposals for action to address these risks have been put forward, but policymakers and financial regulators have not taken definitive actions to implement them.

What Remains to Be Done

These financial regulatory reforms currently underway represent significant steps in this high-risk area. However, many of the rules to implement the new regulatory requirements arising from the act are yet to be completed. As of December 2012, regulators had issued final rules for about 48 percent of the 236 provisions of the act that GAO identified as necessitating regulators to issue rulemakings. However, in some cases the dates by which affected entities had to comply with the rules had yet to be reached. Of the remaining provisions, regulators had proposed rules for about 29 percent, and rulemakings had not occurred for about 23 percent. In some cases, progress has been made but has been slowed to address market participant concerns. For example, the rules implementing new capital requirements for all banks were proposed in June 2012 and were to begin becoming effective by January 2013, but banking regulators announced that this implementation will be postponed to provide more time In light of the volume of comments received and the wide range of views expressed during the comment period.

The reforms that have been implemented also need attention to help ensure their effectiveness. For example, the Financial Stability Oversight Council faces various challenges to ensuring that it achieves its mission, given that identifying risks to financial stability is difficult, vast, and procedurally complex. It also must ensure that it achieves effective collaboration among its many members, almost all of whom come from state and federal agencies with their own specific statutory missions. In a September 2012 report, GAO concluded that whether this council and the Office of Financial Research will fundamentally change the way the federal government monitors threats to financial stability remains to be seen. GAO also made various recommendations to strengthen their accountability and transparency, including having these entities clarify their monitoring responsibilities to better ensure that the monitoring and analysis of the financial system are comprehensive and not unnecessarily duplicative, and systematically sharing key financial risk indicators among member agencies to assist in identifying potential threats for further monitoring or analysis.

The ultimate resolution of the two failed housing enterprises also remains undone. Although various proposals to resolve their role have been issued, no definitive actions have been taken as of yet. Similarly, further actions could be taken to help restore FHA's financial soundness and define its future role. To improve its condition, FHA has implemented fee increases and underwriting changes, but as GAO previously concluded, Congress or FHA needs to determine the economic conditions that FHA's primary insurance fund would be expected to withstand without drawing on the Treasury. Finally, definitive actions to address the risk posed by money market funds and the credit exposures arising in the triparty repo market and within clearinghouses also remain outstanding.

GAO Contact

For additional information about this high-risk area, contact Orice Williams Brown at (202) 512-8678 or williamso@gao.gov.

Related GAO Products

Financial Regulatory Reform: Regulators Have Faced Challenges Finalizing Key Reforms and Unaddressed Areas Pose Potential Risks. GAO-13-195. Washington, D.C.: January 23, 2013.

Financial Regulatory Reform: Financial Crisis Losses and Potential Impacts of the Dodd-Frank Act. GAO-13-180. Washington, D.C.: January 16, 2013.

*Dodd-Frank Act: Agencies' Efforts to Analyze and Coordinate Their
Rules.* GAO-13-101. Washington, D.C.: December 18, 2012.

*Financial Stability: New Council and Research Office Should Strengthen
the Accountability and Transparency of Their Decisions.* GAO-12-886.
Washington, D.C.: September 11, 2012.

*Credit Rating Agencies: Alternative Compensation Models for Nationally
Recognized Statistical Rating Organizations.* GAO-12-240. Washington,
D.C.: January 18, 2012.

*Bank Capital Requirements: Potential Effects of New Changes on Foreign
Holding Companies and U.S. Banks Abroad.* GAO-12-235. Washington,
D.C.: January 17, 2012.

*Dodd-Frank Act Regulations: Implementation Could Benefit from
Additional Analyses and Coordination.* GAO-12-151. Washington, D.C.:
November 10, 2011.

*Federal Housing Administration: Improvements Needed in Risk
Assessment and Human Capital Management.* GAO-12-15. Washington,
D.C.: November 7, 2011.

*Mortgage Financing: Opportunities to Enhance Management and
Oversight of FHA's Financial Condition.* GAO-10-827R. Washington,
D.C.: September 14, 2010.

*Fannie Mae and Freddie Mac: Analysis of Options for Revising the
Housing Enterprises' Long-term Structures.* GAO-10-144T. Washington,
D.C.: October 8, 2009.

*Financial Regulation: Recent Crisis Reaffirms the Need to Overhaul the
U.S. Regulatory System.* GAO-09-1049T. Washington, D.C.: September
29, 2009.

*Financial Regulation: A Framework for Crafting and Assessing Proposals
to Modernize the Outdated U.S. Financial Regulatory System.*
GAO-09-216. Washington, D.C.: January 8, 2009.

*Mortgage Financing: FHA's Fund Has Grown, but Options for Drawing on
the Fund Have Uncertain Outcomes.* GAO-01-460. Washington, D.C.:
February 28, 2001.

Restructuring the U.S. Postal Service to Achieve Sustainable Financial Viability

Why Area Is High Risk

Amid challenging economic conditions, a changing business environment, and declining mail volumes, the U.S. Postal Service (USPS) is facing a deteriorating financial situation in which it does not have sufficient revenues to cover its expenses and financial obligations.

Mail volume has declined from 213 billion pieces in fiscal year 2006 to about 160 billion pieces in fiscal year 2012. USPS has projected that volume will decline to about 144 billion pieces by 2016. Further, volume for First-Class Mail, USPS's most profitable product, has declined by 30 percent since 2006 and USPS has projected that it will decline by another 23 percent by 2016. This trend exposes weaknesses in USPS's business model, which has relied on mail volume growth to help cover USPS expenses. USPS actions to improve its financial condition have been limited in part by legal requirements, such as those related to changing the frequency of mail delivery and closing unneeded facilities. Unless USPS can move more aggressively to reduce the gap between its costs and revenues, its financial losses will continue to grow as its viability becomes more difficult to manage. In July 2009, GAO added USPS's financial condition to the list of high-risk areas needing attention by Congress and the executive branch to achieve broad-based restructuring.

What GAO Found

USPS cannot fund its current level of service and operations from its revenues; has a retiree health benefit liability of about $94 billion; and did not have sufficient cash or borrowing authority to make retiree health benefit prefunding payments totaling $11.1 billion for the last 2 years, which contributed to a net loss of almost $16 billion for fiscal year 2012. Although USPS has reduced its expenses, it has not been able to cut costs fast enough to offset the large decline in mail volume and revenue. Further, although USPS has generated new revenue, primarily from package delivery services, its total revenue continues to decline. USPS reached its $15 billion borrowing limit in fiscal year 2012, thus risking a lack of liquidity. USPS urgently needs to restructure to reflect changes in its customers' use of the mail, to align its costs with revenues, generate sufficient funding for capital investment, and manage its debt (see table 4).

Table 4: USPS Financial Results, Fiscal Years 2006 through 2012

Numbers in billions

Fiscal year	Net income	Year-end debt	Total mail volume
2006	$0.9	$2.1	213
2007	(5.1)	4.2	212
2008	(2.8)	7.2	203
2009	(3.8)	10.2	177
2010	(8.5)	12.0	171
2011	(5.1)	13.0	168
2012	(15.9)	15.0	160

Source: USPS.

Note: Congress reduced USPS's retiree health benefit prefunding payment by $4 billion in fiscal year 2009, and delayed its $5.5 billion prefunding payment for fiscal year 2011 until August 2012. USPS did not make the prefunding payments totaling $11.1 billion for fiscal years 2011 and 2012.

In February 2012, USPS issued a 5-year plan with specific actions to close a projected $21 billion gap between its costs and revenues by 2016 and took actions to implement parts of the plan that did not require congressional approval. These actions included reducing its career workforce by over 55,000 employees and closing 111 mail processing facilities. USPS has also asked Congress to restructure the funding of its pension and retiree health benefit obligations and allow it to reduce the frequency of mail delivery from 6 to 5 days per week. Both the Senate and House of Representatives considered several bills with different approaches to addressing USPS's financial problems, and by the end of 2012, the Senate had passed postal reform legislation, but the House had not. The President's fiscal year 2013 budget request also proposed postal reforms, including restructuring USPS pension and retiree health benefit funding and giving USPS the authority to reduce mail delivery frequency from 6 to 5 days.

GAO has issued a number of reports on strategies and options for USPS to generate revenues, reduce costs, increase efficiency by optimizing its workforce and networks, and restructure the funding of USPS pension and retiree health obligations. GAO has also reported that USPS's actions alone under its existing authority will not be sufficient to achieve sustainable financial viability and that comprehensive legislation is urgently needed.

What Remains to Be Done

Congress needs to approve a comprehensive package of actions to improve USPS's financial viability by (1) modifying its retiree health benefit payments in a fiscally responsible manner; (2) facilitating USPS cost reduction so that USPS can reduce excess capacity, consolidate its networks and workforce, and close redundant facilities; and (3) requiring any binding arbitration in the negotiation process for USPS labor contracts to take USPS's financial condition into account. USPS needs to continue taking action to reduce costs related to its operations, workforce, and facilities as well as increase revenues so that it can eliminate its net losses, repay its debt, and generate capital for investments, such as replacing its aging vehicle fleet.

GAO Contact

For additional information about this high-risk area, contact Lorelei St. James at (202) 512-2834 or stjamesl@gao.gov.

Related GAO Products

U.S. Postal Service: Status, Financial Outlook, and Alternative Approaches to Fund Retiree Health Benefits. GAO-13-112. Washington, D.C.: December 4, 2012.

U.S. Postal Service: Challenges Related to Restructuring the Postal Service's Retail Network. GAO-12-433. Washington, D.C.: April 17, 2012.

U.S. Postal Service: Mail Processing Network Exceeds What Is Needed for Declining Mail Volume. GAO-12-470. Washington, D.C.: April 12, 2012.

U.S. Postal Service: Action Needed to Maximize Cost-Saving Potential of Alternatives to Post Offices. GAO-12-100. Washington, D.C.: November 17, 2011.

U.S. Postal Service: Allocation of Responsibility for Pension Benefits between the Postal Service and the Federal Government. GAO-12-146. Washington, D.C.: October 13, 2011.

U.S. Postal Service:, Actions Needed to Stave off Financial Insolvency. GAO-11-926T. Washington, D.C.: September 6, 2011.

United States Postal Service: Strategy Needed to Address Aging Delivery Fleet. GAO-11-386. Washington, D.C.: May 5, 2011.

U.S. Postal Service: Ending Saturday Delivery Would Reduce Costs, but Comprehensive Restructuring Is Also Needed. GAO-11-270. Washington, D.C.: March 29, 2011.

U.S. Postal Service: Foreign Posts' Strategies Could Inform U.S. Postal Service's Efforts to Modernize. GAO-11-282. Washington, D.C.: February 16, 2011.

U.S. Postal Service: Strategies and Options to Facilitate Progress toward Financial Viability. GAO-10-455. Washington, D.C.: April 12, 2010.

Funding the Nation's Surface Transportation System

Why Area Is High Risk

The nation's surface transportation system—including highways, transit, and rail systems that move both people and freight—is critical to the economy and affects the daily lives of most Americans. However, the system is under growing strain, and the cost to repair and upgrade the system to meet current and future demands is estimated in the hundreds of billions of dollars. Yet, calls for increased investments come at a time when traditional funding sources are eroding. Funding is further complicated by the federal government's financial condition and fiscal outlook. Moreover, spending for surface transportation programs has not commensurately improved system performance because many programs do not effectively address key challenges, federal goals and roles are unclear, programs lack links to performance, and some programs do not use the best tools and approaches to ensure effective investment decisions. GAO added this area to its High Risk List in 2007.

What GAO Found

Motor fuel and other truck-related taxes that support the Highway Trust Fund—the major source of federal surface transportation funding—are eroding. Federal motor fuel tax rates have not increased since 1993, and because of inflation, the 18.4 cent per gallon tax on gasoline enacted in 1993 is worth about 11.5 cents today. This trend will likely continue in the years ahead as vehicles become more fuel efficient and use alternative fuels that are not subject to federal fuel taxes. In August 2012, the Congressional Budget Office estimated that $110 billion in additional revenues would be required to maintain current spending levels plus inflation through 2022. To avoid a shortfall in the Highway Trust Fund, Congress transferred more than $34 billion in general revenues to the Highway Trust Fund from fiscal years 2008 to 2010, and in 2012, appropriated an additional $18.8 billion in general revenues for fiscal years 2013 and 2014. This approach has effectively broken the link between highway taxes paid and benefits received by users.

There has been progress in clarifying federal goals and roles and linking federal programs to performance, as GAO has recommended. In July 2012, President Obama signed into law the Moving Ahead for Progress in the 21st Century Act (MAP-21) that included provisions to move toward a more performance-based highway and transit program and to establish a framework to address key challenges in the area of freight movement. For example, for highways, the act identified seven national performance goals for pavement and bridge conditions, injuries and fatalities, traffic congestion, and other areas; requires the Secretary of Transportation, in consultation with states and others, to establish performance measures for these goals; and requires states and other grantees to establish performance targets for those measures and to report their progress in achieving these targets. In addition, MAP-21 links funding to performance by requiring states to take corrective action should progress toward their targets be insufficient, and to spend a specified portion of their annual federal funding to improve bridge conditions and Interstate-system pavement should conditions fall below minimum standards set by the Secretary. For freight movement, including freight rail, the act establishes national goals and directs the Secretary to establish a national freight network, a strategic plan, and tools to support a performance-based approach to evaluate, select, and fund new freight projects.

Passenger rail, which has historically been funded through general revenues and not through the Highway Trust Fund, also presents challenges. The federal government has recently begun to pursue investment in high speed passenger rail through the Federal Railroad Administration's High Speed Intercity Passenger Rail grant program, and to date has obligated about $9.9 billion for 150 high speed intercity passenger rail projects—with more than one-third of the amount obligated designated for a single project in California. While this funding will allow many projects to begin construction, it is not sufficient to complete them. For example, California's high speed rail system is planning to seek as much as $38 billion in additional federal funds to complete its Phase I San Francisco to Los Angeles construction effort. In December 2012, GAO testified before Congress on its preliminary assessment of the California high speed rail project. GAO found some weaknesses in the project's cost estimates and a number of challenges, including identifying funding beyond the first 130-mile construction segment.

In addition to challenges in funding high speed rail projects, the federal government finances nearly all of Amtrak's capital costs. Further, Amtrak's revenues typically do not meet its operating expenses and the federal government subsidizes a portion of these costs. For example, in fiscal year 2011 Amtrak reported that ticket revenue covered about 79 percent of its operating expenses. In fiscal year 2011 the federal government provided about $1.5 billion to Amtrak—about $922 million for capital and debt service and an additional $562 million for operating grants. Amtrak's reliance on federal financial support is likely to continue given its estimated capital needs of about $52 billion for Northeast Corridor improvements through 2030 and an additional $23 billion for locomotive and passenger car replacement by 2040. While Amtrak has taken measures to improve its financial management, such as implementing a Strategic Asset Management System in 2011, these actions are too recent to determine how they will affect Amtrak's financial performance, the need for continued federal subsidies, and the targeting of subsidies to achieve public benefits.

What Remains to Be Done

Congress and the administration need to agree on a long-term plan for funding surface transportation. Continuing to fund the Highway Trust Fund through general revenues may not be sustainable given competing demands and the federal government's fiscal challenges. A sustainable solution is based on balancing revenues to and spending from the Highway Trust Fund. New revenues from users can come only from taxes and fees, and ultimately major changes in transportation spending, revenues, or both will be needed to bring the two into balance. For passenger rail, legislation authorizing federal investments in Amtrak and high speed rail will be up for reauthorization in 2013. With California alone seeking as much as $38 billion for high speed rail, and additional Amtrak investment needs looming, Congress will need to decide how and to what extent to continue to invest in these systems in light of competing demands and the federal government's fiscal challenges.

Successfully implementing a more goal-oriented, performance-based approach to highways may require a clearer definition of the federal role and the responsibilities of the Federal Highway Administration (FHWA). A performance-based program represents substantial new responsibilities for FHWA, and GAO has reported that FHWA's responsibilities have expanded over the years and left the agency, to a large extent, with a broad mandate in an increasingly constrained budget environment. GAO has also reported that opportunities exist to narrow the scope of FHWA's responsibilities—areas where national interests may be less evident or where FHWA expends considerable time and resources yet exercises little effective control. Some programs or activities may better be devolved to state and local governments, if they are better suited to perform them.

GAO Contact

For additional information about this high-risk area, contact Susan Fleming at (202) 512-2834 or flemings@gao.gov.

Related GAO Products

Highway Trust Fund: Pilot Program Could Help Determine Viability of Mileage Fees for Certain Vehicles. GAO-13-77. Washington, D.C.: December 13, 2012.

*Surface Transportation: Financing Program Could Benefit from Increased
Performance Focus and Better Communication.* GAO-12-641.
Washington, D.C.: June 21, 2012.

*Highway Infrastructure: Federal-State Partnership Produces Benefits and
Poses Oversight Risks.* GAO-12-474. Washington, D.C.: April 26, 2012.

Transportation: Key Issues and Management Challenges. GAO-12-581T.
Washington, D.C.: March 29, 2012.

*Highway Trust Fund: All States Received More Funding Than They
Contributed in Highway Taxes from 2005 to 2009.* GAO-11-918.
Washington, D.C.: September 8, 2011.

*Surface Transportation: Competitive Grant Programs Could Benefit from
Increased Performance Focus and Better Documentation of Key
Decisions.* GAO-11-234. Washington, D.C.: March 30, 2011.

*Intercity Passenger Rail: Recording Clearer Reasons for Awards
Decisions Would Improve Otherwise Good Grantmaking Practices.*
GAO-11-283. Washington, D.C.: March 10, 2011.

*Surface Freight Transportation: A Comparison of the Costs of Road, Rail,
and Waterways Freight Shipments That Are Not Passed on to
Consumers.* GAO-11-134. Washington, D.C.: January 26, 2011.

*Statewide Transportation Planning: Opportunities Exist to Transition to
Performance-Based Planning and Federal Oversight.* GAO-11-77.
Washington, D.C.: December 15, 2010.

*Federal Transit Programs: Federal Transit Administration Has
Opportunities to Improve Performance Accountability.* GAO-11-54.
Washington, D.C.: November 17, 2010.

*High Speed Rail: Learning From Service Start-ups, Prospects for
Increased Industry Investment, and Federal Oversight Plans.*
GAO-10-625. Washington, D.C.: June 17, 2010.

*High Speed Passenger Rail: Future Development Will Depend on
Addressing Financial Challenges and Establishing a Clear Federal Role.*
GAO-09-317. Washington, D.C.: March 19, 2009.

*Surface Transportation: Clear Federal Role and Criteria-Based Selection
Process Could Improve Three National and Regional Infrastructure
Programs.* GAO-09-219. Washington, D.C.: February 6, 2009.

*Surface Transportation Programs: Proposals Highlight Key Issues and
Challenges in Restructuring the Programs.* GAO-08-843R. Washington,
D.C.: July 29, 2008.

*Surface Transportation: Restructured Federal Approach Needed for More
Focused, Performance-Based, and Sustainable Programs.* GAO-08-400.
Washington, D.C.: March 6, 2008.

*Freight Transportation: National Policy and Strategies Can Help Improve
Freight Mobility.* GAO-08-287. Washington, D.C.: January 7, 2008.

Strategic Human Capital Management

Why Area Is High Risk	Addressing complex challenges such as disaster response, national and homeland security, and economic stability requires a high-quality federal workforce able to work seamlessly with other agencies, levels of government, and across sectors. However, current budget and long-term fiscal pressures, coupled with a potential wave of employee retirements that could produce gaps in leadership and institutional knowledge, threaten the government's capacity to effectively address these and many other evolving, national issues. The Office of Personnel Management (OPM), individual agencies, and Congress have all taken important steps over the last few years that will better position the government to close current and emerging critical skills gaps that are undermining agencies' abilities to meet their vital missions. Although progress has been made, the area remains high risk because more work is needed in implementing specific corrective strategies for addressing critical skills gaps and evaluating their results. GAO added this area to its High Risk List in 2001.
What GAO Found	In February 2011, GAO reported that closing on-going and emerging critical skills gaps would require agencies to continue to address their specific human capital needs, as well as work with OPM and through the Chief Human Capital Officers (CHCO) Council to address critical skills gaps that cut across several agencies. In particular, actions are needed in three broad areas:

- *Planning.* Identifying the causes of and solutions for skills gaps and steps to implement those solutions.

- *Implementation.* Defining and implementing corrective actions to narrow skills gaps through talent management and other strategies.

- *Measurement and evaluation.* Assessing the effects and evaluating the performance of initiatives to close skills gaps.

Since then, OPM, individual agencies, and Congress have continued to make progress on this issue and have demonstrated top-level leadership involvement. For example, in September 2011, OPM and the CHCO Council—as part of ongoing discussions between OPM, the Office of Management and Budget, and GAO on the steps needed to address the federal government's human capital challenges—established the Chief Human Capital Officers Council Working Group (Working Group) to identify and mitigate critical skills gaps. Underscoring the top leadership commitment to this task, the Working Group is led by OPM and the Department of Defense (DOD); agencies' Chief Human Capital Officers and their representatives were involved in forming the Working Group and are participating in its deliberations. Further, the Working Group's efforts were designated a cross-agency priority goal within the administration's fiscal year 2013 federal budget.

Although much remains to be done, using a multi-faceted approach, including a literature review and an analysis of various staffing gap indicators, the Working Group has thus far identified the following government-wide mission-critical occupations:

- Information technology management/cybersecurity

- Auditor

- Human resources specialist

- Contract specialist

- Economist

- Science, technology, engineering, and mathematics occupational groups

The Working Group also identified seven mission critical competencies, including data analysis, strategic thinking, influencing and negotiating, and problem solving, as well as three grants management competencies. At the same time, individual agencies identified agency-specific mission critical occupations, such as nurses at the Department of Veterans Affairs. The Working Group plans to complete its efforts by March 2013 by which time it intends to implement the strategies to address the skills gaps, monitor and report progress of those strategies, and write a closeout report on its efforts.

OPM and the CHCOs will need to continue their efforts to identify and address critical skills gaps on an ongoing basis once the Working Group completes its initial efforts. In January 2013, OPM reported that the director of OPM—as leader of the cross-agency priority goal to close critical skills gaps—had identified key federal officials from each of the six government-wide mission critical occupations to serve as "sub-goal leaders." OPM noted that in working with their occupational communities, the sub-goal leaders have selected specific strategies to decrease skills gaps in the occupations they represent. OPM also noted that the Director meets quarterly with these officials to monitor their progress.

Additional steps OPM and the CHCOs could take include creating a readily-accessible mechanism to assemble and disseminate lessons learned and leading practices, and developing collaborative actions such as shared training to help address skills gaps affecting multiple agencies. These steps, among others, could further help OPM and agencies sustain and improve their efforts to identify and address current and evolving critical skills gaps while simultaneously avoiding any duplication of effort.

In addition to the Working Group, OPM has taken steps to improve the federal hiring process, with the aim of making it easier for people to apply for a federal job and strengthen the ability of agencies to compete with the private sector for filling entry-level positions. One such effort is the Pathways Program, which created two new conduits into federal service and modified an existing program. The final rule implementing Pathways took effect in July 2012.

Congress continued its oversight as well. For example, in September 2012, the Senate Subcommittee on Oversight of Government Management, the Federal Workforce, and the District of Columbia held a hearing on the state of the federal workforce in which representatives from OPM, GAO, federal labor unions, and other stakeholders testified on the progress being made in modernizing the government's human capital policies and procedures. This hearing, along with research requests made to GAO and other initiatives, helped policymakers oversee and inform decision-making on the efforts of OPM and individual agencies to acquire, develop, and retain employees with the skills needed to carry out the government's vital work.

Strategic human capital planning that is integrated with broader organizational strategic planning is essential for ensuring that agencies have the talent, skill, and experience mix they need to cost-effectively execute their mission and program goals. Such planning is especially important now because, as shown in figure 2, agencies are facing a wave of potential retirements. Government-wide, around 30 percent of federal employees on board at the end of fiscal year 2011 will become eligible to retire by 2016. At some agencies, however, such as the Department of Housing and Urban Development and the Small Business Administration, at least 40 percent of those on board at the end of fiscal year 2011 are already eligible or will become eligible to retire by 2016.

The government's top leadership and management ranks also face potentially high levels of retirement. About 58 percent of senior executives and 45 percent of GS-15s who were on board at the end of fiscal year

2011 will be eligible to retire by 2016. Likewise, certain occupations also face the potential of large numbers of retirements. For example, 46 percent of air traffic controllers could be eligible to retire by 2016.

Figure 2: Agencies are Facing a Retirement Wave

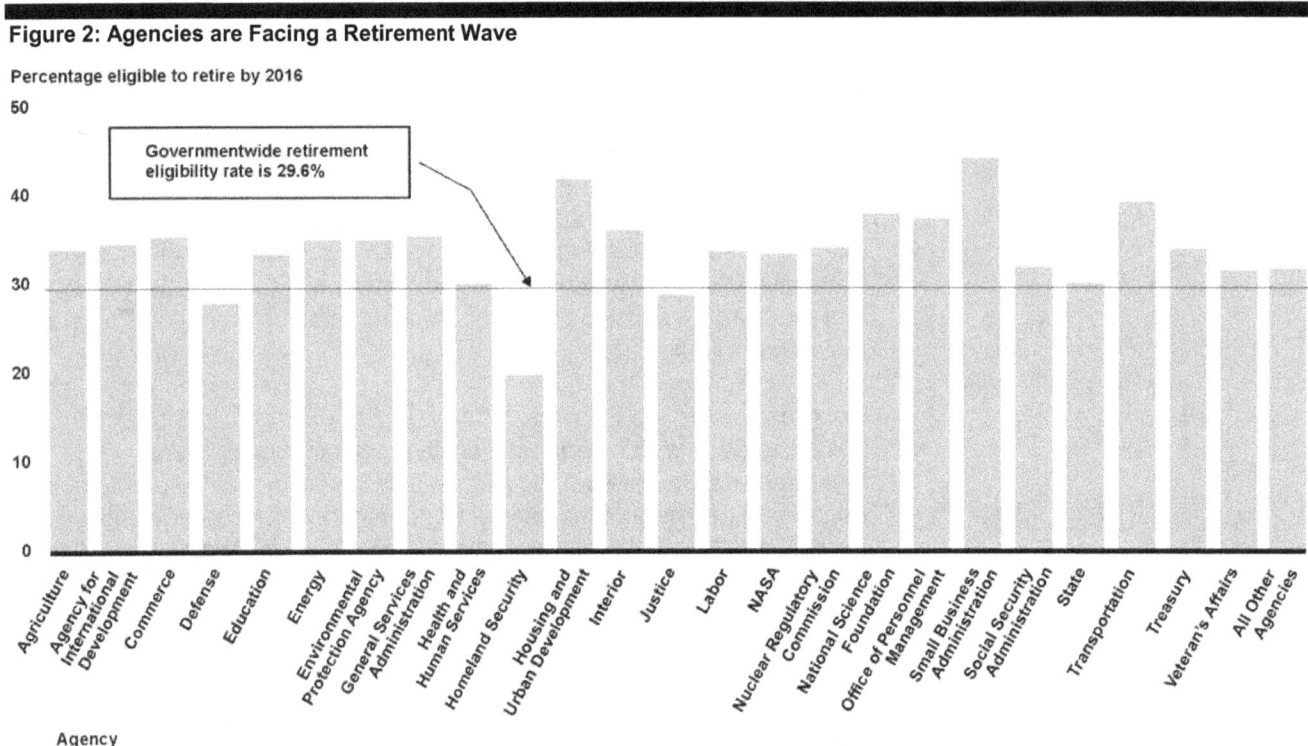

Percentage eligible to retire by 2016

Governmentwide retirement eligibility rate is 29.6%

Agency

Source: GAO analysis of Office of Personnel Management data

Underscoring these broad demographic trends, GAO's work has identified both government-wide and agency-specific skills gaps in several areas, including the following:

Cybersecurity. In a November 2011 report, GAO found that even as threats to federal information technology infrastructure and systems continue to grow in number and sophistication, federal agencies' progress in implementing key workforce planning practices for cybersecurity personnel has been mixed. For example, five of the eight agencies GAO reviewed, including the largest, DOD, have established cybersecurity workforce plans or other agency-wide activities addressing cybersecurity workforce planning. However, all of the agencies GAO reviewed faced challenges determining the size of their cybersecurity workforce because of variations in how work is defined and the lack of an occupational series specific to cybersecurity. GAO recommended, among other actions, that OPM should finalize and issue guidance to agencies on how to track the use and effectiveness of incentives for cybersecurity and other hard-to-fill positions. OPM agreed with this recommendation and identified steps it is taking to address federal agencies' use of incentives.

Acquisition management. Agencies such as DOD and the Department of Homeland Security (DHS) need to address shortages of trained acquisition personnel to oversee and manage contracts that have become more expensive and increasingly complex. For example, in September 2012, GAO reported that 51 of the 71 DHS acquisition programs GAO surveyed reported workforce shortfalls in government personnel serving in program management, business functions, and engineering and technical positions. GAO found that the workforce shortfalls led to insufficient program planning, hindering the development of key acquisition documents intended to inform senior-level decision making, and that 29 of the 51 programs that identified workforce shortfalls had also experienced cost growth or schedule slips. In a 2008 report, GAO recommended DHS take several actions to better manage its acquisition workforce challenges, such as establishing a coordinated planning process across DHS component agencies and improving workforce data. DHS generally agreed with GAO's recommendations and has taken steps to more effectively manage and strategically plan for its acquisition workforce, including establishing a strategic human capital planning initiative to improve coordination between the Chief Procurement Officer, DHS components, the Chief Human Capital Officer, and other stakeholders to develop a Fiscal Year 2013 Acquisition Workforce Strategic Human Capital Plan. DHS has begun collecting and tracking data on the department's acquisition workforce but not yet on the department's use of contractor acquisition support.

Department of Interior's oversight of oil and gas activities. In its July 2012 report, GAO found that the Department of the Interior continues to face workforce planning challenges following a reorganization effort to improve its oversight of offshore oil and gas activities in the wake of the April 2010 oil spill in the Gulf of Mexico. In particular, GAO found that Interior has not developed a strategic workforce plan that outlines specific strategies to help it address the recruitment, retention, and training challenges to oversee offshore oil and gas activities, particularly for engineers and inspectors. Interior has also not specifically determined when it will develop such a plan. To address this, GAO recommended that the relevant components of Interior develop a strategic workforce plan that, among other actions, determines the critical skills and competencies that will be needed to achieve current and future programmatic results and to develop strategies to address critical skills gaps. Interior agreed with this recommendation, noting that its Bureau of Ocean Energy Management will pilot and evaluate a workforce planning tool to institutionalize workforce planning and guide the long-term strategic planning process. Similarly, Interior stated that its Bureau of Safety and Environmental Enforcement will develop a comprehensive bureau-wide strategic human capital plan to address anticipated workforce changes and gaps in critical skills and competencies. The target dates for these efforts are the summer and fall of 2013, respectively.

DOD's large, diverse civilian workforce. In March 2012, DOD included a list of 22 mission critical occupations in its most recent congressionally-mandated civilian strategic workforce plan. DOD first identified 17 of these occupations as mission critical in 2007 and an additional 5 in 2009. GAO's September 2012 report found that DOD had reported conducting gap assessments for 8 of these 22 mission critical occupations it had identified as part of strategic workforce planning efforts for its civilian workforce of about 780,000 personnel. Examples of occupations where DOD did not report conducting gap analyses included budget analysis, information technology management, and logistics management. GAO noted that having a fully developed workforce plan, with completed gap assessments, would help DOD make informed decisions about its workforce and develop strategies to mitigate skill shortages and thus recommended that DOD complete competency gap analyses for its mission-critical occupations and report the results of these analyses. DOD partially concurred with this recommendation noting that competency gaps are to be assessed in the future using a tool that is expected to be available by fiscal year 2014. In January 2013, GAO reported that DOD's Office of the Secretary of Defense and military services had been directed to freeze—or cap—their full-time equivalent civilian positions, but that it was unclear the extent to which DOD had taken into account department-wide priorities for critical skills and competencies when implementing the civilian cap. In that report, GAO recommended that to the extent possible, DOD use the results of its critical skills and competencies gap assessments to make informed decisions for changes to the workforce. DOD generally concurred with GAO's recommendation noting that it is aggressively working towards fully meeting the congressionally mandated requirements of its Strategic Workforce Plan.

Aviation safety. As GAO noted in its September 2012 report, the Federal Aviation Administration (FAA) is implementing its Safety Management Systems (SMS) initiative to shift to a data-driven, risk-based, safety oversight approach that is required for the FAA and several of its business lines, and will be required for the aviation industry. FAA officials have stated that implementing this system will require some skills that agency employees lack. However, FAA has not yet assessed the skills of its workforce to identify specific gaps in employee expertise. GAO recommended that to better leverage existing resources and to facilitate SMS implementation, FAA should conduct a workforce analysis to inventory existing employee skills and abilities and develop strategies for addressing any SMS-related gaps. The Department of Transportation agreed to consider the recommendations.

What Remains to Be Done

Over the last 2 years, executive agencies and Congress have continued their leadership and commitment to ensuring the government takes a more strategic and efficient approach to the recruitment, hiring, development, and retention of individuals with the skills needed to cost-effectively carry out the nation's business. At the same time, GAO has recommended numerous actions agencies should take to address their specific human capital challenges, and has also made recommendations to OPM to address government-wide human capital issues.

Going forward, further progress will depend on the extent to which OPM and agencies sustain their planning, implementation, and monitoring efforts using a strategic approach that (1) involves top management, employees, and other stakeholders; (2) identifies the critical skills and competencies that will be needed to achieve current and future programmatic results; (3) develops strategies that are tailored to address skills gaps; (4) builds the internal capability needed to address administrative, training, and other requirements important to support workforce planning strategies; and (5) includes plans to monitor and evaluate progress toward closing skills gaps and meeting other human capital goals using a variety of appropriate metrics.

OPM and agencies need to implement refinements to the approaches the Working Group used to identify and address critical skills gaps in order to enhance their effectiveness in the future. These refinements can include:

- identifying ways to document and assemble lessons learned, leading practices, and other useful information for addressing skill gaps into a readily-accessible clearinghouse or database so agencies can draw on one another's experiences and avoid duplicating efforts;

- examining the cost-effectiveness of delivering tools and shared services such as online training for workforce planning to address issues affecting multiple agencies;

- reviewing the extent to which new capabilities are needed to give OPM and other agencies greater visibility over skills gaps government-wide to better identify which agencies may have surpluses of personnel in those positions and which agencies have gaps, as well as the adequacy of current mechanisms for facilitating the transfer of personnel from one agency to another to address those gaps as appropriate; and

- determining whether existing workforce planning and other tools can be used to help streamline the processes developed by the Working Group.

OPM agreed that these were important areas for consideration.

GAO Contact

For additional information about this high-risk area, contact Robert N. Goldenkoff at (202) 512-2757 or goldenkoffr@gao.gov, or Yvonne D. Jones at (202) 512-2717 or jonesy@gao.gov.

Related GAO Products

Acquisition Workforce: DOT Lacks Data, Oversight, and Strategic Focus Needed to Address Significant Workforce Challenges. GAO-13-117. Washington, D.C.: January 23, 2013.

Human Capital: Critical Skills and Competency Assessments Should Help Guide DOD Civilian Workforce Decisions. GAO-13-188. Washington, D.C.: January 17, 2013.

Human Capital: DOD Needs Complete Assessments to Improve Future Civilian Strategic Workforce Plans. GAO-12-1014. Washington, D.C.: September 27, 2012.

Human Capital Management: Effectively Implementing Reforms and Closing Critical Skills Gaps Are Key to Addressing Federal Workforce Challenges. GAO-12-1023T. Washington, D.C.: September 19, 2012.

Homeland Security: DHS Requires More Disciplined Investment Management to Help Meet Mission Needs. GAO-12-833, Washington, D.C.: September 18, 2012.

Oil and Gas Management: Interior's Reorganization Complete, but Challenges Remain in Implementing New Requirements. GAO-12-423. Washington, D.C.: July 30, 2012.

Human Capital: HHS and EPA Can Improve Practices Under Special Hiring Authorities. GAO-12-692. Washington, D.C.: July 9, 2012.

Disaster Assistance Workforce: FEMA Could Enhance Human Capital Management and Training. GAO-12-538. Washington, D.C.: May 25, 2012.

Modernizing the Nuclear Security Enterprise: Strategies and Challenges in Sustaining Critical Skills in Federal and Contractor Workforces. GAO-12-468. Washington, D.C.: April 26, 2012.

OPM Retirement Modernization: Progress Has Been Hindered by Longstanding Information Technology Management Weaknesses. GAO-12-430T. Washington, D.C.: February 1, 2012.

Cybersecurity Human Capital: Initiatives Need Better Planning and Coordination. GAO-12-8. Washington, D.C.: November 29, 2011.

Foreign Language Capabilities: Departments of Homeland Security, Defense, and State Could Better Assess Their Foreign Language Needs and Capabilities and Address Shortfalls. GAO-10-715T. Washington, D.C.: July 29, 2010.

Department of Homeland Security: A Strategic Approach Is Needed to Better Ensure the Acquisition Workforce Can Meet Mission Needs. GAO-09-30. Washington, D.C.: November 19, 2008.

Managing Federal Real Property

Why Area Is High Risk

The federal government faces long-standing problems in managing federal real property, including effectively managing excess and underutilized property, an overreliance on leasing, and protecting federal facilities. The government has given high level attention to this issue and has made progress in real property management, but the underlying challenges that hamper reform remain. Specifically, the government continues to lack consistent, accurate, and useful data to support decision making. In addition, competing stakeholder interests regarding the disposition of excess real property, and legal requirements such as those related to environmental cleanup also present challenges. The Federal Protective Service (FPS) has struggled to effectively target limited resources for protecting federal facilities. Additionally, challenges persist with the Department of Defense's management of its real property (see *DOD Support Infrastructure Management* for an update on this topic).

What GAO Found

The federal government holds excess and underutilized property, relies extensively on costly leasing practices, and faces numerous challenges in securing real property. The government has made progress reforming real property management after GAO designated it high risk in 2003. For example, the 2004 Executive Order 13327 established the Federal Real Property Council (FRPC), composed of members from real property-holding agencies to promote reform efforts. However, the federal government has not yet fully addressed the underlying challenges that hamper reform, including legal requirements, a lack of accurate and useful data to support decision-making, and competing stakeholder interests. For example, although GAO recognized data improvement efforts in its 2011 high risk update, the government still has limited data that support strategic decision making. In addition, competing stakeholder interests, and legal requirements agencies must adhere to, such as those related to environmental cleanup and historic preservation, present a challenge to disposing of real property. In May 2011, the administration proposed legislation, referred to as the Civilian Property Realignment Act (CPRA). CPRA would, among other things, establish a legislative framework for disposing of and consolidating civilian real property. However, this and other real property reform legislation introduced in Congress have not been enacted.

The federal government continues to retain more real property than it needs. In June 2010, the President directed federal civilian agencies were to have achieved $3 billion in cost savings by 2012 through a number of methods, one of which was better management of excess properties. Although the Office of Management and Budget (OMB) and federal agencies believe they will reach their savings targets, the actual savings associated with selling excess and better managing underutilized property are not transparent and may be overstated. The lack of reliable data is a significant challenge to identifying and reducing the government's unneeded and underutilized property. FRPC developed the Federal Real Property Profile (FRPP) database to collect key inventory information on the government's real property holdings. However, FRPC has not followed sound data collection practices in designing and maintaining the FRPP, which raises concerns that the database is not a useful tool for describing the nature, use, and extent of excess and underutilized federal real property.

The federal government continues to rely heavily on leasing. The government often leases space from private landlords in the same real estate market where it also owns underutilized real property. This practice is inefficient, resulting in millions of dollars of additional costs to federal agencies. From 2006 to 2011, the amount of space that the General Service Administration (GSA), the leasing agent for many federal agencies, leased from the private sector grew more than 12 percent, while also losing millions of dollars on these leased assets. Even though agencies pay rent and fees to GSA that are designed to cover the costs, GSA has lost $200 million on leases since 2005, including $75 million in 2011 alone. As a result, GSA had to use funds generated from its owned inventory to offset the losses, which decreases the funds available to invest in GSA's owned assets. In some cases, federal agencies in the same market could consolidate into other government-owned properties. However, agencies do not have a strong understanding of real property held by other agencies and may lack the authority or expertise to lease underutilized property to other federal agencies.

Federal agencies also continue to face challenges in securing real property. For example, FPS management and funding challenges have hampered the agency's ability to protect about 9,000 federal facilities managed by GSA. In particular, FPS has limited ability to allocate resources using a risk management strategy and lacks appropriate oversight and enforcement to manage its growing contract guard program. In addition, while GAO found that FPS's approach to collaborating with state and local law enforcement was reasonable and consistent with key practices, FPS lacked the data needed to fully put these collaboration efforts into practice.

What Remains to Be Done

Sustained progress is needed to address the conditions and underlying challenges that make this area high risk. Multiple administrations have committed to a more strategic approach toward managing real property. However, their efforts have not yet fully addressed the underlying challenges that GAO identified. GAO has recommended as a corrective action plan that OMB, in consultation with FRPC, develop a national strategy for managing federal excess and underutilized real property. Additionally, FRPP is not yet a useful tool for describing the nature, use, and extent of excess and underutilized federal real property. Accordingly, GAO has recommended that GSA and FRPC take action to improve the FRPP to increase federal capacity to implement and monitor corrective measures. Finally, to better protect facilities, agencies such as FPS should develop a comprehensive program to increase its capacity to allocate budget-limited physical security resources to the highest needs.

GAO Contact

For additional information about this high-risk area, contact David Wise at (202) 512-2834 or wised@gao.gov, or Mark L. Goldstein at (202) 512-2834 or goldsteinm@gago.gov.

Related GAO Products

Federal Real Property: Improved Data Needed to Strategically Manage Historic Buildings, Address Multiple Challenges. GAO-13-35. Washington, D.C.: December 11, 2012

Federal Real Property Security: Interagency Security Committee Should Implement A Lessons Learned Process. GAO-12-901. Washington, D.C.: September 10, 2012

Critical Infrastructure: DHS Needs to Refocus Its Efforts to Lead the Government Facilities Sector. GAO-12-852. Washington, D.C.: August 13, 2012.

Federal Protective Service: Actions Needed to Assess Risk and Better Manage Contract Guards at Federal Facilities. GAO-12-739. Washington, D.C.: August 10, 2012.

Federal Real Property: Strategic Partnerships and Local Coordination Could Help Agencies Better Utilize Space. GAO-12-779. Washington, D.C.: July 25, 2012.

Federal Protective Service: Preliminary Results on Efforts to Assess Facility Risks and Oversee Contract Guards. GAO-12-943T. Washington, D.C.: July 24, 2012.

Federal Buildings Fund: Improved Transparency and Long-term Plan Needed to Clarify Capital Funding Priorities. GAO-12-646. Washington, D.C.: July 12, 2012.

Federal Real Property: National Strategy and Better Data Needed to Improve Management of Excess and Underutilized Property. GAO-12-645. Washington, D.C.: June 20, 2012.

Federal Protective Service: Better Data on Facility Jurisdictions Needed to Enhance Collaboration with State and Local Law Enforcement. GAO-12-434. Washington, D.C.: March 27, 2012.

Excess Facilities: DOD Needs More Complete Information and a Strategy to Guide Its Future Disposal Efforts. GAO-11-814. Washington, D.C.: September 19, 2011.

Federal Protective Service: Progress Made but Improved Schedule and Cost Estimate Needed to Complete Transition. GAO-11-554. Washington, D.C.: July 15, 2011.

Federal Real Property: Proposed Civilian Board Could Address Disposal of Unneeded Facilities. GAO-11-704T. Washington, D.C.: June 9, 2011.

Budget Issues: Better Fee Design Would Improve Federal Protective Service's and Federal Agencies' Planning and Budgeting for Security. GAO-11-492. Washington, D.C.: May 20, 2011.

DOD Approach to Business Transformation

Why Area Is High Risk

The Department of Defense (DOD) spends billions of dollars each year to maintain key business operations intended to support the warfighter, including systems and processes related to the management of contracts, finances, the supply chain, support infrastructure, and weapons systems acquisition. Weaknesses in these areas adversely affect DOD's efficiency and effectiveness, and hinder its ability to free up resources for higher priority needs. As a result, GAO has designated many of DOD's key business areas as high risk due to their vulnerability to waste, fraud, abuse, and mismanagement. In 2005, GAO added DOD's overall approach to managing business transformation as a high-risk area because (1) DOD had not established clear and specific management responsibility, accountability, and control over business transformation-related activities and applicable resources and (2) DOD lacked a clear strategic and integrated plan for business transformation with specific goals, measures and accountability mechanisms to monitor progress and achieve improvements.

Because of the complexity and long-term nature of DOD's transformation efforts, GAO has reported the need for a chief management officer (CMO) position and a comprehensive, enterprise-wide business transformation plan. In May 2007, DOD designated the Deputy Secretary of Defense as the CMO. In addition, the National Defense Authorization Acts for fiscal years 2008 and 2009 contained provisions that codified the CMO and deputy CMO (DCMO) positions, required DOD to develop a strategic management plan, and required the Secretaries of the military departments to designate their Under Secretaries as CMOs and to develop business transformation plans.

What GAO Found

GAO found that DOD has met two of the five criteria for removing the high-risk designation on its business management approach. Specifically, through various actions, DOD has demonstrated top leadership support for improving its business operations and the capacity to focus oversight on reform efforts. For example, over the past several years, DOD has issued directives outlining broad CMO and DCMO responsibilities, issued its first strategic management plan and subsequent updates, filled key positions such as the DCMO and military department CMOs, and established governance structures intended to provide a forum for discussing business-related topics and serve as oversight mechanisms. However, more remains to be done to fully address limitations in the department's management approach. In particular, DOD has not yet fully met the remaining three criteria, which involve developing a comprehensive strategic plan to guide transformation efforts, implementing an approach for monitoring and validating the effectiveness of reform initiatives, and demonstrating sustained progress in addressing longstanding systemic weaknesses in key business areas. These areas are discussed in the following paragraphs.

Strategic Management Plan

DOD's current Strategic Management Plan (SMP), which was issued in September 2011, represents an improvement over previous plans. However, the plan continues to lack key information that would make it more effective in guiding business transformation efforts and helping DOD achieve needed improvements. DOD issued its first SMP in 2008 and has updated the plan three times, further defining goals, initiatives, and performance measures for achieving business transformation. For example, the current plan identifies seven business goals and, unlike prior versions, shows how these goals align with DOD's overall strategic goals and contains performance measures that generally include milestones or target data. In some cases, it also shows linkages to other plans for certain business areas, such as financial management and information technology, and assigns accountability to senior leaders within the Office of the Secretary of Defense for achieving results for specific goals. However, the plan continues to lack key information, such as a description of the specific business-related challenges that each goal is intended to address, sufficient context to explain the basis for why specific goals were chosen, measures that fully reflect core activities needed to assess progress, and funding priorities linked to goals. The following examples illustrate these points.

- *Acquisition.* The goal related to strengthening DOD's acquisition processes is aimed at obtaining greater efficiency and productivity in defense spending; however, the narrative accompanying this goal does not provide any information on what is causing the cost growth for DOD's major defense acquisition programs, or on how the measures and initiatives associated with the goal may address those causes. GAO's work shows that many factors contribute to cost growth, including the lack of well defined requirements and sufficient information on technology at key points in the procurement process. Unless the underlying root causes of these issues are addressed, substantive improvements are unlikely.

- *Supply chain.* The plan includes a business goal to re-engineer business processes to reduce transaction times, drive down costs, and improve services. Associated with this goal is an initiative to "improve the supply chain end to end process" and measures that relate to percentage of filling orders accurately and customer wait time; however, the narrative describing the goal does not discuss what aspects of the supply chain process need improvement. GAO's work shows that deficiencies exist in several areas of the supply chain, such as material distribution, requirements forecasting, and asset visibility.

- *Contracting.* The plan includes a business goal to create agile business operations that plan for, support, and sustain contingency missions and an initiative to "institutionalize operational contract support;" however, the plan does not identify the areas where DOD faces challenges and needs to focus its reform efforts. GAO's work shows that challenges include insufficient capacity to oversee contractors and inadequate planning for contractor support during contingency operations.

With additional information on the scope and root causes of challenges, DOD would more effectively communicate business priorities and focus initiatives to ensure that the department is addressing long-term systemic weaknesses in its business areas. Such information is necessary to establish a clear and common understanding of key problems and gaps and would make the strategic management plan a more useful tool for decision makers by setting strategic direction for targeting reform efforts and making investment decisions.

In addition, the plan identifies specific business goals but does not explain why the business areas identified in these goals were considered to be priorities compared to other areas or what criteria DOD used to determine when to remove goals that had been included in earlier plans. For example, DOD included the high-risk area of support infrastructure management among the business priorities in prior SMPs. However, the current plan omits this area without providing a rationale for doing so, such as whether sufficient progress had been made to warrant its removal. GAO's work shows that, while DOD has made progress in some areas of managing its support infrastructure, it continues to face significant challenges in others, such as reducing excess facilities and achieving efficiencies from joint basing. As a result, support infrastructure remains on GAO's High Risk List of issue areas vulnerable to waste, fraud, abuse, and mismanagement or in need of broad transformation.

The plan also includes some measures for its seven business goals; however, in some key business areas, the measures do not reflect all core activities needed to assess progress in addressing underlying challenges. GAO's prior work has shown that performance measures should focus on core activities that would help managers assess whether they are achieving organizational goals. For example:

- *Workforce needs.* DOD's plan includes a goal to strengthen and right-size DOD's total workforce and a related initiative to recruit and retain the right quality skilled personnel to meet mission requirements. The plan includes measures related to DOD's progress in recruiting sufficient numbers of military personnel against prescribed end-strength goals, and the percentage of military recruits that have high school diplomas and meet other criteria. However, the plan does not include additional measures to assess whether DOD is recruiting and retaining civilian staff with the right mix of skills and competencies such as financial management and acquisition skills. GAO's past work has shown that this is an important business transformation challenge and that DOD has not yet completed statutorily-mandated gap assessments of its skills and competencies needed to develop the right recruiting and retention goals. Further, DOD's plan does not have a set of measures that reflect the core activities needed to assess progress toward right-sizing DOD military, civilian, and contractor personnel who comprise the total workforce.

- *Contract management.* The current plan identifies measures related to planning for contractor support, but does not address other core activities such as those related to addressing challenges in providing sufficient numbers of trained personnel to perform contractor oversight. GAO's work has shown that DOD faces significant challenges in building a workforce of trained personnel to manage and oversee contractors.

Finally, the plan lists key initiatives for achieving each business goal, but it does not include any information on resource needs or investment priorities so that activities can be linked to funding decisions. GAO's prior work has shown that agencies are successful in achieving business management transformation when they strive to establish strategic plans that prioritize initiatives and resources, and therefore, GAO has previously recommended that the strategic management plan include funding priorities. Without including a description of funding priorities or resource needs, DOD decision makers cannot be assured that they are developing plans and budget requests that reflect business priorities.

Assessing Performance and Demonstrating Results

DOD has broadly outlined a performance management approach, but greater clarity is needed to fully define how the department will measure progress, address long-term systemic challenges in key business areas, and demonstrate tangible results. Since GAO last reported in January 2011, DOD has continued to measure its performance in achieving business goals and established new governance structures intended to provide management oversight. For example, the Under Secretaries of

Defense report performance results on measures in the SMP and on the goal related to business reform in DOD's annual performance plan. The Office of the DCMO summarizes these results on a quarterly basis. The DCMO periodically meets with the CMO to discuss some of this information, such as measures that are not on target. The Under Secretaries also internally collect and report on measures against separate business-related areas, such as the Logistics Strategic Plan and the Financial Improvement and Audit Readiness Plan, which may contain additional measures than those in the SMP. Similarly, the military department CMOs collect information on the business priorities in their respective plans.

In addition, DOD has established two governance structures intended, in part, to monitor business transformation progress. These include the Deputy's Management Action Group (a high level forum for senior leaders to discuss business-related topics and other issues) and the Defense Business Council (a recently established body that is responsible for recommending certification of business system investments and broadly improving DOD's business activities). Although the Council has met several times, DOD has not yet demonstrated how the Council will integrate and use performance information from various sources to assess progress on a department-wide basis and identify corrective actions or issues to raise to the higher level Deputy's Management Action Group.

Through its governance efforts, DOD has clearly increased senior leadership involvement in overseeing transformation efforts, and has continued to implement a significant number of reform activities, including in areas that GAO has designated as high risk. However, these efforts have not yet produced tangible and sustained results in addressing longstanding deficiencies in key business areas. GAO's work shows that many of same fundamental weaknesses that cause these areas to be at high risk for fraud, waste, abuse, and mismanagement still remain. For example:

- *Business systems modernization.* In the area of business systems modernization, DOD has taken steps such as establishing and implementing guidance, structures and processes to provide investment management oversight and control for the acquisition, modernization and sustainment of systems. However, these efforts have yet to yield significant results in materially improving the cost, schedule, and performance of its major automated information systems and eliminating duplicative investments.

- *Weapons acquisition.* Regarding weapons acquisition, DOD has undertaken several reforms, including significantly revising acquisition policies and implementing initiatives intended to improve affordability and control cost growth. However it has yet to demonstrate sustained improvements in cost and schedule outcomes on major defense acquisitions programs, such as reducing the number of programs that exceed statutory thresholds for cost growth, increasing the number of programs meeting the cost performance targets that GAO uses to measure progress in the weapon systems acquisition high-risk area, and increasing the number of programs with mature critical technologies, stable designs, and proven production processes at key points in the acquisition process.

- *Financial management.* In the area of financial management, DOD now has a Financial Improvement and Audit Readiness Plan that lays out a strategy and methodology for achieving auditability. DOD has also issued guidance to DOD components for developing financial improvement plans to implement the Financial Improvement and Audit Readiness Plan, which GAO believes provides a reasonable methodology. While DOD continues to focus its efforts on improving the processes and systems that produce budgetary information, it has not yet achieved auditability of any of its financial statements. The department has also not made significant progress in addressing some of the key weaknesses, such as reversing the trend of continuing delays in its deployment of its Enterprise Resource Planning systems, which are intended to replace existing outdated systems and which DOD considers critical to its financial improvement efforts and achieving audit readiness.

GAO recognizes that transforming DOD's business operations is a complex undertaking and will be a continuous process, and therefore, would not expect that DOD's management oversight would have prompted reforms to address all of the challenges in any given area. However, in order for DOD to demonstrate that its management approach has matured to the point where DOD is able to achieve and sustain progress, GAO would expect to see more tangible results in resolving some fundamental weaknesses in some key business areas, including those on GAO's High Risk List.

What Remains to Be Done

DOD needs to demonstrate that its management oversight of reform efforts is producing tangible results in addressing longstanding deficiencies in key business areas. To better achieve these results and guide its oversight, it will be important for DOD to further refine its strategic management plan and approach for measuring progress on a department-wide basis. Taking these steps will further enhance DOD's ability to strategically focus the department's transformation efforts on the highest priority areas, assess progress against business goals, take corrective action to stay on course in correcting the root causes undermining its ability to achieve needed reforms, and ultimately demonstrate tangible results in addressing longstanding business challenges. Specifically,

- DOD needs to further refine its Strategic Management Plan to ensure that it:

    - identifies the scope of business challenges and underlying root causes to be addressed;

    - describes the underlying rationale for business goals, including any changes in goals from prior plans;

    - includes a set of measures that reflects core activities for each business area; and

    - links activities to resource needs and funding priorities.

- DOD needs to further define how the CMO, DCMO, Under Secretaries of Defense, military department CMOs, and other senior leaders, supported by existing governance structures, will:

    - integrate various sources of performance information on business—related activities;

    - monitor and assess this information to measure department-wide progress against business goals; and

    - identify corrective actions and monitor implementation.

GAO Contact

For additional information about this high-risk area, contact Sharon Pickup at (202) 512-9619 or pickups@gao.gov.

Related GAO Products

Defense Business Transformation: Improvements Made but Additional Steps Needed to Strengthen Strategic Planning and Assess Progress. GAO-13-267. Washington, D.C: February 12, 2013.

DOD Joint Bases: Management Improvements Needed to Achieve Greater Efficiencies. GAO-13-134. Washington, D.C.: November 15, 2012.

DOD Business Systems Modernization: Governance Mechanisms for Implementing Management Controls Need to Be Improved. GAO-12-685. Washington, D.C.: June 1, 2012.

Defense Inventory: Actions Underway to Implement Improvement Plan, but Steps Needed to Enhance Efforts. GAO-12-493. Washington, D.C.: May 3, 2012.

DOD Financial Management: Improvement Needed in DOD Components' Implementation of Audit Readiness Effort. GAO-11-851. Washington, D.C.: September 13, 2011.

Excess Facilities: DOD Needs More Complete Information and a Strategy to Guide Its Future Disposal Efforts. GAO-11-814. Washington, D.C.: September 19, 2011.

High-Risk Series: An Update. GAO-11-278. Washington, D.C.: February 2011.

Defense Business Transformation: DOD Needs to Take Additional Actions to Further Define Key Management Roles, Develop Measurable Goals, and Align Planning Efforts. GAO-11-181R. Washington, D.C.: January 26, 2011.

Defense Business Transformation: Status of Department of Defense Efforts to Develop a Management Approach to Guide Business Transformation. GAO-09-272R. Washington, D.C.: January 9, 2009.

Organizational Transformation: Implementing Chief Operating Officer/Chief Management Officer Positions in Federal Agencies. GAO-08-34. Washington, D.C.: November 1, 2007.

Defense Business Transformation: Achieving Success Requires a Chief Management Officer to Provide Focus and Sustained Leadership. GAO-07-1072. Washington, D.C.: September 5, 2007.

DOD Business Systems Modernization

Why Area Is High Risk

The Department of Defense (DOD) is spending billions of dollars each year to acquire modern systems that are fundamental to achieving its business transformation goals. While DOD's capability and performance relative to business systems modernization has improved, significant challenges remain. The department has not fully defined and established business systems modernization management controls, which are vital to ensuring that it can effectively and efficiently manage an undertaking with the size, complexity, and significance of its business systems modernization and minimize the associated risks.

What GAO Found

DOD reports that its business systems environment includes about 2,200 investments, which are funded by billions of dollars in annual expenditures and are intended to support business functions and operations. Since GAO designated this area as high risk in 1995, it has made about 250 recommendations aimed at strengthening DOD's institutional approach to modernization and reducing the risk associated with key investments. For example, since 2001, GAO has provided a series of recommendations relative to developing and using a business enterprise architecture and establishing effective investment management controls to guide and constrain DOD's multibillion-dollar business systems and services. In addition, since 2002, Congress has included provisions consistent with GAO's recommendations in National Defense Authorization Acts.

Between 2005 and 2008, GAO reported that DOD had made progress toward implementing key institutional modernization management controls in response to statutory provisions and GAO recommendations. For example, DOD had continued to develop updates to its architecture—a modernization blueprint that is intended to provide a clear and comprehensive picture of the department. These updates had addressed important elements related to the requirements of the National Defense Authorization Acts and practices that GAO has identified as missing. However, notwithstanding this progress, in May 2009, GAO reported that DOD's efforts to modernize its management controls (both institutional and program specific) had slowed compared with previous years, leaving much to be accomplished. Since that time, DOD has continued to take steps to comply with statutory provisions and satisfy relevant system modernization management guidance. However, while DOD has initiated numerous management activities aimed at modernizing its business systems environment, it has been limited in its ability to demonstrate results.

In this regard, GAO's work has highlighted challenges that DOD has continued to face in aligning its business enterprise architecture at all levels of the department, leveraging the architecture to avoid investments that provide similar but duplicative functionality in support of common DOD activities, and institutionalizing the business systems investment process. In addition, ensuring that effective system acquisition management controls are implemented for each business system investment also remains a formidable challenge. Examples of progress and challenges in these areas are described in the following paragraphs.

- DOD has defined a federated approach to its architecture, where member architectures conform to an overarching corporate or parent architecture and utilize a common vocabulary. This approach is to provide governance across all business systems, functions, and activities within the department and improve visibility across DOD's respective efforts. However, adopting this approach continues to be a challenge. While DOD is making improvements, its corporate architecture has yet to be federated through the development of aligned subordinate architectures for each of the military departments. In this regard, the military departments have made little or no progress. Moreover, DOD has yet to include common definitions of key terms and concepts to help ensure that these architectures will be properly linked and aligned.

- DOD has recently initiated plans to address duplicative investments; however, these plans have yet to result in the consolidation or elimination of duplicative investments or functionality. In February 2012, GAO reported that while DOD had information technology (IT) investment management processes in place that are, in part, intended to prevent, identify, and eliminate unnecessary duplicative investments, GAO identified 31 potentially duplicative IT investments accounting for about $1.2 billion in DOD's IT spending for fiscal years 2007 through 2012. DOD officials have stated that operational activities identified by programs in its systems repository can be compared by the investment review board to identify those investments that provide duplicative functionality in support of common DOD activities. However, this process depends on self-reported data from the programs and there continues to be little or no validation or verification of the information. GAO recommended that DOD utilize or correct existing mechanisms to identify and eliminate, where appropriate, potentially duplicative investments. While DOD officials stated that they are working on automating the compliance review process, the department has more work to do in this area. For example, DOD has identified 15 end-to-end business processes to be defined in the architecture. However, only two of these processes were to be fully defined by the end of fiscal year 2012, thus enabling only a fraction of activities to be available for comparison during compliance reviews.

- In June 2011, GAO reported that DOD had made limited progress in defining and implementing investment management policies and procedures outlined in GAO's Information Technology Investment Management framework and consistent with the investment management provisions of the Clinger-Cohen Act of 1996. More recently, in June 2012, GAO reported that DOD and the military departments had yet to address GAO's related recommendations and implement many critical processes associated with selecting investments and providing investment oversight and had made little progress in addressing additional elements of GAO's framework that it previously reported as unsatisfied. According to DOD, slow progress on its investment management policies and procedures across the department and its military components was due, in part, to the department's activities to address new requirements in the *National Defense Authorization Act for Fiscal Year 2012*. Specifically, in June 2012, DOD issued investment review guidance that updated its investment review governance, structure, and certification procedures to address the new requirements. Following this guidance, DOD retired its four functional investment review boards in 2012 and replaced them with the Defense Business Council, a senior-level board that is to meet as the corporate investment review board to review and certify systems for fiscal year 2013 within a series of functional portfolios. These portfolios are to include all business systems budgeted to spend more than $1 million, including those in operations and maintenance. While this new approach may provide the Office of the Deputy Chief Management Officer the opportunity to improve transparency for a greater number of systems throughout DOD and manage systems using tradeoffs among its portfolios of investments, the new investment management approach is still in transition and details for how systems will be reviewed and the extent to which this new approach will provide measurement against planned outcomes has not yet been demonstrated.

As part of its investment review and certification process, DOD also has performed various business process reengineering activities related to its business systems investments and underlying end-to-end business process. However, the department has not yet begun to measure associated results. Thus, the extent to which these efforts have streamlined and improved the efficiency of the underlying business processes remains uncertain. As a result, GAO has recommended that DOD begin to report on the status and results of its reengineering efforts to ensure oversight and promote department accountability.

- In 2010, GAO reported that DOD's large-scale, software-intensive system acquisitions continued to fall short of cost, schedule, and performance expectations. Specifically, GAO reported that six of nine enterprise resource planning systems had experienced schedule delays ranging from 2 to 12 years, and five had incurred cost increases ranging from $530 million to $2.4 billion. Despite this, in October 2012, GAO reported that DOD rated no investments at high or moderately high risk levels on the federal IT Dashboard. Rather, it reported 85 percent at low and moderately low risk levels. GAO reported that DOD did not rate any of its investments as high risk due, in part, to departmental officials' views that such ratings could lead to an Office of Management and Budget review. In addition, these ratings did not always reflect significant schedule delays, cost increases, and other weaknesses that GAO and the DOD Inspector General continued to identify. The following are examples of selected investments that continue to experience significant performance problems but were all rated as low or moderately low risk by DOD.

  - In 2012, GAO reported that Air Force's Defense Enterprise Accounting and Management System (DEAMS), which is the Air Force's target accounting system designed to provide accurate, reliable, and timely financial information, faced a 2-year deployment delay and an estimated cost increase of about $500 million for an original life-cycle cost estimate of $1.1 billion (an increase of approximately 45 percent). GAO also reported that assessments by DOD users had identified operational problems with the system, such as data accuracy issues, an inability to generate auditable financial reports, and the need for manual workarounds. In July 2012, the DOD Inspector General reported that the DEAMS' schedule delays were likely to diminish the cost savings it was to provide, and would jeopardize the department's goals for attaining an auditable financial statement. DOD's Chief Information Officer rated DEAMS low risk or moderately low risk from July 2009 through March 2012.

  - Army's General Fund Enterprise Business System (GFEBS) is an Army financial management system intended to improve the timeliness and reliability of financial information and to support the department's auditability goals. In early 2012, GAO reported that while the GFEBS life cycle cost estimate of about $1.4 billion had not changed, the system faced a 10-month implementation delay, and DOD users reported operational problems, including deficiencies in data accuracy and an inability to generate auditable financial reports. These concerns were reiterated by the DOD Inspector General in July 2012. DOD's Chief Information Officer rated GFEBS as moderately low risk from July 2009 through March 2012.

- Army's Global Combat Support System-Army (GCSS-Army) is intended to improve the Army's supply chain management capabilities and provide accurate equipment readiness status reports, among other things. In March 2012, GAO reported that GCSS-Army was experiencing a cost overrun of approximately $300 million on an original life-cycle cost estimate of $3.9 billion (an increase of approximately 8 percent) and a deployment delay of approximately 2 years. DOD rated GCSS-Army as low or moderately low risk from July 2009 through March 2012.

To ensure that DOD's evaluations of investment risk for its major IT Dashboard investments reflect all available performance assessments, GAO has made recommendations to the department to reassess its considerations for assigning risk levels for Dashboard investments, including assessments of investment performance and risk from outside the programs.

Until DOD fully defines and consistently implements the full range of business systems modernization management controls, it may not be able to adequately ensure that its business system investments are the right solutions for addressing its business needs, nor effectively demonstrate that its business system investments are being managed to streamline business processes, produce expected capabilities efficiently and cost effectively, and deliver planned benefits. GAO plans to continue to monitor DOD's efforts to address these areas and, to this end, has ongoing work focusing on (1) the status of the updates to the federated business enterprise architecture and business system investment management process; (2) GAO's prior recommendations pertaining to business systems modernization; (3) DOD's ability to measure the impact of its modernization efforts and demonstrate results; and (4) the extent to which selected major automated information systems are meeting planned cost and schedule milestones and performance measures.

What Remains to Be Done

Establishing a well-defined, federated architecture along with well-defined investment management policies and procedures for modernizing DOD's business systems and processes are critical to effectively improving the department's business systems environment and essential to managing the thousands of business systems in a consistent, repeatable, and effective manner that, among other things, maximizes mission performance while minimizing or eliminating system overlap and duplication. In this regard, DOD must provide further governance and oversight in these areas and work to demonstrate actual progress made against planned outcomes. In addition, business system investments need to be defined and implemented within the context of DOD's federated architecture, and both the corporate and component investment management process and architecture governance need to be better defined and institutionalized. Further, DOD needs to ensure that its business system investments are managed with the kind of acquisition management rigor and discipline that is embodied in relevant guidance and best practices, so that each investment will deliver expected benefits and capabilities on time and within budget. In addition, DOD's considerations for assigning risk levels for major investments should include assessments of investment performance and risk from outside the programs.

GAO Contacts

For additional information about this high-risk area, contact Carol R. Cha at (202) 512-4456 or chac@gao.gov, or Valerie C. Melvin at (202) 512-6304 or melvinv@gao.gov.

Related GAO Products

Information Technology Dashboard: Opportunities Exist to Improve Transparency and Oversight of Investment Risk at Select Agencies. GAO-13-98. Washington, D.C: October 16, 2012.

Organizational Transformation: Enterprise Architecture Value Needs to Be Measured and Reported. GAO-12-791. Washington, D.C.: September 26, 2012.

DOD Business Systems Modernization: Governance Mechanisms for Implementing Management Controls Need to Be Improved. GAO-12-685. Washington, D.C.: June 1, 2012.

Challenges in Attaining Audit Readiness and Improving Business Processes and Systems. GAO-12-642T. Washington, D.C.: April 18, 2012.

DOD Financial Management: Implementation Weaknesses in Army and Air Force Business Systems Could Jeopardize DOD's Auditability Goals. GAO-12-134. Washington, D.C.: February 28, 2012.

Information Technology: Departments of Defense and Energy Need to Address Potentially Duplicative Investments. GAO-12-241. Washington, D.C.: February 17, 2012.

Organizational Transformation: Military Department Can Improve Their Enterprise Architecture Programs. GAO-11-902. Washington, D.C.: September 26, 2011.

Department of Defense: Further Actions Needed to Institutionalize Key Business System Modernization Management Controls. GAO-11-684. Washington, D.C.: June 29, 2011.

Business Systems Modernization: Scope and Content of DOD's Congressional Report and Executive Oversight of Investments Need to Improve. GAO-10-663. Washington, D.C.: May 24, 2010.

DOD Business Systems Modernization: Recent Slowdown in Institutionalizing Key Management Controls Needs to Be Addressed. GAO-09-586. Washington, D.C.: May 18, 2009.

DOD Support Infrastructure Management

Why Area Is High Risk

The Department of Defense (DOD) manages a global real property portfolio that consists of more than 555,000 facilities—including barracks, commissaries, data centers, office buildings, laboratories, and maintenance depots—located on more than 5,000 sites worldwide and covering more than 28 million acres. With a replacement value of close to $850 billion, this infrastructure is critical to maintaining military readiness, and the cost to build and maintain it represents a significant financial commitment.

Since designating this area as high risk in 1997, GAO has reported on challenges DOD faces in reducing excess and obsolete infrastructure, sustaining facilities, and achieving cost savings and efficiencies in base support by eliminating duplication of support services where bases are in close proximity to one another or adjacent to one another. Because DOD has made significant progress in addressing issues regarding planning and funding to sustain facilities, GAO narrowed the defense infrastructure high-risk area in GAO's 2011 high risk update to focus on two remaining issues: reducing excess infrastructure and achieving cost savings and efficiencies in base support. Since GAO's 2011 update, DOD has made near-term progress in reducing excess facilities but progress on its long-term demolition plans beyond fiscal year 2013 are unclear and DOD believes that it continues to have significant excess capacity relative to the planned force structure. DOD has not made significant progress in realizing the anticipated cost savings and efficiencies envisioned to be gained through joint basing since GAO's last update. Therefore, additional actions by DOD are needed in these two areas, based on GAO's criteria[1] to warrant removing the high-risk designation for DOD's defense support infrastructure management. Challenges also persist with the government-wide management of federal real property (see *Managing Federal Real Property* for an update on this topic).

What GAO Found

While DOD has completed implementation of the 2005 Base Realignment and Closure (BRAC) round and made near-term progress in reducing excess infrastructure, it has not made sufficient progress on developing a long-term disposal plan beyond fiscal year 2013. DOD has stated that two

---

[1]The criteria for removal from the High Risk List consist of: (1) demonstrated top leadership commitment, (2) capacity to resolve the risk, (3) a corrective action plan, (4) monitoring to validate effectiveness of corrective measures, and (5) demonstrated progress.

additional BRAC rounds are needed to reduce its significant excess capacity relative to the planned force structure. Additionally, DOD is limited in its ability to identify potentially excess facilities because it does not maintain complete and accurate data concerning the utilization of facilities. In regard to joint basing, DOD has established 12 joint bases. However, DOD has not developed (1) an implementation plan to guide joint bases in achieving anticipated cost savings and efficiencies goals, (2) a reliable method of collecting information on the net costs or estimated savings and efficiencies, (3) a consistent interpretation and reported use of the common standards by the joint bases, (4) a process to prioritize the review and identify potential revision of those standards, (5) a communication strategy to meet the needs of joint base officials, and (6) guidance to the joint bases on developing training materials to be used to inform incoming personnel about the specifics of how installation services are provided on joint bases.

Reducing Excess and Obsolete Infrastructure

DOD disposes of the majority of its excess infrastructure in two ways. First, DOD can demolish, sell, or otherwise dispose of individual facilities on its installations when the facilities are determined to be excess or surplus. Second, DOD can close entire bases under the BRAC process. Additionally, in managing disposal of its excess infrastructure, DOD needs accurate and complete infrastructure inventory records to ensure that the department has an accurate picture of how much infrastructure, and specifically which facilities, is actually excess to its needs.

DOD has made progress in its current 6-year demolition program (2008 through 2013) for reducing its excess infrastructure. Based on GAO's analysis of DOD's real property inventory database and DOD's demolition plans for the remaining 3 years of its demolition program, DOD is on track to meet its overall department-wide target to demolish 62.3 million square feet and its plant replacement value (for facilities that are not measured in square feet) target of $1,179 million by the end of fiscal year 2013. GAO's analysis of DOD's real property inventory database showed that, as of September 30, 2010, DOD has demolished about 30.8 million square feet—about 49 percent of its department-wide square-footage target during the first 3 years of its 6-year demolition program. According to DOD, as of June 2011, it had spent about $833 million for demolition in fiscal years 2008 through 2010 and plans to spend about an additional $941 million to demolish about 32.7 million square feet of facilities in fiscal years 2011 through 2013. If DOD follows through with its plan to demolish an additional 32.7 million square feet by the end of fiscal year 2013, GAO projects that DOD will exceed its overall department wide square-footage target by about 1.1 million square feet.

While DOD's near-term demolition efforts are encouraging, the department has not made sufficient progress on developing future plans for demolishing additional excess facilities beyond fiscal year 2013. DOD's future plans to eliminate excess facilities after its current demolition program ends are unclear, as are its plans for taking into account external factors that affected the disposal of longstanding excess facilities that were identified before fiscal year 2008 and have consequently prevented DOD from disposing of some of its oldest excess and surplus facilities. Since GAO's last high risk update, DOD has significantly reduced its estimated demolition plans for fiscal years 2014 through 2016 from 222 million square feet of excess facilities to about 31 million square feet because of erroneous estimates in the initial demolition budget plan. According to DOD officials, many of the demolition projects completed to date have been limited to those projects that are easily accomplished because they do not have many restrictions that would increase their cost or the time needed to complete them. DOD officials acknowledge that the demolition of the remaining long-standing excess facilities may require more time and effort to complete because of several external factors, including management of historic preservation requirements, environmental restrictions, host nation agreements, and consolidation efforts.

Also, DOD officials told us that after the current demolition program ends, they intend to explore a broader effort for future facilities management, including other approaches to eliminating excess, such as consolidation and recapitalization, instead of focusing primarily on demolition. However, it is not clear what strategies and measures DOD plans to establish to manage its disposal of excess facilities as part of this broader effort. In September 2011, GAO recommended that DOD develop the strategies and measures needed to enhance its management of excess facilities after the current near term demolition program ends that take into account the external factors that may affect future disposal efforts. DOD concurred with this recommendation but has not yet completed actions to implement it.

Moreover, DOD believes that it has significant excess capacity relative to the planned force structure. DOD has demonstrated strong commitment and top leadership support in addressing this situation by requesting authorization for two more BRAC rounds. DOD officials state that the department's plans to make cuts in force structure to adjust to strategic and fiscal factors will require similar cuts in supporting infrastructure, including military bases. For example, the Army plans to reduce its force levels by 72,000 solders, the Marine Corps is resizing to 182,100 active Marines from 202,100, and the Air Force is eliminating approximately 300 aircraft over 5 years. The Secretary of Defense stated in August 2012 that continuing to maintain and operate infrastructure excess to needs risks diverting scarce resources that should go to maintaining force readiness but instead will be diverted to maintaining unneeded facilities and consequently risks "hollowing out the force."

However, DOD is limited in its ability to identify potentially excess facilities because it does not maintain complete and accurate data concerning the utilization of its facilities. GAO found that as of September 30, 2010, DOD's real property inventory database showed utilization data for less than half of DOD's total inventory of facilities and that much of the data is old and does not reflect the true usage of the structures. DOD acknowledges that its database does not cover its entire inventory but rather just what is needed to be reported to the Federal Real Property Profile, which requires annual reports on only five categories of buildings. However, some problems exist with DOD's reporting to the Federal Real Property Profile. DOD's real property inventory as of September 30, 2010, showed that for 32,999 of the 145,239 buildings in the five building categories for which DOD requires utilization rate reporting, no utilization rate was recorded in DOD's database. Nonetheless, because the Federal Real Property Profile will not accept blank fields, DOD entered a utilization rate into the 32,999 records based on prior reporting or even when there was no data supporting the rate entered into the field. Moreover, even when utilization rate data was recorded in DOD's database the record entry often did not reflect the true usage of the facilities. For example, data for the Air Force showed a utilization rate of zero percent for 22,563 buildings that were in an active status and were being used.

Because DOD does not maintain complete and accurate data concerning the utilization of its facilities, it is unable to determine whether all of its facilities are required in order to meet its mission needs, an inability that limits identification of potentially excess facilities. In September 2011, to address these limitations in facility utilization data, GAO recommended that DOD develop and implement a methodology for calculating and recording utilization data for all types of facilities and modify its processes to update and verify the accuracy of reported utilization data to reflect a facility's true status. DOD partially agreed with GAO's recommendation but has not yet taken any action to improve its utilization data.

Achieving Cost Savings and Efficiencies in Base Support

Since GAO's 2011 high risk update, DOD has demonstrated little further progress in realizing the anticipated cost savings and efficiencies envisioned to be gained through consolidation and elimination of duplicate base support where bases are adjacent to or in close proximity to one another. In 2005, DOD recommended to the BRAC Commission combining 26 installations into 12 joint bases to take advantage of opportunities for efficiencies arising from consolidation and elimination of duplicate support services and, in 2010, completed this consolidation. DOD has also established common standards to define the level of service expected to be provided at each joint base and in order to ensure consistent delivery of installation support services. DOD stated that savings in personnel and facilities costs could be realized by, among other things, reducing duplication of efforts, paring unnecessary management personnel, achieving greater efficiencies through economies of scale, consolidating and optimizing existing and future service contract requirements, establishing a single space management authority that could achieve greater utilization of facilities, and reducing the number of base support vehicles and equipment consistent with the size of the combined facilities. DOD's recommendation to the 2005 BRAC Commission estimated that joint basing would realize a 20-year savings of $2.3 billion, with $601 million in savings by the end of the implementation period in fiscal year 2011. However, the 20-year saving estimate has now decreased by nearly 90 percent, to $249 million.

GAO's work has shown that a key reason installation support costs at the joint bases are expected to increase is that the Office of the Secretary of Defense required that the joint bases deliver installation support in accordance with the new support standards even though the military services had not previously funded installation support in the amounts needed to meet each of the standards. In addition, the military services' approach to joint base implementation will result in some additional administrative costs and the loss of some existing installation support efficiencies. GAO's more recent work has shown that DOD leadership has not provided clear direction to joint basing officials and has not developed an implementation plan to guide joint bases in their efforts to achieve the efficiencies and cost savings goals of joint basing. DOD officials told GAO that the department did not have a plan because joint basing is a relatively new initiative and implementation issues are still being resolved. Additionally, DOD does not have a reliable method of collecting information on the net costs or estimated savings, and efficiencies, specifically resulting from joint basing and excluding other influences on the bases' budgets. DOD has developed a data collection tool, called the Cost and Performance Visibility Framework, through which the joint bases report installation support performance data, including annually reporting on funds obligated to provide base support services. However, because of inconsistencies in the way the joint bases reported data through the framework to date, and because the data reported through the framework includes costs and savings which are not specific to joint basing, DOD is not yet able to accurately isolate the effects of joint basing on the cost of providing support services.

Moreover, while in fiscal years 2010 and 2011 the joint bases reported meeting the common standards more than 70 percent of the time, the lack of clarity in some standards, the fact that unclear standards are not always reviewed and changed in a timely manner, and the fact that the data collection and reporting on the standards in some cases adhere to individual service standards rather than the common standard hinders the effectiveness of the standards as a common framework for managing installation support services.

Furthermore, DOD also has not established a communication strategy that provides information to meet the needs of joint basing officials on how to achieve the joint basing goals of cost savings and efficiencies. GAO found that the joint bases do not have a formal method of routinely sharing information among the joint bases on identified challenges and potential solutions or guidance on developing and providing training for new joint base personnel on how the joint bases provide installation support services.

GAO previously reported that organizational transformations such as merging components and transforming organizational cultures should be driven by top leadership, have implementation goals and a time line to show progress, and include a communication strategy. Although the joint bases anecdotally reported achieving some savings and efficiencies, without an implementation plan to drive savings and a means to collect reliable information on the specific costs, estimated savings, and efficiencies from joint basing, DOD will not be able to facilitate achievement of the goals of cost savings and efficiencies, track the extent to which these goals have been achieved, or evaluate the continuation or expansion of joint basing.

In November 2012, to improve DOD's management of joint basing, GAO recommended that DOD (1) develop and implement a plan that provides measurable goals linked to achieving savings and efficiencies at the joint bases and to provide guidance to the joint bases directing them to identify opportunities for cost savings and efficiencies; (2) continue to develop and refine the Cost and Performance Visibility Framework through which the joint bases report installation support performance data; (3 and 4) compile a comprehensive list of common standards needing clarification and prioritize the review and potential revision of those standards; (5) develop a common strategy that facilitates routine communication between the joint bases, and between the joint bases and the Office of the Secretary of Defense, to encourage joint resolution of common challenges and sharing of best practices and lessons learned; and (6) develop guidance to ensure that all joint bases develop and provide training materials to incoming joint base personnel. DOD stated that it does not agree with the report's principal recommendation regarding the establishment of savings goals because the recommendation reflects a fundamental difference in the way GAO and DOD view prudent management of the joint bases at this point in their development. DOD further stated that the creation of the 12 joint bases from 26 separate installations is equivalent to the mergers of corporations, in which the cultural differences are often the hardest to bridge. While savings targets may be appropriate in the future, DOD stated that it decided to allow an extended transition period and to defer near-term savings to increase the odds that each joint base will succeed over the long run. DOD added that its patient approach should continue. GAO acknowledges that establishing joint basing is a complex undertaking but DOD's current position of taking a patient approach and deliberately deferring near term savings contradicts the position it took when requesting the BRAC Commission approve its joint basing recommendation. Specifically, in its recommendation to the BRAC Commission, DOD stated that joint basing would produce savings immediately with 20 year net present value savings of over $2.3 billion; 20 year savings have now declined by 90 percent to about $249 million. DOD partially concurred with GAO's other recommendations although it did not specify what actions it planned to take to implement most of them.

What Remains to Be Done

To demonstrate sustained progress in defense support infrastructure management, DOD needs to develop strategies and measures to better focus and manage its future disposal efforts after the current demolition program ends in 2013, including taking into account external factors, such as historic preservation requirements, environmental restrictions, host nation agreements, and consolidation efforts, that may affect future disposal efforts. To ensure continued progress after 2013, DOD will need a new corrective action plan, monitoring for performance against the new plan, and a demonstration of progress in implementing the new plan. DOD also needs to continue to focus on other means, such as consolidation and recapitalization, to dispose of facilities that are excess to needs. Additionally, DOD needs to develop and implement a methodology for calculating and recording utilization data for all types of facilities and modify its processes to update and verify the accuracy of reported utilization data to reflect a facility's true status as a first step to identifying property excess to needs and thus being in position to execute the disposal plan.

DOD also needs to develop and implement a plan that provides measurable goals linked to achieving savings and efficiencies at the joint bases and provide guidance to the joint bases that directs them to identify opportunities for cost savings and efficiencies. At a minimum, DOD should consider the items identified in its recommendation to the 2005 BRAC Commission as areas for possible savings and efficiencies, including (1) paring unnecessary management personnel, (2) consolidating and optimizing contract requirements, (3) establishing a single space management authority to achieve greater utilization of facilities, and (4) reducing the number of base support vehicles and equipment. DOD needs to demonstrate top leadership commitment to achieving the savings and efficiencies that were its justification for doing joint basing in the first place. Further, DOD needs to develop and implement a corrective action plan that provides measurable goals linked to achieving savings and efficiencies at the joint bases and monitor performance to ensure achievement of the goals. DOD needs to provide guidance to the joint bases directing them to identify opportunities for savings and efficiencies and demonstrate progress in achieving the savings and efficiencies envisioned in adopting joint basing.

GAO Contact

For additional information about this high-risk area, contact Brian J. Lepore at (202) 512-4523 or leporeb@gao.gov.

Related GAO Products

DOD Joint Bases: Management Improvements Needed to Achieve Greater Efficiencies. GAO-13-134. Washington, D.C.: November 15, 2012.

Military Base Realignments and Closures: Updated Costs and Savings Estimates from BRAC 2005. GAO-12-709R. Washington, D.C.: June 29, 2012.

Military Base Realignments and Closures: Key Factors Contributing to BRAC 2005 Results. GAO-12-513T. Washington, D.C.: March 8, 2012.

Excess Facilities: DOD Needs More Complete Information and a Strategy to Guide Its Future Disposal Efforts. GAO-11-814. Washington, D.C.: September 19, 2011.

Federal Real Property: Proposed Civilian Board Could Address Disposal of Unneeded Facilities. GAO-11-704T. Washington, D.C.: June 9, 2011.

Federal Real Property: Progress Made on Planning and Data, but Unneeded Owned and Leased Facilities Remain. GAO-11-520T. Washington, D.C.: April 6, 2011.

Defense Infrastructure: DOD Needs to Periodically Review Support Standards and Costs at Joint Bases and Better Inform Congress of Facility Sustainment Funding Uses. GAO-09-336. Washington, D.C.: March 30, 2009.

DOD Financial Management

Why Area Is High Risk

The Department of Defense (DOD) is responsible for more than half of the federal government's discretionary spending. Significant financial and related business management systems and control weaknesses have adversely affected DOD's ability to control costs; ensure basic accountability; anticipate future costs and claims on the budget; measure performance; maintain funds control; prevent and detect fraud, waste, and abuse; address pressing management issues; and prepare auditable financial statements. These issues led to GAO's designating DOD financial management as high risk in 1995. DOD is one of the few federal entities that cannot accurately account for its spending or assets and is one of three major impediments that prevent GAO from rendering an opinion on the annual consolidated financial statements of the federal government. Without accurate, timely, and useful financial information, DOD is severely hampered in making sound decisions affecting its operations. Further, to the extent that current budget constraints and fiscal pressures continue, the reliability of DOD's financial information and ability to maintain effective accountability for its resources will be increasingly important to the federal government's ability to make sound resource allocation decisions. Effective financial management is also fundamental to achieving DOD's broader business transformation goals.

What GAO Found

Since the last high risk update in 2011, DOD's senior-level commitment to improving the department's financial management and achieving audit readiness has continued to be encouraging, with statements, testimony, and actions emphasizing the importance of effective financial management and audit readiness to DOD's ability to effectively carry out its stewardship responsibilities over the substantial funding and other resources entrusted to the department.

DOD leadership directives, reinforced by congressional mandates, have set out a strategy and methodology for improving DOD's financial management. DOD's Financial Improvement and Audit Readiness (FIAR) Plan, which provides the strategy for DOD's financial management reform efforts, has evolved since the plan was first issued in 2005. More specifically, in 2009, DOD changed its strategy to focus on two department-wide priorities: (1) strengthening processes, controls, and systems that produce budgetary information and support the department's Statement of Budgetary Resources (SBR) and (2) improving the accuracy and reliability of management information pertaining to mission-critical assets, including military equipment and real property. Congress codified these priorities in the National Defense Authorization Act (NDAA) for fiscal year 2010, which also mandated September 30, 2017, as the date by which DOD is required to validate its financial statements as ready for audit. In 2011, the Secretary of Defense underscored the department's first priority with a directive that set an accelerated interim date of September 30, 2014, for validation of one of DOD's financial statements—its SBR—as audit ready. Congress required that DOD's FIAR Plan be adapted to support this goal in the NDAA for fiscal year 2012.

Implementation of the FIAR strategy department-wide is an ambitious undertaking that will require the commitment of resources and efforts at all levels, in all components, and across all DOD financial and business operations, such as those in the high-risk functional areas of contract management, supply chain management, support infrastructure management, and weapon systems acquisition. Because of the complexity and long-term nature of DOD's financial management and business transformation efforts, GAO has reported that sustained and active involvement of the department's Chief Management Officer (CMO), the Deputy CMO (DCMO), the military departments' CMOs, the DOD Comptroller, and other senior leaders is critical.

Moreover, the results of GAO's and the DOD Inspector General's recent work have raised concerns about the ability of DOD components to effectively implement the department's FIAR Plan. Effective, timely component-level actions are critical if the department is to achieve the plan's objectives within the designated time lines. However, GAO's review of the Navy's Civilian Pay and Air Force's Military Equipment audit readiness efforts identified significant deficiencies in the components' execution of the FIAR Plan. Specifically, GAO found that the components were not following the FIAR methodology as set out in the FIAR Guidance—they conducted insufficient testing and reached conclusions that were not supported by testing results. GAO made 13 recommendations for improving development, implementation, documentation, and oversight of the Navy's and Air Force's improvement plans in accordance with the FIAR Guidance. DOD reported that it has corrective actions under way to address these recommendations.

GAO reviewed the Marine Corps' efforts as DOD's pilot military service for an SBR audit. The Marine Corps received a disclaimer of opinion from the DOD Inspector General on its fiscal years 2010 and 2011 SBRs because it could not provide needed supporting documentation in a timely manner, and the support that was provided for transactions was incomplete. The DOD Inspector General and GAO also reported that the Marine Corps did not have adequate processes, systems controls, and controls over accounting and reporting on the use of budgetary resources. The Marine Corps developed action plans in response to the DOD Inspector General's findings, but GAO found that the plans focused on near-term outcomes and did not adequately specify key actions needed for long-term, sustainable readiness for a full audit. As a result of its difficulties in preparing for a full SBR audit, the Marine Corps altered its plans, beginning with fiscal year 2012, to narrow its focus to undergoing an audit of current-year budget activity and expenditures as an interim step toward achieving an audit of multiple-year budgetary activity and expenditures required for a full SBR audit. DOD officials have stated that they plan to revise the FIAR Guidance so that in preparing the SBR for audit, all components will begin with the current-year focus adopted by the Marine Corps as a building block for assuring that support for transactions can be identified and provided to auditors.

In its 2011 report on the Marine Corps' effort, GAO recommended, among other corrective actions, that the Marine Corps use the results of its audit to develop a comprehensive, risk-based plan for designing and implementing corrective actions that provide sustainable solutions to address the recommendations from the SBR audit efforts. GAO also recommended that the secretaries of the military departments consider these lessons learned in their own financial improvement efforts. A key step in developing reliable financial statements, including the SBR, is the reconciliation of the components' Fund Balance with Treasury (FBWT). GAO found that neither the Marine Corps nor the Navy had implemented effective processes for reconciling their Fund Balance with Treasury. GAO's recommendations included development and implementation of standard operating procedures to guide the reconciliation process and training. DOD has reported that the Navy is coordinating with the Defense Finance and Accounting Service (DFAS) to develop guidance for its FBWT reconciliation process and related training.

In recent reviews of other DOD components, GAO also found internal control weaknesses in DOD's procedures for maintaining accountability for billions of dollars in funds and other resources. For example, the Army and DFAS could not readily identify the full population of payroll accounts associated with the Army's $46 billion active duty military payroll because of deficiencies in existing procedures and nonintegrated personnel and payroll systems. GAO recommended that the Army identify documents needed to support military payroll transactions affecting the pay of millions of active duty Army military personnel and that it develop and implement procedures for maintaining those documents. As a first step, the Army has developed a matrix of supporting documents for its military pay. However, the Army has not yet completed action to populate a central repository with these records. GAO also reported on deficiencies in the DFAS processes for detecting errors in active duty military payroll disbursements. In commenting on the report, DOD officials stated that DFAS plans to complete an assessment of the extent of errors by the end of February 2013 as a basis for determining any corrective actions.

GAO also reviewed DOD's process for monitoring and reporting on its late-payment penalties under the Prompt Payment Act and the loss of early-payment discounts offered in contracts. GAO found that the process had significant flaws and omissions that resulted in incomplete and inaccurate data. Specifically, DOD's performance measure for late-payment penalties did not consider about $54 billion of commercial payments from nine feeder systems, and DOD did not assess the data for accuracy or completeness. In addition, GAO found that DOD was not monitoring or reporting on discounts lost across the department. GAO recommended that DOD establish procedures for (1) assuring that the late-payment penalties data are properly compiled, (2) validating the accuracy and completeness of the data compiled and reported, and (3) monitoring discounts lost. In commenting on the report, DOD officials stated that they plan to implement corrective actions to address these recommendations.

GAO has also reported that substantive results are not yet apparent from DOD's efforts to develop two important resources—modern business information systems and a skilled workforce—for resolving its financial management weaknesses and achieving and sustaining audit readiness. DOD has identified several, multifunctional Enterprise Resource Planning (ERP) systems as critical to its financial management improvement efforts. In a report on four of these ERPs, GAO found deficiencies in their capability to perform essential business functions in areas such as data quality, data conversion, system interfaces, and training. Further, DFAS personnel reported difficulty in using the systems to perform day-to-day activities. If these business systems do not provide the intended capabilities on schedule, DOD's goal of establishing effective financial management operations and becoming audit ready could be jeopardized. GAO recommended that DOD ensure that (1) any future system deficiencies identified through independent assessments are resolved or mitigated prior to further deployment of the systems, (2) time lines are established and monitored for those issues identified by DFAS that are impacting their efficient and effective use, and (3) training on actual job processes are provided in a manner that allows users to understand how the new processes support their job responsibilities and the work they are expected to perform. GAO emphasized prioritization as an important part of an effective, risk-based process for addressing deficiencies. GAO also reported on continuing delays in DOD's deployment of its key ERP systems, which are intended to replace existing outdated systems. In March 2012, GAO reported on the status of twelve ERP systems that DOD has identified as critical to ensuring that the department meets its mandated September 30, 2017, goal of full audit readiness. Specifically, GAO reported that schedules for five critical systems had been delayed from 2 to 4 years. As a result, two of the five systems are not to be fully deployed until fiscal year 2016 and two others not until the end of fiscal year 2017. GAO recommended that DOD follow best practices in cost and schedule management to allow better oversight for timely development, within cost, of systems that deliver the intended capabilities.

Regarding DOD's financial management workforce, GAO reported that, as of September 2012, DOD had not met statutory requirements for assessing the gap between existing and future critical-skill needs. GAO recommended that DOD conduct competency analyses for mission-critical occupations, including the financial management workforce; develop guidance for strategic workforce planning; and improve its performance measures. As provided by the *National Defense Authorization Act for Fiscal Year 2012* and in concert with a financial management workforce competency model, the DOD Comptroller is developing a financial management training and certification program. DOD told GAO that it expects to complete the certification program pilot in late March 2013 and that phased implementation is targeted for completion in March 2014.

Without a competent workforce to implement effective financial management processes, systems, and controls, DOD and its components are at risk of reporting unreliable data, which will impair the department's ability to support well-informed management decision making. To the extent that such weaknesses are not addressed, DOD financial management will continue to be at high risk for waste, fraud, abuse, and mismanagement.

Congressional oversight committees have pressed for increased progress at DOD, through legislation and hearings in 2011 and 2012 in the Senate and House of Representatives, including those of the House Armed Services Committee Panel on Defense Financial Management and Auditability Reform, which conducted eight hearings as part of a 6-month review. GAO will continue to support Congress in its oversight.

What Remains to Be Done

Leadership. DOD will need to ensure the sustained involvement of leadership at all levels of the department in financial management and business transformation.

Audit readiness and accountability. DOD needs to take the following actions in working toward full financial statement auditability.

- The Navy and Air Force need to complete corrective actions in response to GAO's recommendations for improving the development, implementation, documentation, and oversight of their improvement plans in accordance with the FIAR Guidance. Other DOD components also need to consider how these recommendations apply to their own efforts.

- The Marine Corps needs to apply the results of its SBR audit efforts to the development of a comprehensive, risk-based plan for designing and implementing corrective actions.

- The military departments should consider the Marine Corps' lessons learned in conducting their own financial improvement efforts, and DOD needs to provide guidance on how the departments can fully leverage the lessons to facilitate their SBR and other audit readiness efforts.

- The Navy and DFAS need to adopt effective standard-operating procedures for reconciling the Navy's and Marine Corps' Fund Balance with Treasury—a fundamental step in preparing the SBR and other financial statements—to guide the reconciliation process and form the basis of a staff training curriculum.

- To achieve audit readiness for its military pay, the Army should develop a process for identifying the population of payroll transactions by fiscal year. In addition, the Army should establish procedures for identifying personnel and key finance documents needed to support the pay of military personnel. Further, DFAS needs to develop processes for detecting errors in active duty military payroll disbursements.

- DOD needs to improve its process for monitoring and reporting on late-payment penalties under the Prompt Payment Act and the loss of discounts offered when a contract or invoice allows an economically justified discount for early payment.

Business information systems. DOD needs to adopt best practices in cost estimation and scheduling to address cost, schedule, and capability issues and the resolution of identified deficiencies in the development and implementation of its ERPs. Also, DOD needs to establish procedures to help ensure that (1) any system deficiencies identified through independent assessments, including DOD Inspector General audits, are resolved or mitigated prior to further deployment of the systems, and (2) deficiencies are prioritized for correction on the basis of relative risk. DOD also needs to augment procedures and provide guidance to include specific time lines for tracking and monitoring the progress of corrective actions. Finally, DOD needs to establish training on how these systems capture and process data and information.

Workforce planning. DOD needs to fulfill the mandated critical-skill requirements for financial management workforce planning and improvement. In particular, DOD needs to conduct competency gap analyses of its current and expected future financial management workforce, develop guidance for strategic workforce planning, and improve its related performance measures.

GAO Contact

For additional information about this high-risk area, contact Asif Khan at (202) 512-9869 or khana@gao.gov.

Related GAO Products

DOD Financial Management: Actions Needed to Address Deficiencies in Controls over Army Active Duty Military Payroll. GAO-13-28. Washington, D.C.: December 12, 2012.

DOD Financial Management: Improvements Needed in Prompt Payment Monitoring and Reporting. GAO-12-662R. Washington, D.C.: June 26, 2012.

DOD Financial Management: Challenges in Attaining Audit Readiness and Improving Business Processes and Systems. GAO-12-642T. Washington, D.C.: April 18, 2012.

DOD Financial Management: Reported Status of Department of Defense's Enterprise Resource Planning Systems. GAO-12-565R. Washington, D.C.: March 30, 2012.

DOD Financial Management: The Army Faces Significant Challenges in Achieving Audit Readiness for Its Military Pay. GAO-12-406. Washington, D.C.: March 22, 2012.

DOD Financial Management: Implementation Weaknesses in Army & Air Force Business Systems. GAO-12-134. Washington, D.C.: February 28, 2012.

DOD Financial Management: Ongoing Challenges with Reconciling Navy and Marine Corps Fund Balance with Treasury. GAO-12-132. Washington, D.C.: December 20, 2011.

Human Capital: DOD Needs Complete Assessments to Improve Future Civilian Strategic Workforce Plans. GAO-12-1014. Washington, D.C.: September 27, 2012.

DOD Financial Management: Improved Controls, Processes, and Systems Are Needed for Accurate and Reliable Financial Information. GAO-11-933T. Washington, D.C.: September 23, 2011.

DOD Financial Management: Weaknesses in Controls over the Use of Public Funds and Related Improper Payments. GAO-11-950T. Washington, D.C.: September 22, 2011.

DOD Financial Management: Marine Corps Statement of Budgetary Resources Audit Results and Lessons Learned. GAO-11-830. Washington, D.C.: September 15, 2011.

DOD Financial Management: Improvement Needed in DOD Components' Implementation of Audit Readiness Effort. GAO-11-851. Washington, D.C.: September 13, 2011.

DOD Financial Management: Numerous Challenges Must Be Addressed to Achieve Auditability. GAO-11-864T. Washington, D.C.: July 28, 2011.

DOD Supply Chain Management

Department of Defense (DOD) supply chain management has experienced weaknesses in the management of supply inventories, materiel distribution, and asset visibility. For example, DOD's most recent available data shows that in September 2011 it had $9.2 billion worth of on-hand excess inventory, categorized for potential reuse or disposal, and $523 million worth of on-order excess inventory, already purchased but likely to be excess due to changes in requirements. Also, a number of challenges, including incomplete delivery data for many surface shipments to Afghanistan, have hindered the distribution of supplies and equipment to the warfighter, and will likely continue to affect operations in Afghanistan and limit DOD's visibility and oversight of the supply chain. GAO added this area to the High Risk List in 1990.

What GAO Found

DOD has made moderate progress in addressing supply chain management weaknesses, but several long-standing problems have not yet been resolved. GAO found that DOD has met two of the five criteria for removing the high-risk designation in the supply chain management area. Specifically, DOD has demonstrated top leadership support for improving supply chain management, and the department has the capacity to resolve risks in this area. For example, DOD leadership has developed and begun implementing a congressionally mandated plan for improving inventory management. In addition, DOD has directed time and resources to reduce distribution costs and improve distribution services, as well as undertaking efforts to improve asset visibility.

However, DOD has not yet fully met the remaining three criteria, which include developing a corrective action plan for materiel distribution and asset visibility, monitoring and independently validating the effectiveness and sustainability of corrective measures, and demonstrating sustained progress in implementing corrective measures. With respect to inventory management, DOD has not yet implemented all the activities associated with its improvement plan that runs through fiscal year 2015. For example, DOD is in the early stages of implementing numerous actions to improve demand forecasting, such as establishing improved methods and techniques for demand forecasting. In the areas of materiel distribution and asset visibility, DOD has not established integrated, comprehensive approaches for overseeing and addressing problems across the department and implementing associated initiatives; however, DOD has begun developing a strategy to coordinate efforts to improve asset tracking and in-transit visibility. Finally, DOD's development of enterprise-wide performance metrics for monitoring the effectiveness and efficiency of supply chain management remains a work in progress. Each of these areas is discussed in more detail below.

Inventory management. In the area of inventory management, prior GAO work reviewing spare parts management at the military services and the Defense Logistics Agency (DLA) found ineffective and inefficient inventory management practices. Problems with accurately forecasting demand for spare parts was a major factor contributing to mismatches between inventory levels and requirements, resulting in purchasing and storing excess inventory. In response to a provision of the National Defense Authorization Act for fiscal year 2010, DOD submitted a corrective action plan to Congress in November 2010 aimed at reducing excess inventory by improving inventory management practices. DOD established overarching goals in the plan to reduce on-order excess inventory, those items already purchased but likely to be excess due to changes in requirements, and on-hand excess inventory, those items categorized for potential reuse or disposal. Additionally, DOD developed actions to improve inventory management in nine key areas, including improving demand forecasting for spare parts.

GAO reported in 2012 that DOD had made progress in implementing its inventory improvement plan and was tracking reductions to its excess inventory, but the department was only 18 months into a 4-year implementation period and many planned activities still remained to be completed. DOD reported that from fiscal years 2009 to 2011 it had reduced on-order excess inventory by approximately $832 million—a reduction that achieved its initial target 4 years early. With respect to on-hand excess inventory, since fiscal year 2009 DOD had met its fiscal year 2012 target of having no more than 10 percent of its inventory categorized as on-hand excess. Since DOD was exceeding its initial targets for reducing excess inventory, GAO observed in its 2012 report that DOD's inventory management improvement efforts would benefit from establishing challenging, but achievable targets for reducing excess inventory and recommended the department periodically reexamine and update its targets. In response to the recommendation, DOD reexamined its on-order and on-hand targets and revised its on-hand excess inventory target to 8 percent by fiscal year 2016. However, DOD did not make any changes to its on-order excess inventory targets.

GAO also found overall implementation of the plan was generally on schedule, but some activities remained to be implemented. For example, DOD was in the early stages of implementing numerous actions to improve demand forecasting, such as identifying improved methods and techniques for demand forecasting. Most but not all of the progress at that time had been in gathering and analyzing data, and reviewing guidance and practices from the services and DLA. For example, DOD, as part of the plan, was revising DOD guidance to standardize and strengthen inventory management practices across DOD. Additionally, DOD demonstrated progress in other areas of the plan's implementation, such as reviewing regularly items that have had no demand for 5 or more years and increasing participation among the services in an in-storage visibility program that is designed to prevent unnecessary procurements. Over time, implementation of these and other planned activities could enable DOD to demonstrate progress in implementing corrective measures and to achieve sustained results in improving inventory management.

Materiel distribution and asset visibility. DOD has had individual efforts under way to improve materiel distribution and asset visibility. These efforts have been positive steps; however, GAO for many years has encouraged DOD to take a more integrated, comprehensive approach to overseeing and addressing problems across the department and implementing associated initiatives. One indication of progress in this area is that DOD is developing a strategy to guide its collective efforts to improve asset tracking and in-transit visibility throughout its supply chain. Such a strategy, once completed and implemented, could provide a basis for DOD to integrate its corrective measures and ultimately demonstrate progress in improving asset visibility.

In 2011, GAO found that DOD had taken steps to mitigate some of the challenges concerning supplying the warfighter in Afghanistan, but it continues to face several challenges in delivering and maintaining visibility of supplies and equipment. Problems include unmet delivery standards and time lines for cargo shipments, as well as incomplete delivery data for many surface shipments, inadequate radio-frequency identification information to track all cargo movements, lack of a common-operating picture for distribution data that integrates DOD's many transportation information systems and processes, difficulties in collecting information on all incidents of pilferage and damage of cargo, and ineffective tracking and managing of cargo containers. GAO made a number of recommendations to address these specific concerns. Furthermore, GAO found that DOD's oversight of materiel distribution is fragmented. Although U.S. Transportation Command oversees the distribution of supplies and equipment into a theater of operations, no single entity is responsible for overseeing the global distribution pipeline, including the tactical movement of items from major bases in Afghanistan to the warfighter. This fragmented nature of DOD's chain of command for distribution to Afghanistan ultimately limits visibility, control, and accountability for items needed by the warfighter. DOD's lack of full oversight for delivery to the warfighter in Afghanistan somewhat limits its ability to identify where delays in the distribution system exist and to take corrective actions to improve DOD's logistics response time.

Over the last few years, DOD implemented several improvement efforts—under an umbrella initiative known as Distribution Process Owner Strategic Opportunities—to reduce distribution costs and improve distribution service to the warfighter. According to DOD, these efforts led to more than $490 million in cost avoidances through increasing utilization of containers, pallets, and aircraft; shifting more cargo to larger containers; and positioning supplies closer to overseas customers. Furthermore, DOD reported that these efforts led to better shipment delivery times for a limited number of customers.

Although DOD achieved some positive results from these improvement efforts, they were not developed with the intent to address all challenges that DOD faces in its materiel distribution system, including some that GAO has identified in its prior work. For example, GAO reported in 2012 that the Distribution Process Owner Strategic Opportunities initiative was designed to improve segments of DOD's distribution system, but its scope did not include efforts specifically targeting the tactical movement of supplies and equipment within theaters of operation, such as Afghanistan. As discussed earlier, GAO's work on distribution challenges in Afghanistan found that DOD's oversight of its entire distribution system was fragmented, and DOD officials acknowledged that the design and scope of Distribution Process Owner Strategic Opportunities limits its ability to optimize DOD's entire distribution system. An absence of comprehensive oversight for materiel distribution limits DOD's ability to measure and evaluate the effectiveness of the entire process and influence change across the spectrum of DOD's operations.

In 2012, a GAO review of DOD's efforts to incorporate Item Unique Identification (IUID) technology into supply chain management found a number of implementation challenges. IUID technology allows DOD to label an item and assign a unique number to the item, could improve the accountability of property and equipment, and could enable DOD to track equipment as it moves between its components. Challenges GAO identified include incomplete information on the number of items that need to be marked with IUID labels, difficulties in collecting information on IUID implementation costs, and the lack of an overarching schedule for the integration of IUID into DOD's information technology systems. For example, DOD does not have complete information on the total number of legacy items its components have marked with IUID labels and must mark in the future, does not have a full set of quantifiable goals or interim milestones that correspond to the criteria for marking items with IUID, and does not use consistent criteria among its components to track progress. Without the components reporting complete and comparable data, DOD's ability to assess progress in marking legacy items will remain limited.

Also, DOD's ability to track and share data on uniquely identified items across its components is hampered by the lack of full integration of data into certain information technology systems. DOD is revising its supply chain management policy and guidance to better include IUID use, but has not fully defined requirements for using these data, nor developed complete, integrated master schedules for integrating IUID department-wide and within components' systems.

Enterprise-wide supply chain performance metrics. As GAO has reported previously and most recently in 2012, the department continues to lack additional performance measures to assess the overall effectiveness and efficiency of the supply chain across the enterprise. DOD logistics officials currently provide performance information—customer wait time by military service, perfect order fulfillment for DLA, and the on-order and on-hand excess inventory measures—to the DOD Deputy Chief Management Officer for inclusion in the department's performance budget. In addition, the Office of the Secretary of Defense is leading the development of a supply chain metrics strategy designed to identify key department-wide metrics to monitor the performance of the supply chain and serve as a basis for making supply chain guidance and resource decisions. The development of department-wide metrics is based on one outcome—readiness—and four attributes—responsiveness, reliability, cost, and planning and precision—of the supply chain. To support the measurement of the outcome and attributes, DOD identified potential department-wide metrics to be collected and assessed. However, DOD has not made final decisions and the effort is a work in progress, as it has been since 2007.

What Remains to Be Done

Inventory management. DOD's plan to reduce excess inventory and improve inventory management practices covers fiscal years 2010 through 2015 and many actions in the plan remain to be completed. As implementation continues, DOD needs to continue to monitor its progress achieving the targets for on-order and on-hand excess inventory and update the targets, as necessary, to ensure the department has challenging, yet achievable targets to guide continued improvement. Additionally, several areas of the plan present considerable implementation challenges due to their complexity. These areas include improving demand forecasting, accelerating the use of modeling to determine the optimal number and types of parts needed at the wholesale and retail levels to achieve readiness and cost goals, and implementing the revised DOD guidance on the processes and procedures for retaining inventory. As it implements the remainder of the plan, DOD will need to address these areas and demonstrate sustained progress in implementing corrective measures.

Materiel distribution and asset visibility. DOD needs to take a number of additional actions to address problems and challenges with materiel distribution and asset visibility that affect delivery of critical items to the warfighter, and to ensure that its improvement efforts are integrated and comprehensive.

- To address materiel distribution and asset visibility challenges such as those identified in Afghanistan, DOD needs to take steps to implement prior GAO recommendations that include investigating cases of undelivered cargo shipments, ensuring sufficient data is entered on radio frequency identification tags, better integrating its many transportation information systems to establish a common operating picture, improving visibility of the incidence and cost of pilferage and damage to cargo, and improving container management.

- To address DOD's fragmented oversight of its materiel distribution system, DOD needs to revise several of its distribution policies to provide clear guidance on how it will oversee the overall effectiveness, efficiency, and alignment of DOD-wide distribution activities. Such changes could reduce fragmentation by helping to ensure comprehensive oversight over the entire DOD-wide global distribution pipeline, including the tactical movement of items on the battlefield.

- DOD also needs to take additional actions to improve asset visibility, to include completing and implementing its strategy for coordinating improvement efforts across the department for asset tracking and in-transit visibility.

- With respect to IUID, DOD needs to, among other steps, take actions to improve management of IUID implementation, enable the components to report complete data for marking items with IUID labels, and enable the components to share data across DOD enterprise information systems.

Enterprise-wide supply chain performance metrics. DOD needs to complete the development of a comprehensive, standardized set of department-wide supply chain metrics, incorporate these metrics into guidance, and employ these metrics in monitoring the effectiveness and efficiency of its supply chains, including inventory management, materiel distribution, and asset visibility. The metrics also should be incorporated into the existing inventory management improvement plan, the new strategy being developed for asset visibility, and any similar efforts in the area of materiel distribution.

GAO Contact

For additional information about this high-risk area, contact Zina Merritt at (202) 512-5257 or merrittz@gao.gov, or Cary Russell at (202) 512-5431 or russellc@gao.gov.

Related GAO Products

Defense Logistics: DOD Has Taken Actions to Improve Some Segments of the Materiel Distribution System. GAO-12-883R. Washington, D.C.: August 3, 2012.

Defense Inventory: Actions Underway to Implement Improvement Plan, but Steps Needed to Enhance Efforts. GAO-12-493. Washington, D.C.: May 3, 2012.

Defense Logistics: Improvements Needed to Enhance DOD's Management Approach and Implementation of Item Unique Identification Technology. GAO-12-482. Washington, D.C.: May 3, 2012.

Warfighter Support: DOD Has Made Progress, but Supply and Distribution Challenges Remain in Afghanistan. GAO-12-138. Washington, D.C.: October 7, 2011.

Defense Logistics: DOD Needs to Take Additional Actions to Address High-Risk Challenges in Supply Chain Management. GAO-11-569. Washington, D.C.: July 28, 2011.

DOD Weapon Systems Acquisition

Why Area Is High Risk

Congress and the Department of Defense (DOD) have long explored ways to improve the acquisition of major weapon systems, yet many DOD programs are still falling short of cost and schedule expectations. The results are unanticipated cost overruns, reduced buying power, and in some cases a reduction in the capability ultimately delivered to the warfighter. Over the next 5 years, DOD expects to invest more than $300 billion (fiscal year 2013 dollars) on the development and procurement of major defense acquisition programs. With the prospect of slowly growing or flat defense budgets for years to come, DOD must get better returns on its weapon system investments and find ways to deliver capability to the warfighter for less than it has in the past. GAO added this area to its High Risk List in 1990.

What GAO Found

GAO's work continues to reveal significant cost and schedule growth in DOD's portfolio of major defense acquisition programs. In 2012, GAO reported that the total acquisition cost of DOD's fiscal year 2011 portfolio of 96 major defense acquisition programs grew by more than $74.4 billion, or 5 percent, in the past year. About $31.1 billion of that amount can be attributed to factors such as inefficiencies in production, $29.6 billion to quantity changes, and $13.7 billion to research and development cost growth. DOD's largest weapon system acquisition program—the Joint Strike Fighter program—accounted for most of the cost growth, but it is not the only program to experience management and execution problems. As shown in figure 3, less than half of the programs in the 2011 portfolio met two of the three cost-growth targets GAO uses to measure DOD's progress in the weapon system acquisition high-risk area.[1] GAO also reported that a majority of programs lost buying power in the last year and planned to deliver capabilities at higher unit costs.

---

[1]In December 2008, DOD, GAO, and the Office of Management and Budget discussed a set of cost growth metrics and goals to evaluate DOD's progress on improving program performance for purposes of GAO's high-risk report. These metrics were designed to capture total cost-growth performance over 1- and 5-year periods as well as from the original program estimate on a percentage basis as opposed to dollar amount to control for the disparity in the amount of funding among programs. DOD no longer supports the use of these metrics. GAO continues to believe that the current metrics have value.

Figure 3: Percentage of Programs Meeting Total Acquisition Cost Growth Targets

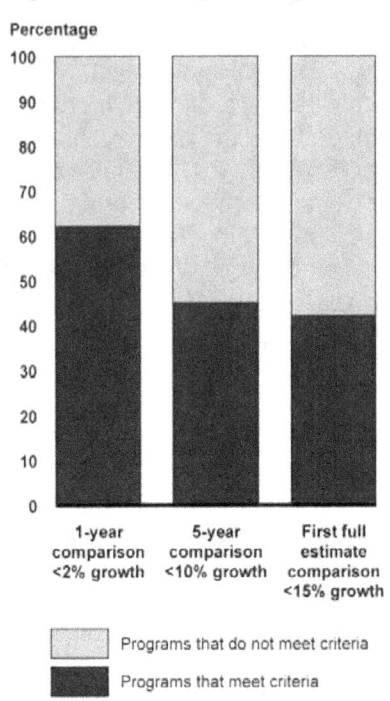

Percentage

1-year
comparison
<2% growth

5-year
comparison
<10% growth

First full
estimate
comparison
<15% growth

Programs that do not meet criteria

Programs that meet criteria

Source: GAO analysis of DOD data.

The implementation of knowledge-based acquisition practices that might prevent or mitigate the potential for cost growth has been uneven across the portfolio. GAO's 2012 assessment of weapon programs found that programs are still proceeding through the acquisition process with high levels of technology, design, and manufacturing risks. Of the eight programs GAO assessed that had recently passed through one of three key decision points in the acquisition process, only one had implemented all of the applicable knowledge-based practices. The rest of these programs will carry technology, design, and production risks, as well as the resulting cost and schedule risks, into subsequent phases of the acquisition process.

DOD continues to demonstrate a strong commitment, at the highest levels, to improving the management of its weapon system acquisitions. Over the past 2 years, DOD has made progress in (1) addressing the prioritization of its weapon system investments through changes to its process for validating new requirements; (2) reinforcing the importance of cost estimating, systems engineering, and testing by implementing key tenets of the Weapon Systems Acquisition Reform Act of 2009; and (3) promoting affordability and increasing the productivity of defense spending through its "Better Buying Power" initiatives.

- *Prioritizing weapon system investments.* GAO has recommended that DOD assign priority levels to its capability needs and proposed weapon programs and align those priorities with available budgetary resources. In response, DOD revised the policy and guidance for its Joint Capabilities and Integration and Development System to require the prioritization of capability requirements within portfolios. In May 2012, the Joint Requirements Oversight Council also issued guidance to the military services and other stakeholders outlining areas that it assessed as priorities for additional investment and areas of lower priority where risk can be more easily accommodated. These efforts, if sustained, should help DOD shape a more affordable portfolio of weapon systems that balances risks and resources.

- *Reinforcing the importance of cost estimating, systems engineering, and testing.* In 2012, GAO reported that the Weapon Systems Acquisition Reform Act of 2009 has had a significant influence on programs in the 3 years since it was enacted, particularly in areas, such as (1) requirement setting, (2) cost and schedule estimating, (3) testing, and (4) system reliability planning, all of which have been sources of problems in the past. Moving forward, DOD faces challenges in extending the influence of the Weapons Systems Acquisition Reform Act. These challenges include: limited organizational capacity to support cost estimating, performance assessment, systems engineering, and developmental testing; lack of guidance in certain areas; limited dissemination of lessons learned related to systematic problems and best practices; and differences between the Office of the Secretary of Defense and the military services about what constitutes an appropriate level of risk and whether the benefits of certain reform provisions are worth the cost.

- *Promoting affordability and productivity.* In 2012, DOD unveiled its second set of "Better Buying Power" initiatives to improve the return on investment it receives from its weapon system spending. These initiatives include measures such as setting and enforcing affordability targets, instituting a long-term investment plan for portfolios of weapon systems, implementing "should cost" management, and eliminating redundancies within portfolios. These actions are consistent with GAO's past findings and recommendations. If these initiatives are going to have a lasting, positive effect, however, decision makers need to be held accountable for implementing them. GAO's recent work shows there is much ground yet to cover. In 2012, GAO reported that 4 of the 16 future and 19 of the 37 current major defense acquisition programs GAO assessed had established affordability targets. In addition, 6 of the 16 future and 23 of the 37 current major defense acquisition programs GAO assessed had completed "should cost" analyses as part of DOD's first set of "Better Buying Power" initiatives.

DOD also plans to improve its ability to assess the root causes of poor weapon system acquisition outcomes and monitor the effectiveness of its actions to improve its management of weapon systems acquisition, in part as a result of congressional action. The fiscal year 2011 National Defense Authorization Act requires that DOD's Office of Performance Assessment and Root Cause Analysis, among other offices, issue guidance to provide for periodic performance assessments of elements of the defense acquisition system. In 2012, DOD announced its plans to institute a system to measure the cost performance of programs and governmental and nongovernmental institutions, such as military departments and contractors, and assess the effectiveness of its acquisition policies. As part of this effort, DOD's Office of Performance Assessment and Root Cause Analysis is examining a wide range of acquisition-related information from the past 40 years, such as contract type, stability of key performance requirements, and program manager tenure to determine if there is any statistical correlation between these factors and good or poor acquisition outcomes. DOD expects the first set of data derived from this initiative to be published in early 2013.

What Remains to Be Done

In the past few years, a number of acquisition reforms have been introduced both through legislation and efforts undertaken by DOD, such as the Weapon Systems Acquisition Reform Act of 2009 and the Under Secretary of Defense for Acquisition, Technology and Logistics' "Better Buying Power" initiatives. These reforms have the potential to improve outcomes on individual weapon system acquisition programs, as well as the affordability of DOD's entire portfolio of weapon programs. They also demonstrate a commitment by Congress and DOD leadership to address long-standing problems with weapon system acquisition. However, DOD must still take actions to ensure it has developed adequate capacity to address weapon system acquisition issues; identified the right corrective actions to address the root causes of issues; and implemented mechanisms to monitor performance and demonstrate progress. Specifically, DOD needs to:

- ensure that key activities, such as cost estimating, program assessment, systems engineering, and developmental testing, are prioritized by the acquisition communities within DOD and the military services and that these entities have adequate capacity to perform their designated roles;

- follow through on its efforts to develop a system to measure the performance of programs and the effectiveness of its acquisition policies;

- set goals for and regularly report on the results of its "Better Buying Power" initiatives to track and assess their implementation;

- support well-planned programs by providing them the resources they need, while holding all programs accountable for policy implementation via milestone reviews, funding decisions, and performance metrics.

GAO Contact

For additional information about this high-risk area, contact Michael J. Sullivan at (202) 512-4841 or sullivanm@gao.gov.

Related GAO Products

Weapons Acquisition Reform: Reform Act Is Helping DOD Acquisition Programs Reduce Risk, but Implementation Challenges Remain. GAO-13-103. Washington, D.C.: December 14, 2012.

Joint Strike Fighter: DOD Actions Needed to Further Enhance Restructuring and Address Affordability Risks. GAO-12-437. Washington, D.C: June 14, 2012.

Missile Defense: Opportunity Exists to Strengthen Acquisitions by Reducing Concurrency. GAO-12-486. Washington, D.C.: April 20, 2012.

Defense Acquisitions: Assessments of Selected Weapon Programs. GAO-12-400SP. Washington, D.C.: March 29, 2012.

KC-46 Tanker Aircraft: Acquisition Plans Have Good Features but Contain Schedule Risk. GAO-12-366. Washington, D.C: March 26, 2012.

Space Acquisitions: DOD Faces Challenges in Fully Realizing Benefits of Satellite Acquisition Improvements. GAO-12-563T. Washington, D.C: March 21, 2012.

Defense Management: Guidance and Progress Measures Are Needed to Realize Benefits from Changes in DOD's Joint Requirements Process. GAO-12-339. Washington, D.C.: February 24, 2012.

Arleigh Burke Destroyers: Additional Analysis and Oversight Required to Support the Navy's Future Surface Combatant Plans. GAO-12-113. Washington, D.C.: January 24, 2012.

Defense Acquisitions: Future Ground-Based Vehicles and Network Initiatives Face Development and Funding Challenges. GAO-12-181T. Washington, D.C: October 26, 2011.

Defense Acquisitions: DOD Can Improve Its Management of Configuration Steering Boards. GAO-11-640. Washington, D.C.: July 7, 2011.

Mitigating Gaps in Weather Satellite Data

Why Area Is High Risk

The United States relies on two complementary types of satellite systems for weather observations and forecasts: (1) polar-orbiting satellites that provide a global perspective every morning and afternoon and (2) geostationary satellites that maintain a fixed view of the United States. Both types of systems are critical to weather forecasters, climatologists, and the military to map and monitor changes in weather, climate, the oceans, and the environment. Federal agencies are currently planning and executing major satellite acquisition programs to replace existing polar and geostationary satellite systems that are nearing the end of their expected life spans. However, these programs have troubled legacies of cost increases, missed milestones, technical problems, and management challenges that have resulted in reduced functionality and slips to planned launch dates. As a result, the continuity of satellite data is at risk.

Officials from the Department of Commerce's National Oceanic and Atmospheric Administration (NOAA) acknowledge that there is a substantial risk of a gap in polar satellite data in the afternoon orbit, between the time that the current polar satellite is expected to reach the end of its life and the time when the next satellite is expected to be in orbit and operational. This gap could span from 17 to 53 months or more, depending on how long the current satellite lasts and any delays in launching or operating the new one. There is also a risk of a gap in the early morning orbit if the Department of Defense's next satellites do not work as intended. According to civilian and military satellite experts, this is a possibility because the two remaining satellites have been in storage for over a decade and will be quite old by the time they are launched. Similarly, while federal agencies do not anticipate gaps in geostationary satellite observations, such a gap could occur if satellites currently in orbit do not last as long as anticipated or if the major satellite acquisition currently underway encounters schedule delays.

According to NOAA program officials, a satellite data gap would result in less accurate and timely weather forecasts and warnings of extreme events, such as hurricanes, storm surges and floods. Such degradation in forecasts and warnings would place lives, property, and our nation's critical infrastructures in danger. Given the criticality of satellite data to weather forecasts, the likelihood of significant gaps and the potential impact of such gaps on the health and safety of the U.S. population and economy, GAO has concluded that the potential gap in weather satellite data is a high-risk area and added it to the High Risk List in 2013.

What GAO Found

NOAA faces ongoing challenges in ensuring the continuity of satellite operations in both the polar-orbiting and geostationary environmental satellite programs.

- *Polar-orbiting satellites.* NOAA officials anticipate a gap in the afternoon orbit from 18 to 24 months between the time that the current polar satellite reaches the end of its lifespan and when the first satellite in its Joint Polar Satellite System (JPSS) program is ready for operational use. GAO identified other scenarios where the gap could last from 17 to 53 months. In addition, there is the possibility of satellite data gaps in the Department of Defense's early morning orbit. The final two Defense Meteorological Satellite Program satellites may not work as intended after they are launched because they were built in the late 1990s and will be quite old by the time they are launched. If the satellites do not perform as expected, a data gap in the early morning orbit could occur as early as 2014. Satellite data gaps in the morning or afternoon polar orbits would lead to less accurate and timely weather forecasting, and as a result, advanced warning of extreme events—such as hurricanes, storm surges, and floods—would be affected.

In June 2012, GAO reported that while NOAA officials communicated publicly and often about the risk of a polar satellite data gap, the agency had not established plans to mitigate the gap. At the time, NOAA officials stated that the agency would continue to use existing satellites as long as they provide data and that there were no viable alternatives to the JPSS program. However, GAO's report noted that a more comprehensive mitigation plan was essential since it is possible that other governmental, commercial, or foreign satellites could supplement the polar satellite data. Further, because it could take time to adapt ground systems to receive, process, and disseminate an alternative satellite's data, GAO noted that any delays in establishing mitigation plans could leave the agency little time to leverage its alternatives. GAO recommended that NOAA establish mitigation plans for pending satellite gaps in the afternoon orbit as well as potential gaps in the early morning orbit.

In September 2012, the Under Secretary of Commerce for Oceans and Atmosphere reported that NOAA had several actions under way to address polar satellite data gaps, including (1) an investigation on how to maximize the life of the current operational satellite, (2) an investigation on how to accelerate the development of the second JPSS satellite, and (3) the development of a mitigation plan to address potential data gaps until the first JPSS satellite becomes operational. The Under Secretary also directed NOAA's Assistant Secretary to conduct an enterprise-wide examination of contingency options and to develop a written, descriptive, end-to-end plan that considers the entire flow of data from possible alternative sensors through data assimilation and on to forecast model performance.

NOAA subsequently issued a mitigation plan for a potential gap in the afternoon orbit, between the current polar satellite and the first JPSS satellite. The plan identifies and prioritizes options for obtaining critical observations, including alternative satellite data sources and improvements to data assimilation in models. It also lists technical, programmatic, and management steps needed to implement these options.

However, it is not clear when decisions will be made to implement the steps needed to ensure that the options are viable. Moreover, it is not yet clear how this mitigation plan will be integrated with the Under Secretary's directive to begin developing an overarching end-to-end plan for sustaining weather forecasts. GAO has ongoing work assessing NOAA's efforts to limit and mitigate potential polar satellite data gaps.

- *Geostationary satellites.* While NOAA's policy is to have two operational geostationary satellites and one backup satellite in orbit at all times, continued delays in the launch of the first satellite in the Geostationary Operational Environmental Satellite-R (GOES-R) series could lead to a gap in satellite coverage. NOAA's policy proved useful in December 2008 and again in September 2012, when NOAA experienced problems with one of its operational satellites, but was able to move its backup satellite into place until the problems were resolved. However, beginning in April 2015, NOAA expects to have two operational satellites in orbit, but it will not have a backup satellite until GOES-R is launched and completes an estimated 6-month post-launch test period.

As a result, there could be a year or more gap during which time a backup satellite would not be available. If NOAA were to experience a problem with either of its operational satellites before GOES-R is in orbit and operational, it would need to rely on older satellites that are beyond their expected operational lives and may not be fully functional. Any further delays in the launch of the first satellite in the GOES-R program would likely increase the risk of a gap in satellite coverage.

In September 2010, GAO reported that NOAA had not established adequate continuity plans for its geostationary satellites. Specifically, in the event of a satellite failure, with no backup available, NOAA planned to reduce its operations to a single satellite and if available, rely on a satellite from a foreign nation. However, the agency did not have plans that included processes, procedures, and resources needed to transition to a single or foreign satellite. Without such plans, there would be an increased risk that users would lose access to critical data. GAO recommended that NOAA develop and document continuity plans for the operation of geostationary satellites that included implementation procedures, resources, staff roles, and timetables needed to transition to a single satellite, a foreign satellite, or other solution.

One year later, in September 2011, NOAA developed an initial continuity plan that generally includes these elements. Specifically, NOAA's plan identifies steps it would take in transitioning to a single or foreign satellite, the amount of time this transition would take, roles of product area leads, and resources such as imaging product schedules, disk imagery frequency, and staff to execute the changes. In December 2012, NOAA issued an updated plan that provides additional contingency scenarios.

However, it is not evident that critical steps have been implemented, including simulating continuity situations and working with the user community to account for differences in products under different continuity scenarios. GAO has ongoing work assessing NOAA's actions to ensure that its plans are viable and that continuity procedures are in place and have been tested.

What Remains to Be Done

In response to GAO recommendations to establish contingency and continuity plans, NOAA has established plans to address potential gaps in satellite data for both its polar-orbiting and geostationary satellite systems. However, these plans are only the beginning. NOAA must make difficult decisions on which technical, programmatic, and management steps it will implement to ensure that its mitigation plans are viable when needed. For example, for the polar-orbiting satellites, NOAA must make decisions about (1) whether and how to extend support for legacy satellite systems so that their data might be available if needed, (2) how much time and resources to invest in improving satellite models so that they assimilate data from alternative sources, (3) whether to pursue international agreements for access to additional satellite systems and how best to resolve any security issues with the foreign data, (4) when and how to test the value and integration of alternative data sources, and (5) how these preliminary mitigation plans will be integrated with the agency's broader end-to-end plans for sustaining weather forecasting capabilities. NOAA must also identify time frames for when these decisions will be made.

For the geostationary satellites, NOAA must demonstrate its progress in conducting training and simulations for contingency scenarios, evaluating the status of viable foreign satellites, and working with the user community to account for differences in product coverage under contingency scenarios. These steps are critical for NOAA to move forward in documenting the processes it will take to implement its contingency plans. Once these activities are completed, NOAA should also update its contingency plan to provide more details on its contingency scenarios, associated time frames, and any preventative actions it is taking to minimize the possibility of a gap.

GAO has ongoing work assessing NOAA's actions on both its polar-orbiting and geostationary satellite programs to determine whether its plans are viable and its continuity procedures are in place and have been tested.

GAO Contact

For additional information about this high-risk area, contact David A. Powner at (202) 512-9286 or pownerd@gao.gov.

Related GAO Products

Environmental Satellites: Focused Attention Needed to Mitigate Program Risks. GAO-12-841T. Washington, D.C.: June 27, 2012.

Geostationary Weather Satellites: Design Progress Made, but Schedule Uncertainty Needs to be Addressed. GAO-12-576. Washington, D.C.. June 26, 2012.

Polar-Orbiting Environmental Satellites: Changing Requirements, Technical Issues, and Looming Data Gaps Require Focused Attention. GAO-12-604. Washington, D.C.: June 15, 2012.

NASA: Assessments of Selected Large-Scale Projects. GAO-12-207SP. Washington, D.C.: March 1, 2012.

Polar Satellites: Agencies Need to Address Potential Gaps in Weather and Climate Data Coverage. GAO-11-945T. Washington, D.C.: September 23, 2011.

Geostationary Operational Environmental Satellites: Improvements Needed in Continuity Planning and Involvement of Key Users. GAO-10-799. Washington, D.C.: September 1, 2010.

Environmental Satellites: Planning Required to Mitigate Near-term Risks and Ensure Long-term Continuity. GAO-10-858T. Washington, D.C.: June 29, 2010.

Polar-Orbiting Environmental Satellites: Agencies Must Act Quickly to Address Risks That Jeopardize the Continuity of Weather and Climate Data. GAO-10-558. Washington, D.C.: May 27, 2010.

Environmental Satellites: Strategy Needed to Sustain Critical Climate and Space Weather Measurements. GAO-10-456. Washington, D.C.: April 27, 2010.

Strengthening Department of Homeland Security Management Functions

Why Area Is High Risk

In 2003, GAO designated implementing and transforming the Department of Homeland Security (DHS) as high risk because DHS had to transform 22 agencies—several with major management challenges—into one department. Further, failure to effectively address DHS's management and mission risks could have serious consequences for U.S. national and economic security. Given the significant effort required to build and integrate a department as large and complex as DHS, GAO's initial high-risk designation addressed the department's initial transformation and subsequent implementation efforts, to include associated management and programmatic challenges. At that time, GAO reported that the creation of DHS was an enormous undertaking that would take time to achieve, and that the successful transformation of large organizations, even those undertaking less strenuous reorganizations, could take years to implement.

Over the past 10 years, the focus of this high-risk area has evolved in tandem with DHS's maturation and evolution. The overriding tenet has consistently remained the department's ability to build a single, cohesive and effective department that is greater than the sum of its parts—a goal that requires effective collaboration and integration of its various components and management functions. In 2007, in reporting on DHS's progress since its creation, as well as in GAO's 2009 high risk update, GAO reported that DHS had made more progress in implementing its range of missions rather than its management functions, and that continued work was needed to address an array of programmatic and management challenges. DHS's initial focus on mission implementation was understandable given the critical homeland security needs facing the nation after the department's establishment, and the challenges posed by its creation, integration and transformation.

As DHS continued to mature, and as GAO reported in its assessment of DHS's progress and challenges 10 years after 9/11, GAO found that the department implemented key homeland security operations and achieved important goals in many areas to create and strengthen a foundation to reach its potential.[1] For example, DHS developed strategic and operational plans to guide its efforts, such as the National Response Framework that outlines disaster response guiding principles; successfully hired, trained, and deployed workforces, including the federal screening workforce to assume screening responsibilities at airports nationwide; and established new, or expanded existing, offices and programs to implement its homeland security responsibilities, such as the National Cybersecurity and Communications Integration Center to help coordinate efforts to address cybersecurity threats. However, GAO also identified that more work remained for DHS to address weaknesses in its operational and implementation efforts, and to strengthen the efficiency and effectiveness of those efforts. GAO further reported that continuing weaknesses in DHS's management functions had been a key theme impacting the department's implementation efforts. Recognizing DHS's progress in transformation and mission implementation, GAO's 2011 high risk update focused on the continued need to strengthen DHS's management functions and integrate those functions within and across the department, as well as the impact of these challenges on the department's ability to effectively and efficiently carry out its missions.

While challenges remain for DHS to address across its range of missions, the department has made considerable progress in transforming its original component agencies into a single cabinet-level department and positioning itself to achieve its full potential. Important strides have also been made in strengthening the department's management functions and in integrating those functions across the department, particularly in recent years. However, continued progress is needed in order to mitigate the risks that management weaknesses pose to mission accomplishment and the efficient and effective use of the department's resources. In particular, the department needs to demonstrate continued progress in implementing and strengthening key management initiatives and addressing corrective actions and outcomes. Therefore, GAO is

---

[1]GAO, *Department of Homeland Security: Progress Made and Work Remaining in Implementing Homeland Security Missions 10 Years after 9/11*, GAO-11-881 (Washington, D.C.: Sept. 7, 2011). This report addressed DHS's progress in implementing its homeland security missions since it began operations, work remaining, and issues affecting implementation efforts. Drawing from over 1,000 GAO reports and congressional testimony issued related to DHS programs and operations, and approximately 1,500 recommendations made to strengthen mission and management implementation, this report addressed progress and remaining challenges in such areas as border security and immigration, transportation security, and emergency management, among others.

narrowing the scope of the high-risk area and changing the name from
*Implementing and Transforming DHS to Strengthening DHS Management
Functions* to reflect this focus.

What GAO Found

As outlined in the following paragraphs, DHS has made important
progress in implementing, transforming, strengthening, and integrating its
management functions, including taking numerous actions specifically
designed to address GAO's criteria for removing areas from the High Risk
List; however, this area remains high risk because the department has
significant work ahead.

Leadership commitment: The Secretary, Deputy Secretary, and Under
Secretary for Management of Homeland Security and other senior
officials have continued to demonstrate commitment and top leadership
support for addressing the department's management challenges. They
have also taken actions to institutionalize this commitment to help ensure
the long-term success of the department's efforts. For example, in May
2012, the Secretary of Homeland Security modified the delegations of
authority between the Management Directorate and its counterparts at the
component level to clarify and strengthen the authorities of the Under
Secretary for Management across the department. Senior DHS officials
have also periodically met with GAO over the past 4 years to discuss the
department's plans and progress in addressing this high-risk area, during
which GAO provided feedback on the department's efforts. According to
these officials, and as demonstrated through their progress, the
department is committed to demonstrating measurable, sustained
progress in addressing this high-risk area.

Corrective action plan: DHS has established a plan for addressing this
high-risk area. Specifically, in a September 2010 letter to DHS, GAO
identified and DHS agreed to achieve 31 actions and outcomes that are
critical to addressing the challenges within the department's management
areas and in integrating those functions across the department. These
key actions and outcomes include, among others, validating required
acquisition documents in accordance with a department-approved,
knowledge-based acquisition process, and obtaining and then sustaining
unqualified audit opinions for at least 2 consecutive years on the
department-wide financial statements. In January 2011, DHS issued its
initial *Integrated Strategy for High Risk Management*, which included key
management initiatives and related corrective action plans for addressing
its management challenges and the outcomes GAO identified. DHS
provided updates of its progress in implementing these initiatives and
corrective actions in its later versions of the strategy—June 2011,

December 2011, June 2012, and September 2012. The comprehensive strategy, if implemented and sustained, provides a path for DHS to be removed from GAO's High Risk List.

Framework to monitor progress: DHS has established a framework for monitoring its progress in implementing its corrective actions and addressing the 31 actions and outcomes. In the June 2012 update to the *Integrated Strategy for High Risk Management*, DHS included, for the first time, performance measures to track its progress in implementing all of its key management initiatives. Additionally, the Under Secretary for Management holds quarterly internal progress review meetings with senior officials from each management function to discuss progress toward achieving milestones and meeting performance goals. It will be important for DHS to continue to track progress toward achieving its goals and monitor and refine its measures and corrective actions, as needed.

Capacity: In June 2012, DHS identified the resources needed to implement most (154 of 173) of its corrective actions, but needs to continue to identify resources for the remaining corrective actions; determine that sufficient resources and staff are committed to initiatives; work to mitigate shortfalls and prioritize initiatives, as needed; and communicate to senior leadership critical resource gaps. DHS also identified ways in which it is leveraging resources to implement corrective actions, which is particularly important in light of constrained budgets. For example, in October 2012, DHS reported that it is pooling resources and working across functional lines to create cross functional, matrixed teams and executive steering committees to ensure timely implementation of the strategy. However, it is too soon to determine whether this approach is a sustainable way for DHS to address the resource challenges and capacity gaps that have affected its implementation efforts at the department and component levels.

Demonstrated, sustained progress: DHS has made important progress in implementing corrective actions across its management functions, but it has not yet demonstrated sustainable, measurable progress in addressing key challenges that continue to remain within these functions and in the integration of those functions. DHS has implemented a number of actions demonstrating the department's progress in improving its management functions. For example, DHS established the Office of Program Accountability and Risk Management in October 2011 to be responsible for the department's overall acquisition governance process. DHS also established a formal IT Program Management Development Track and staffed Centers of Excellence with subject matter experts to assist major and nonmajor programs. In September 2012, GAO reported that as of March 2012, approximately two-thirds of the department's major IT investments GAO reviewed (47 of 68) were meeting current cost and schedule commitments (i.e., goals). Additionally, in the financial management area, DHS has reduced the number of material weaknesses in internal controls and obtained a qualified audit opinion on its fiscal year 2012 financial statements. DHS has also implemented common policies, procedures, and systems, such as those related to human capital, across its management functions.

However, DHS continues to face significant management challenges that hinder the department's ability to meet its missions. Specifically, challenges within acquisition, information technology, financial, and human capital management have resulted in performance problems and mission delays. For example, because of acquisition management challenges, some currently deployed technologies were not appropriately tested and evaluated or do not meet intended requirements, such as Advanced Imaging Technology and explosives detection systems. Additionally, DHS does not have modernized financial management systems, affecting its ability to have ready access to reliable information for informed decision making. Further, human capital management challenges at DHS's Federal Protective Service, such as the lack of assurance that its contract guards received the training and certifications required to stand post at federal facilities, hampered the agency's ability to protect federal facilities. Moving forward, addressing such management challenges will be critical for DHS's success.

Key to addressing the department's management challenges and this high-risk area is DHS demonstrating continued progress implementing its high-risk plan and the ability to achieve sustained progress across the 31 actions and outcomes GAO identified. DHS has made important progress across all of its management functions and significant progress in the area of management integration. However, DHS still has considerable work ahead in many areas. Specifically, GAO believes DHS has fully addressed 6, mostly addressed 2, partially addressed 16, and initiated 7 of the 31 key actions and outcomes (see table 5).

Table 5: GAO's Assessment of DHS's Progress in Addressing Key Actions and Outcomes

Key Outcomes	Fully addressed[a]	Mostly addressed[b]	Partially addressed[c]	Initiated[d]	Total
Acquisition management			2	3	5
IT management	1	1	4		6
Financial management	2		3	4	9
Human capital management		1	6		7
Management integration	3		1		4
Total	6	2	16	7	31

Source: GAO analysis of DHS documents, interviews, and prior GAO reports.

[a]"Fully addressed": outcome is fully addressed.

[b]"Mostly addressed": progress is significant and a small amount of work remains.

[c]"Partially addressed": progress is measurable, but significant work remains.

[d]"Initiated": activities have been initiated to address outcome, but it is too early to report progress.

Acquisition Management

DHS has partially addressed two of the five outcomes GAO identified in the acquisition management area and initiated actions to address the remaining three. For example, in March 2012, DHS created a Procurement Staffing Model to determine optimal numbers of personnel to properly award and administer contracts. Additionally, as of August 2012, DHS had chartered eight Centers of Excellence to enhance component acquisition capabilities and improve insight into program management challenges before they become major problems, and has also taken some steps to improve investment management. Each DHS component also established a Component Acquisition Executive to provide oversight and support to programs within the component's portfolio. Additionally, in October 2011, DHS began to operate a business intelligence system, known as the Decision Support Tool, which integrates information from multiple source databases. This tool is intended to improve the flow of information from component program offices to the Management Directorate to support its governance efforts. However, according to DHS, senior executives are not confident enough in the reliability of the database to use it to help make acquisition decisions.

Further, in September 2012, GAO reported that DHS's acquisition policy reflects many key management practices that could help mitigate risks and increase chances for successful outcomes. However, most of DHS's major acquisition programs continue to cost more than expected, take longer to deploy than planned, or deliver less capability than promised. GAO identified 42 programs that experienced cost growth, schedule slips, or both, with 16 of the programs' costs increasing from a total of $19.7 billion in 2008 to $52.2 billion in 2011—an aggregate increase of 166 percent. GAO found that these outcomes are largely the result of DHS's lack of adherence to key knowledge-based program management practices, even though many are reflected in the department's own acquisition policy.

Finally, while DHS has initiated efforts to validate required acquisition documents in a timely manner at major milestones, GAO reported in September 2012 that DHS leadership has authorized and continued to invest in major acquisition programs even though the vast majority of those programs lack foundational documents demonstrating the knowledge needed to help manage risks and measure performance. GAO recommended that DHS modify acquisition policy to better reflect key program and portfolio management practices and ensure acquisition programs fully comply with DHS acquisition policy. DHS concurred with GAO's recommendations and reported taking actions to address some of them.

IT Management

DHS has fully addressed one, mostly addressed one, and partially addressed the remaining four of the six IT management outcomes GAO identified. DHS has taken steps to strengthen its enterprise architecture program (or blueprint) to guide IT acquisitions. Specifically, a recent independent assessment of the department's enterprise architecture program showed that DHS has achieved stage four of GAO's *Enterprise Architecture Framework* (that is, completing and using an enterprise architecture for targeted results)—fully addressing this outcome. DHS has also continued to improve and strengthen its information security program by developing and implementing the *Fiscal Year 2012 Information Security Performance Plan*, which, among other areas, identified plans of action and milestones weakness remediation. It will be important for the department to fully implement its plan and ensure that progress can be sustained over time. DHS's financial statement auditor reported in November 2012 that weaknesses in the security controls over the department's financial systems were a material weakness for financial reporting purposes.

DHS has also defined and begun to implement a vision for a tiered governance structure intended to improve IT program and portfolio management, which is generally consistent with best practices. However, the governance structure covers less than 20 percent (about 16 of 80) of DHS's major IT investments and 3 of its 13 portfolios, and the department has not yet finalized the policies and procedures associated with this structure. In July 2012, GAO recommended that DHS finalize the policies and procedures and continue to implement the structure. DHS agreed with these recommendations and estimated it would address them by September 2013. It will be important for DHS to continue to strengthen its investment management and systems acquisition practices for progress to be sustained. Further, DHS developed an IT human capital plan and implementation roadmap in response to a 2007 GAO recommendation, and has begun to demonstrate progress in implementing this plan.

Financial Management

DHS has fully addressed two, partially addressed three, and initiated four of the nine financial management outcomes GAO identified. Specifically, DHS has maintained top management commitment to addressing weaknesses in this management area, implemented a corrective action plan process, and demonstrated measurable progress in correcting reported audit qualifications and internal control deficiencies—fully addressing two outcomes. Additionally, DHS reduced the number of material weaknesses in internal controls from 10 in 2005 to 5 in 2012, and obtained a qualified audit opinion on its fiscal year 2012 financial statements. In fiscal year 2011, the department established a goal of obtaining an unqualified audit opinion on all of its financial statements for fiscal year 2013. DHS has efforts underway to resolve certain elements of Coast Guard's general property, plant, and equipment and heritage and stewardship assets, which were the main obstacles to DHS obtaining an unqualified or "clean" audit opinion for fiscal year 2012. However, it has been unable to obtain an audit opinion on its internal controls over financial reporting because of the remaining material weaknesses in internal controls.

Further, although DHS has initiated actions to achieve the outcomes related to financial systems modernization, much work remains to be done. DHS components are currently in the early planning stages of their financial systems modernization efforts, and until these efforts are complete, their current systems will continue to inadequately support effective financial management, in part because of their lack of substantial compliance with key federal financial management requirements. Without sound controls and systems, DHS faces long-term challenges in obtaining and sustaining an audit opinion on internal controls over financial reporting, and ensuring its financial management systems generate reliable, useful, and timely information for day-to-day decision making.

Human Capital Management

DHS has mostly addressed one of the seven human capital management outcomes and partially addressed the remaining six. For example, DHS has developed and demonstrated progress in implementing a strategic human capital plan, mostly addressing this outcome. Specifically, DHS issued a workforce strategy and a revised workforce planning guide to help the department plan for its workforce needs, and its components are in various stages of implementing these workforce planning efforts. However, in December 2012, GAO identified several factors that have hampered DHS's strategic workforce planning efforts and recommended that DHS, among other things, identify and document additional performance measures to assess workforce planning efforts, integrate audit results with components' operational plans, and provide timely feedback on those plans. DHS agreed with these recommendations and stated that it plans to take actions to address them.

Additionally, DHS has taken steps to seek employees' input to strengthen human capital approaches and activities. For example, DHS established an Employee Engagement Executive Steering Committee in January 2012 to identify actions for improving employee engagement, but these actions are not yet under way. Moreover, DHS has made efforts to improve employee morale, such as determining the root causes of morale problems. Despite these efforts, federal surveys have consistently found that DHS employees are less satisfied with their jobs than the government-wide average. In September 2012, GAO recommended, among other things, that DHS improve its root cause analysis efforts of morale issues. DHS agreed with these recommendations and noted actions it plans to take to address them.

Management Integration

DHS has made substantial progress integrating its management functions, fully addressing three of the four outcomes GAO identified as key to the department's management integration efforts. Specifically, as mentioned above, DHS issued a comprehensive plan to guide its management integration efforts—the *Integrated Strategy for High Risk Management*—in January 2011, and has generally improved upon this plan with each update. In addition, the department has implemented mechanisms to promote accountability for management integration among department and component management chiefs, such as requiring department management chiefs to provide input into component chiefs' annual performance evaluations. Further, DHS has put into place common policies, procedures, and systems within individual management functions, such as human capital, that help to integrate its component agencies. Additionally, according to DHS, the modified delegations of authority between the Management Directorate and its counterparts at the component level should provide increased standardization of operating guidelines, policies, structures, and oversight of programs; and clarify the roles between the department and components.

To achieve the last and most significant outcome—implement actions and outcomes in each management area to develop consistent or consolidated processes and systems within and across its management functional areas—DHS needs to continue to demonstrate sustainable progress integrating its management functions within and across the department and its components and take additional actions to further and more effectively integrate the department. For example, DHS recognizes the need to better integrate its lines of business and is establishing an initiative to manage investments across the department's components and management functions. In September 2012, DHS reported that it has developed draft policy and procedural guidance to support implementation of the initiative and now plans to begin using aspects of this new approach to develop portions of the department's fiscal years 2015 through 2019 budget. However, the effectiveness of this key integration effort is dependent upon DHS following through with its plans, and it is therefore too early to assess its impact.

What Remains to Be Done

In recognition of the evolution of this high-risk area, GAO is narrowing its scope and changing the name from *Implementing and Transforming the Department of Homeland Security* to *Strengthening Department of Homeland Security Management Functions* to reflect a focus on the department's remaining management challenges.

Going forward, DHS needs to continue implementing its *Integrated Strategy for High Risk Management* and show measurable, sustainable progress in implementing its key management initiatives and corrective actions and achieving outcomes. In doing so, it will be important for DHS to

• make continued progress in addressing the 31 actions and outcomes and demonstrate that systems, personnel, and policies are in place to ensure that progress can be sustained over time;

- maintain its current level of top leadership support and sustained commitment to ensure continued progress in executing its corrective actions through completion;

- continue to implement its plan for addressing this high-risk area and periodically report its progress to Congress and GAO;

- closely track and independently validate the effectiveness and sustainability of its corrective actions and make midcourse adjustments, as needed; and

- monitor the effectiveness of its efforts to establish reliable resource estimates at the department and component levels, address and work to mitigate any resource gaps, and prioritize initiatives as needed to ensure it has the capacity to implement and sustain its corrective actions.

GAO will continue to monitor DHS's efforts in this high-risk area to determine if the actions and outcomes are achieved and sustained.

GAO Contact

For additional information about this high-risk area, contact David C. Maurer at (202) 512-9627 or maurerd@gao.gov.

Related GAO Products

DHS Strategic Workforce Planning: Oversight of Departmentwide Efforts Should be Strengthened. GAO-13-65. Washington, D.C.: December 3, 2012.

Department of Homeland Security: Taking Further Action to Better Determine Causes of Morale Problems Would Assist in Targeting Action Plans. GAO-12-940. Washington, D.C.: September 28, 2012.

Information Technology: DHS Needs to Enhance Management of Cost and Schedule for Major Investments. GAO-12-904. Washington, D.C.: September 26, 2012.

Department of Homeland Security: Continued Progress Made Improving and Integrating Management Areas, but More Work Remains. GAO-12-1041T. Washington, D.C.: September 20, 2012.

Homeland Security: DHS Requires More Disciplined Investment Management to Help Meet Mission Needs. GAO-12-833. Washington, D.C.: September 18, 2012.

Information Technology: DHS Needs to Further Define and Implement Its New Governance Process. GAO-12-818. Washington, D.C.: July 25, 2012.

Federal Emergency Management Agency: Workforce Planning and Training Could Be Enhanced by Incorporating Strategic Management Principles. GAO-12-487. Washington, D.C.: April 26, 2012.

DHS Human Capital: Senior Leadership Vacancy Rates Generally Declined, but Components' Rates Varied. GAO-12-264. Washington, D.C.: February 10, 2012.

Department of Homeland Security: Progress Made and Work Remaining in Implementing Homeland Security Missions 10 Years after 9/11. GAO-11-881. Washington D.C.: September 7, 2011.

Financial Management Systems: DHS Faces Challenges to Successfully Consolidating Its Existing Disparate Systems. GAO-10-76. Washington, D.C.: December 4, 2009.

Establishing Effective Mechanisms for Sharing and Managing Terrorism-Related Information to Protect the Homeland

Why Area Is High Risk

GAO designated terrorism-related information sharing as high risk in 2005 because the government faces significant challenges in analyzing and disseminating this information in a timely, accurate, and useful manner. GAO has since monitored federal efforts to implement the Information Sharing Environment (Environment)—an approach that is intended to serve as an overarching solution to strengthening the sharing of intelligence, terrorism, law enforcement, and other information among federal, state, local, tribal, international, and private sector partners.[1] Recent homeland security incidents and the changing nature of domestic threats make continued progress in improving information sharing critical to reducing the risks of threats to the homeland.

What GAO Found

The Office of the Program Manager for the Environment (Program Manager) is situated within and funded through amounts appropriated to the Office of the Director of National Intelligence (ODNI). GAO has reported that the Program Manager, as well as key departments—the Departments of Homeland Security (DHS), Justice, State, and Defense, as well as ODNI—are critical to developing and implementing the Environment and have taken steps to address the five criteria that GAO uses to determine whether an area should be removed from the high risk list. The Program Manager and departments have also taken steps to address action items that GAO identified in a June 2011 letter to the Program Manager that need to be addressed to resolve the high-risk designation.[2] GAO has found that the federal government's leadership structure is committed to enhancing the sharing and management of terrorism-related information and has made significant progress defining a governance structure to implement the Environment. However, the federal government has not yet estimated and planned for the resources needed to resolve risks or fill gaps in the planning they have undertaken to implement the Environment. Also, the Program Manager and key departments need to more fully develop and implement some actions they have underway, such as continuing to mature a performance measurement system that focuses on results achieved in terms of improved sharing and overall homeland security. The Program Manager and key departments will also need to work collaboratively to ensure that

---

[1] See 6 U.S.C. § 485(a)(3), (b).

[2] GAO letter to the Program Manager for the Information Sharing Environment (Washington, D.C.: June 29, 2011).

departments' terrorism-related information sharing initiatives, such as departments' efforts to identify important terrorism-related data, are being appropriately leveraged to reduce gaps in sharing throughout the Environment. As a result, this issue remains high risk.

Within the context of addressing GAO's high-risk designation, the Program Manager and key departments will also need to address actions GAO identified in its June 2011 letter to the Program Manager. As shown in table 5, the Program Manager and key departments have fundamentally met two action items, made progress in addressing six of the action items, and made no substantial progress in addressing one action item. Table 6 contains the action items as well as the current status of each action item.

Table 6: Status of Action Items

Action items	Action item status
Demonstrate that the Information Sharing and Access Interagency Policy Committee has needed authority, is leveraging participating departments, and is producing results.	Fundamentally met
Update the vision for the Environment—the information sharing capabilities and procedures that need to be in place to help ensure terrorism-related information is access ble and identifiable to relevant federal, state, local, private, and foreign partners.	Fundamentally met
Demonstrate that departments are defining incremental costs they will need to fund in order to complete their responsibilities and activities to substantially achieve the Environment.	Progress made
Continue to identify technological capabilities and services that can be shared collaboratively within and across the Environment, consistent with a federated architecture approach.	Progress made
Demonstrate that initiatives within individual departments are, or will be, leveraged to benefit all relevant federal, state, local, and private security stakeholders participating in the Environment.	Progress made
Establish an enterprise architecture management capability and demonstrate that it will be used to guide selection of projects for substantially achieving the Environment.	No substantial progress
Demonstrate that stakeholders generally agree with the strategy, plans, time frames, and their responsibilities and activities for substantially achieving the Environment.	Progress made
Demonstrate that the federal government can show the extent to which sharing has improved under the Environment, or has actions underway to more fully develop a set of metrics and processes to measure results achieved, both from individual projects and activities, as well as from the overall Environment.	Progress made

Action items	Action item status
Demonstrate that established milestones and time frames are being used as baselines to track and monitor progress on individual projects and in substantially achieving the overall Environment.	Progress made

Source: GAO.

Leadership commitment. The federal government has a sustainable leadership structure for information sharing in place consistent with law and executive policy. In accordance with section 1016 of the Intelligence Reform and Terrorism Prevention Act of 2004 (Intelligence Reform Act), as amended, the President created the Environment.[3] Pursuant to this provision, the President designated a Program Manager to, among other things, plan for, oversee the implementation of, and manage the Environment. Also, in July 2009, the administration established the Information Sharing and Access Interagency Policy Committee (Policy Committee)—composed of senior department officials—to develop policies, procedures, guidelines, roles, and standards necessary to establish, implement, and maintain the Environment. The Program Manager and the National Security Staff Senior Director for Information Sharing and Security co-chair the Policy Committee, and the five key departments participate in the committee. As co-chair, the Program Manager has influenced the departments' information sharing priorities, which has helped to ensure that the leadership structure has sufficient authority to direct departments' participation in the Environment.

In addition, in October 2011—in response to concerns about securing data after the Wikileaks breach—the President issued an executive order that established the Senior Information Sharing and Safeguarding Steering Committee (Steering Committee).[4] The Steering Committee is intended to exercise overall responsibility and ensure senior-level accountability for the coordinated interagency development and implementation of policies and standards regarding the sharing and safeguarding of classified information on computer networks. According

---

[3]See Pub. L. No. 108-458, § 1016, 118 Stat. 3638, 3664-70 (2004) (codified as amended at 6 U.S.C. § 485). See also 6 U.S.C. § 482 (requiring the establishment of procedures for the sharing of homeland security information).

[4]See Exec. Order No. 13,587, *Structural Reforms to Improve the Security of Classified Networks and the Responsible Sharing and Safeguarding of Classified Information*, 76 Fed. Reg. 63,811 (Oct. 13, 2011).

to department officials, both committees collaborated on the National Information Sharing and Safeguarding Strategy to reflect this dual focus. As the leadership structure continues to evolve, it will be important to ensure that stakeholders, including executives from the key departments, continue to work together to implement Environment priorities.

Further, in 2008, GAO reported that the Program Manager had yet to determine the desired results to be achieved by the Environment and recommended that the Program Manager work with stakeholders to define the Environment's vision.[5] The Program Manager generally agreed and has since defined the Environment's vision and overall mission and included it in the Information Sharing Environment 2012 Annual Report to Congress, providing stakeholders with a high-level understanding of what the Environment is intended to achieve. All five key departments concurred with the 2012 report, including the Environment's vision and overall mission.

Capacity to resolve risks. In a constrained budget environment, departments are facing challenges in funding information sharing priorities. In 2011, GAO recommended that the Program Manager—in coordination with the Policy Committee and the Office of Management and Budget (OMB)—task the key departments to define the incremental costs needed to help ensure successful implementation of the Environment.[6] The Office of the Program Manager generally agreed with the recommendation. Departments are submitting estimates of some related costs to OMB, such as those related to planned technology investments.[7] However, the Program Manager and key departments have not yet identified other incremental costs they will realize in designing and implementing specific Environment initiatives, such as program management and training activities. Also, while the Office of the Program Manager can provide small amounts of startup funds for information sharing initiatives, agencies are ultimately responsible for funding most of these initiatives, and funding constraints have delayed some department

---

[5]GAO, *Information Sharing Environment: Definition of the Results to Be Achieved in Improving Terrorism-Related Information Sharing Is Needed to Guide Implementation and Assess Progress*, GAO-08-492 (Washington, D.C.: June 25, 2008).

[6]GAO, *Information Sharing Environment: Better Road Map Needed to Guide Implementation and Investments*, GAO-11-455 (Washington, D.C.: July 21, 2011).

[7]OMB Circular A-11, *Preparation, Submission, and Execution of the Budget* (July 2010).

efforts. For example, at least one key department has faced funding shortfalls that have delayed information sharing initiatives. DHS officials explained that information sharing initiatives are considered integral to, and not separate from, the department's fundamental mission activities and are to be funded through the DHS components' respective budgets. However, in September 2012, GAO reported that five of DHS's top eight priority information sharing initiatives faced funding shortfalls, and DHS had to delay or scale back at least four of them.[8] Thus, according to the DHS component officials, in a constrained budget environment, the department's components were faced with difficult decisions regarding how to spread funding among information sharing and other mission activities. Until the Program Manager and the key departments define the incremental costs for building out the Environment, and plan for these costs in future budget cycles or otherwise determine how initiatives will be funded or how budget shortfalls will be mitigated, it will be difficult for them to ensure that they have the needed funding capacity to implement the Environment.

The Program Manager and key departments have also taken steps to define and develop technological capabilities and services to improve information sharing and safeguarding. For example, the Office of the Program Manager is participating in efforts to develop an automated means to determine who is authorized to access data and establish a shared service for verifying user identities. The Program Manager is also promoting the adoption of standards to improve information sharing and enable improved interoperability among systems and networks. It will be important for the Program Manager and key departments to continue to develop and refine these capabilities and services, as needed.

Plans that provide corrective measures. The Program Manager and key departments have made progress in developing plans to correct shortcomings that pose risks to information sharing, but have not ensured that all department information sharing initiatives are being leveraged to benefit sharing throughout the government, or established an enterprise

---

[8]GAO, *Information Sharing: DHS Has Demonstrated Leadership and Progress, but Additional Actions Could Help Sustain and Strengthen Efforts*, GAO-12-809 (Washington, D.C.: Sept. 18, 2012).

architecture management plan for the Environment.[9] Specifically, they have defined projects and activities to guide Environment planning efforts—including an implementation roadmap and related guidance—as well as department priorities and responsibilities to address known information sharing gaps. For example, the implementation roadmap calls for the development and implementation of a fusion center performance framework to guide resource allocation.[10] Further, the Program Manager works with OMB to identify annual information sharing priorities to guide department planning efforts. OMB communicates higher-level priorities through its annual programmatic guidance, then the Program Manager issues corresponding guidance—developed in collaboration with the five key departments—to provide specific actions for implementing information sharing priorities.[11] The Program Manager has acknowledged gaps in the plans, however, including how the government will improve sharing with private sector owners and operators of critical infrastructure. In addition, according to the 2012 annual report to Congress, about half of the agencies that participate in the Environment have not implemented plans for interconnecting certain information networks that carry sensitive information for use in assessing threats. GAO recognizes that the Program Manager and key departments will need to continue developing plans and guidance as new priorities emerge. For example, the National Strategy for Information Sharing and Safeguarding (Strategy) was published in December 2012 and identified a number of priority objectives, including the top five priorities, which are intended to guide

---

[9]An enterprise architecture, or modernization blueprint, provides a clear and comprehensive picture of an entity, whether it is an organization (e.g., federal department or agency) or a functional or mission area that cuts across more than one organization (e.g., financial management). This picture consists of snapshots of the enterprise's current and target operational and technological environments and contains a road map for transitioning from the current to the target environment. An enterprise architecture program management plan would, among other things, (1) reflect Environment enterprise architecture program work activities, events, and time frames for improving Environment enterprise architecture management practices and addressing needed architecture content and (2) define accountability mechanisms to help ensure that the plan is implemented.

[10]A fusion center is as a collaborative effort of two or more federal, state, local, or tribal government agencies that combines resources, expertise, or information with the goal of maximizing the ability of such agencies to detect, prevent, investigate, apprehend, and respond to criminal or terrorist activity.

[11]Although the Program Manager issues milestones and time frames that the departments agree to, officials at the Office of the Program Manager explained that the Program Manager does not have the authority to hold departments accountable for these activities.

stakeholders as they work to develop corresponding implementation plans.

In its 2011 report, GAO found that the Environment could benefit from leveraging individual department's information sharing initiatives and recommended that the Program Manager—in consultation with the Policy Committee and key departments—determine to what extent the Environment could better leverage such initiatives to realize benefits government-wide.[12] The Program Manager generally agreed with the recommendation and initiated an effort to catalogue departments' "high value" terrorism-related data. More specifically, the Program Manager asked departments to identify their "high value" terrorism-related information and datasets to determine the extent to which they could be shared and leveraged with Environment partners. One of the key departments, however, did not participate in this effort. Until all key departments are participating in key Environment initiatives, stakeholders cannot ensure that the departments have comprehensively defined and are implementing the corrective actions needed to reduce risks from gaps in sharing terrorism-related information.

The Program Manager and key departments also have not yet developed an enterprise architecture management plan for the Environment.[13] In 2011, GAO recommended that the Program Manager—in consultation with appropriate stakeholders—establish such a plan that, among other things, reflects time frames for improving enterprise architecture management practices and defines accountability mechanisms to help ensure that this plan is implemented. The Program Manager generally agreed, and officials from the Office of the Program Manager have since noted that they expect to issue a plan to address this recommendation by the end of fiscal year 2013. Establishing this plan is critical to improving collaboration and coordination of departments' activities, and driving the planning and management of operational and technological capabilities and services for the nationwide Environment. These capabilities and services include a federated search capability—the ability for users to effectively and efficiently query and search for terrorism-related information across multiple departments' databases.

---

[12]GAO-11-455.

[13]GAO-11-455.

Monitor and validate effectiveness of corrective measures. The Program Manager established a framework in 2011 to measure the performance of key departments in completing corrective measures included in the Environment implementation plan, which is aligned with the Executive Office of the President's priorities for information sharing. Although departments, to some extent, have their own measures to assess the performance of individual initiatives they are implementing, the Program Manager has established a performance framework that is intended to provide a collective measurement of the impacts that the overall Environment is having on the sharing of terrorism-related information. All five of the key departments—in addition to other Environment stakeholders—participated in the 2012 Performance Assessment Questionnaire, which is designed to allow the Program Manager to assess department performance across several priorities. For example, through the annual questionnaire, the Program Manager measures participation in key Environment initiatives, such as the Nationwide Suspicious Activity Reporting Initiative.[14] As the Environment matures, it will be important for the Program Manager and key departments to continue to develop outcome-based metrics that evolve from counting the number of departments that participate in Environment initiatives to measuring the information sharing results achieved from these initiatives. Information on results can help to inform future funding and program decisions.

More recently, officials from the Office of the Program Manager and departments have developed a set of homeland security scenarios to help define what effective information sharing capabilities look like and target levels of capabilities departments should have in place over set time frames, thereby providing a way to monitor the effectiveness of corrective measures. For example, one scenario describes how departments need to mature their capabilities over the next 7 years from the situation where an analyst has to manually check numerous databases to see if there is information related to a suspicious activity to the situation where the analyst has a single point of entry and can conduct one, federated search of linked databases. GAO found, however, that some key departments are not yet using these scenarios, which were established in the fall of 2011, to assess performance. It will be important to monitor the extent to

---

[14]The Nationwide Suspicious Activity Reporting Initiative is to establish a national capacity for gathering, documenting, processing, analyzing, and sharing reports of suspicious activity that is potentially terrorism-related.

which the scenarios provide a useful means to hold departments accountable for improved capabilities and result in improved sharing.

Demonstrate progress implementing corrective measures. The Program Manager, OMB, and departments use a mix of methods—such as programmatic and implementation guidance with time frames and goals for specific department initiatives and the annual performance questionnaire, among other things—to track progress in implementing corrective measures. The Program Manager publicly accounts for this progress in the annual reports the Program Manager submits to Congress.[15] The report is evolving from a catalogue of information sharing activities to an account of progress against goals, objectives, and baselines that can help to inform future decisions. However, the Program Manager and departments have not yet fully developed an integrated way to measure and demonstrate progress in implementing corrective actions and key initiatives. More specifically, all of the plans and corrective actions that GAO has called for, such as the enterprise architecture management plan, as well as emerging priorities, such as those published in the December 2012 National Strategy for Information Sharing and Safeguarding, have yet to be fully defined. The Program Manager, Policy Committee, Steering Committee, and key departments will then need to define corresponding implementation plans and ways to demonstrate progress against those plans. It will be important to monitor how well the Program Manager, OMB, the Policy and Steering committees, and the departments can measure and demonstrate progress against the new Strategy, plans, and priorities.

What Remains to Be Done

Going forward, the Program Manager and key departments, with OMB oversight and support, need to continue working to address remaining action items informed by GAO's five high-risk criteria, thereby helping to reduce risks and enhance the sharing and management of terrorism-related information:

- Capacity to resolve risks.
    - The Program Manager and Policy Committee should demonstrate that departments are defining incremental costs they will need to fund in order to complete their responsibilities and activities to

---

[15]See 6 U.S.C. § 485(h).

substantially achieve the Environment, consistent with the Intelligence Reform Act, as amended.[16] In addition, the Program Manager, in coordination with the key departments, should define the strategies being taken to mitigate the risks that potential funding shortfalls could have on key Environment initiatives and information sharing priorities.

- The Program Manager and key departments, in coordination with OMB, should continue to identify technological capabilities and services that can be shared collaboratively within and across the Environment, consistent with the Environment enterprise architecture approach that the office of the Program Manager expects to issue in fiscal year 2013.

- Plans that provide corrective measures.

  - The Policy Committee should develop methods to help ensure that important sharing initiatives within individual departments are, or will be, leveraged to benefit all relevant federal, state, local, private sector, and international stakeholders participating in the Environment.[17] In addition, the Program Manager, along with key departments, should work to identify and address remaining gaps in sharing information, including gaps in sharing information with private sector owners and operators of critical infrastructure.

  - The Program Manager, along with the Policy Committee and OMB, should issue an Environment enterprise architecture program management plan that (1) reflects Environment enterprise architecture program work activities, events, and time frames for improving enterprise architecture management practices and addressing missing architecture content and (2) defines accountability mechanisms to help ensure that this program management plan is implemented.

- Monitor and validate effectiveness of corrective measures.

  - The Program Manager, in coordination with the Policy Committee and key departments, should continue to develop the Environment's performance framework by developing metrics that measure the performance of, and results achieved by, the overall

---

[16]See, e.g., 6 U.S.C. § 485(e)(3).

[17]GAO-11-455.

Environment and individual departments' projects and activities. More specifically, the performance metrics used by the Program Manager will need to evolve from measuring department participation in key initiatives to the results achieved by key initiatives.

- Demonstrate progress implementing corrective measures.

  - The Program Manager, in conjunction with the Policy and Steering committees, should demonstrate how the new Strategy, plans, guidance, and priorities are linked and integrated in a way that provides the means to track, monitor, and publicly account for progress on individual projects and in substantially achieving the overall Environment, including setting baselines, milestones, and time frames.

GAO Contact

For additional information about this high-risk area, contact Eileen Larence at (202) 512-6510 or larencee@gao.gov.

Related GAO Products

Information Sharing: DHS Has Demonstrated Leadership and Progress, but Additional Actions Could Help Sustain and Strengthen Efforts. GAO-12-809. Washington, D.C.: September 18, 2012.

Terrorist Watchlist: Routinely Assessing Impacts of Agency Actions since the December 25, 2009, Attempted Attack Could Help Inform Future Efforts. GAO-12-476. Washington, D.C.: May 31, 2012.

Maritime Security: Coast Guard Needs to Improve Use and Management of Interagency Operations Centers. GAO-12-202. Washington, D.C.: February 13, 2012.

Transportation Security Information Sharing: Stakeholders Generally Satisfied but TSA Could Improve Analysis, Awareness, and Accountability. GAO-12-44. Washington, D.C.: November 21, 2011.

Information Sharing Environment: Better Road Map Needed to Guide Implementation and Investments. GAO-11-455. Washington, D.C.: July 21, 2011.

Protecting the Federal Government's Information Systems and the Nation's Cyber Critical Infrastructures

Why Area Is High Risk

As computer technology has advanced, federal agencies and our nation's critical infrastructures-such as power distribution, water supply, telecommunications, and emergency services have become increasingly dependent on computerized information systems and electronic data to carry out operations and to process, maintain, and report essential information. The security of these systems and data is essential to protecting national and economic security, and public health and safety. Safeguarding federal computer systems and the systems that support critical infrastructures—referred to as cyber critical infrastructure protection (cyber CIP)—is a continuing concern. Federal information security has been on GAO's list of high-risk areas since 1997; in 2003, GAO expanded this high-risk area to include cyber CIP. Risks to information and communication systems include insider threats from disaffected or careless employees and business partners, escalating and emerging threats from around the globe, the ease of obtaining and using hacking tools, the steady advance in the sophistication of attack technology, and the emergence of new and more destructive attacks.

What GAO Found

Cyber threats and incidents are increasingly prevalent. Threats to systems supporting critical infrastructure and government information systems are evolving and growing. These threats come from a variety of sources and vary in terms of the types and capabilities of the actors, their willingness to act, and their motives. For example, advanced persistent threats—where adversaries possess sophisticated levels of expertise and significant resources to pursue their objectives—pose increasing risks.

Cyber incidents affecting computer systems and networks continue to rise. Over the past 6 years, the number of cyber incidents reported by federal agencies to the U.S. Computer Emergency Readiness Team (US-CERT) has increased from 5,503 in fiscal year 2006 to 48,562 in fiscal year 2012, an increase of 782 percent (see fig. 4). In addition, reports of cyber incidents affecting national security, intellectual property, and individuals have been widespread, with reported incidents involving data loss or theft, economic loss, computer intrusions, and privacy breaches.

Protecting the Federal Government's
Information Systems and the Nation's Cyber
Critical Infrastructures

Figure 4: Incidents Reported to US-CERT, Fiscal Years 2006-2012

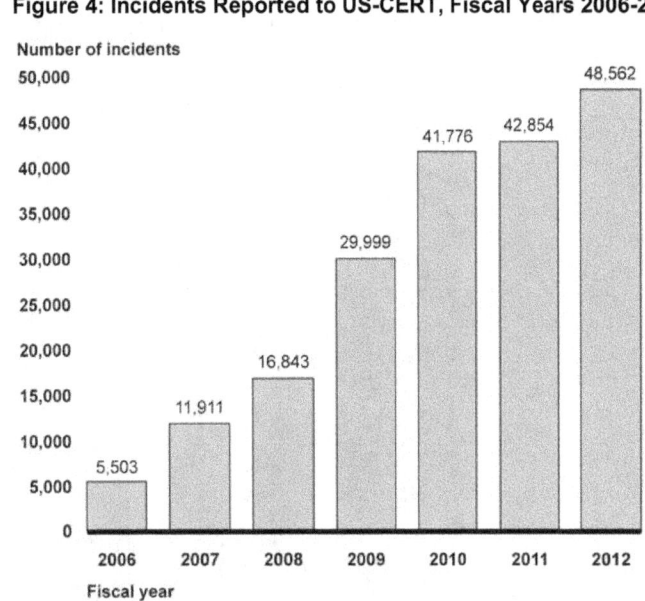

Source: GAO analysis of US-CERT data for fiscal years 2006-2012.

The federal government continues to face challenges in effectively implementing cybersecurity. GAO and agency inspector general reports have identified challenges in a number of key areas of the government's approach to cybersecurity, including those related to protecting the nation's critical infrastructure. While actions have been taken to address aspects of these challenges, issues remain in each of following areas.

- *Designing and implementing risk-based cybersecurity programs at federal agencies.* Shortcomings persist in assessing risks, developing and implementing security controls, and monitoring results at federal agencies. Specifically, for fiscal year 2012, 19 of 24 major federal agencies reported that information security control deficiencies were either a material weakness or significant deficiency in internal controls over financial reporting. Further, inspectors general at 22 of 24 agencies cited information security as a major management challenge for their agency. Most of the 24 major agencies had information security weaknesses in most of five key control categories: limiting, preventing, and detecting inappropriate access to computer resources; managing the configuration of software and hardware; segregating duties to ensure that a single individual does not control all key aspects of a computer-related operation; planning for continuity of operations in the event of a disaster or disruption; and implementing agency-wide information security

Protecting the Federal Government's
Information Systems and the Nation's Cyber
Critical Infrastructures

management programs that are critical to identifying control deficiencies, resolving problems, and managing risks on an ongoing basis (see fig. 5).

Figure 5: Information Security Weaknesses at Major Federal Agencies for Fiscal Year 2012

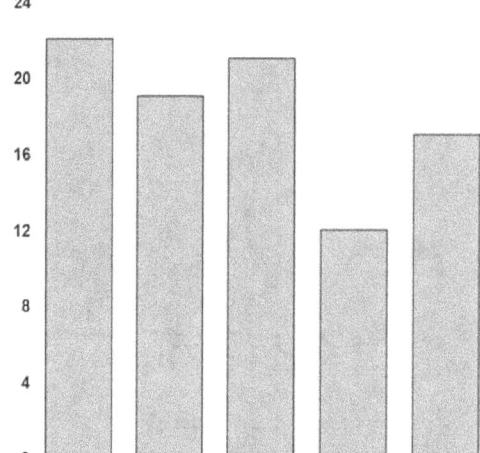

Number of agencies

Information security weaknesses

Source: GAO analysis of agency, inspectors general, and GAO reports as of December 13, 2012.

- *Establishing and identifying standards for critical infrastructures.* The Department of Homeland Security (DHS) and other agencies with responsibilities for specific critical infrastructure sectors have not yet identified cybersecurity guidance applicable to or widely used in each of the sectors. Moreover, sectors vary in the extent to which they are required by law or regulation to comply with specific cybersecurity requirements. Regarding regulatory jurisdiction in securing the U.S. electricity grid, experts GAO spoke with expressed concern that there was a lack of clarity in the division of responsibility between federal and state regulators, particularly regarding cybersecurity.

- *Detecting, responding to, and mitigating cyber incidents.* DHS has made incremental progress in coordinating the federal response to cyber incidents, but challenges remain in sharing information among federal

**Protecting the Federal Government's
Information Systems and the Nation's Cyber
Critical Infrastructures**

agencies and key private sector entities, including critical infrastructure owners, as well as in developing a timely analysis and warning capability.

- *Promoting education, awareness, and workforce planning.* In November 2011, GAO reported that agencies leading strategic planning efforts for education and awareness, including the Department of Commerce, the Office of Management and Budget (OMB), the Office of Personnel Management, and DHS, had not developed details on how they were going to achieve planned outcomes and that the specific tasks and responsibilities were unclear.

- *Promoting research and development (R&D).* The goal of supporting targeted cyber R&D has been impeded by implementation challenges among federal agencies. For example, effectively targeting R&D initiatives has been hindered by limited sharing of detailed information about ongoing research, including the lack of a repository to track R&D projects and funding, as required by law.

- *Managing risks to the global information technology supply chain.* Reliance on a global supply chain for information technology products and services introduces risks to systems, and federal agencies have not always addressed these risks. Specifically, in March 2012, GAO reported that four national security-related agencies varied in the extent to which they had defined supply chain protection measures for their information systems and were not in a position to develop implementing procedures and monitoring capabilities for such measures.

- *Addressing international cybersecurity challenges.* While progress has been made in identifying the importance of international cooperation and assigning roles and responsibilities related to it, the government's approach to addressing international aspects of cybersecurity has not yet been completely defined and implemented.

Until the administration and executive branch agencies implement the hundreds of recommendations made by GAO and agency inspectors general to address cyber challenges, resolve identified deficiencies, and fully implement effective security programs, a broad array of federal assets and operations will remain at risk of fraud, misuse, and disruption, and the nation's most critical federal and private sector infrastructure systems will remain at increased risk of attack from adversaries.

The government has issued a variety of strategy-related documents over the last decade, many of which address aspects of the above challenge

Protecting the Federal Government's
Information Systems and the Nation's Cyber
Critical Infrastructures

areas. The documents address priorities for enhancing cybersecurity within the federal government as well as for encouraging improvements in the cybersecurity of critical infrastructure within the private sector. Since the February 2011 update to GAO's high-risk series, the administration has issued several strategies and planning documents to address aspects of national and federal cybersecurity. For example, in 2011, the administration issued the National Strategy For Trusted Identities In Cyberspace to outline a strategy to make online transactions more secure for business and consumers; the International Strategy for Cyberspace to lay out an approach to engage with international partners on a range of cyber issues and communicate our nation's priorities and how to reduce the threats faced in cyberspace; and Trustworthy Cyberspace: Strategic Plan for the Federal Cybersecurity Research and Development Program, to provide a set of coordinated research priorities that could result in a trustworthy cyberspace.

The administration has also taken steps to enhance various cybersecurity security capabilities. For example, in 2012, in coordination with experts from DHS and the Department of Defense, the National Institute of Standards and Technology, and OMB, it established agency performance goals and a tracking mechanism to monitor performance in three cross-agency priority areas for improving the cybersecurity capabilities of the federal government (see table 7).

Table 7: Descriptions of Priority Areas

Priority area	Description
Trusted Internet connections	Consolidate external telecommunication access points and establish a set of baseline security capabilities for situational awareness and enhanced monitoring.
Continuous monitoring of federal information systems	Transform static security control assessment and authorization process into a dynamic risk mitigation program that provides essential, near real-time security status and remediation.
Strong authentication	Increase the use of federal smartcard credentials such as Personal Identity Verification and Common Access Cards that provide multi-factor authentication and digital signature and encryption capabilities.

Source: GAO.

Improving these capabilities is a step in the right direction and their effective implementation can enhance federal information security.

However, while these and other strategy documents have included certain characteristics of a comprehensive strategic approach that can enhance the usefulness of national strategies, such as setting goals and

**Protecting the Federal Government's
Information Systems and the Nation's Cyber
Critical Infrastructures**

subordinate objectives, they generally lacked other key elements. These missing elements include:

- *Milestones and performance measures.* The government's strategy documents include few milestones or performance measures, making it difficult to track progress in accomplishing stated goals and objectives.

- *Cost and resources.* Past strategy documents linked certain activities to budget submissions; however, none have fully addressed cost and resources.

- *Roles and responsibilities.* Cybersecurity strategy documents have assigned high-level roles and responsibilities but have left important details unclear. For example, OMB and DHS roles and responsibilities for overseeing agencies information security programs have not been clearly defined.

- *Linkage with other key strategy documents.* Existing cybersecurity strategy documents vary in terms of priorities and structure, and they don't specify how they link to or supersede other documents, nor do they describe how they fit into the overall national cybersecurity strategy.

The many continuing cybersecurity challenges faced by the government highlight the need for a more clearly defined oversight process to ensure agencies are held accountable for implementing effective information security programs. Further, until an overarching national cybersecurity strategy is developed that addresses all key elements of desirable characteristics, overall progress in achieving the government's objectives is likely to remain limited.

What Remains to Be Done

The administration needs to prepare an overarching cybersecurity strategy that includes all desirable characteristics of a national strategy, including milestones and performance measures; cost, sources, and justification for needed resources; specific roles and responsibilities of federal organizations; guidance, where appropriate, regarding how this strategy relates to priorities, goals, and objectives stated in other national strategy documents; and demonstrate progress in implementing the strategies and achieving measureable and appropriate outcomes. The strategy should include a roadmap for making significant improvements in cybersecurity challenge areas listed above and better ensure that federal departments and agencies are held accountable for making significant improvements in those cybersecurity challenge areas.

Protecting the Federal Government's
Information Systems and the Nation's Cyber
Critical Infrastructures

Congress should also consider legislation to better define roles and responsibilities for implementing and overseeing federal information security programs and for protecting the nation's critical cyber assets. For example, better defining roles and responsibilities for DHS and OMB oversight of federal information security.

Executive branch agencies, in particular DHS, also need to continue to enhance their cyber analytical and technical capabilities, expand oversight of federal agencies' implementation of information security, and demonstrate progress in strengthening the effectiveness of public-private sector partnerships in securing cyber critical infrastructures.

Agencies also need to (1) develop and implement remedial action plans for resolving known security deficiencies of government systems; (2) fully develop and effectively implement agency-wide information security programs, as required by the Federal Information Security Management Act of 2002; and (3) demonstrate measurable, sustained progress in improving security over federal systems. Such progress should include having the government-wide material weakness in information security upgraded to a significant deficiency for 2 consecutive years and reducing the factors that contribute to the significant deficiency, as reported by GAO in its annual audit of the financial statements for the United States government.

GAO Contact

For additional information about this high-risk area, contact Gregory C. Wilshusen at (202) 512-6244 or wilshuseng@gao.gov.

Related GAO Products

Information Security: Federal Communications Commission Needs to Strengthen Controls over Enhanced Secured Network Project. GAO-13-155. Washington, D.C.: January 25, 2013.

Information Security: Better Implementation of Controls for Mobile Devices Should Be Encouraged. GAO-12-757. Washington, D.C.: September 18, 2012.

Medical Devices: FDA Should Expand Its Consideration of Information Security for Certain Types of Devices. GAO-12-816. Washington, D.C.: August 31, 2012.

Information Security: Environmental Protection Agency Needs to Resolve Weaknesses. GAO-12-696. Washington, D.C.: July 19, 2012.

Protecting the Federal Government's
Information Systems and the Nation's Cyber
Critical Infrastructures

Cybersecurity: Threats Impacting the Nation. GAO-12-666T. Washington, D.C.: April 24, 2012.

Cybersecurity: Challenges in Securing the Electricity Grid. GAO-12-926T. Washington, D.C.: July 17, 2012.

Cybersecurity Human Capital: Initiatives Need Better Planning and Coordination. GAO-12-8. Washington, D.C.: November 29, 2011.

Information Security: Additional Guidance Needed to Address Cloud Computing Concerns. GAO-12-130T. Washington, D.C.: October 6, 2011.

Information Security: Weaknesses Continue Amid New Federal Efforts to Implement Requirements. GAO-12-137. Washington, D.C.: October 3, 2011.

Information Security: State Has Taken Steps to Implement a Continuous Monitoring Application, but Key Challenges Remain. GAO-11-149. Washington, D.C.: July 8, 2011.

Ensuring the Effective Protection of Technologies Critical to U.S. National Security Interests

Why Area Is High Risk

Technological superiority is critical to U.S. military strategy. As such, the Department of Defense (DOD) spends billions of dollars each year to develop and acquire sophisticated weapons to provide an advantage for the warfighter during combat or other missions. Many of these weapons and military technologies are sold overseas to promote U.S. economic, foreign policy, and national security interests. They also are targets for theft, espionage, and illegal export.

The U.S. government has a number of programs to identify and protect technologies critical to U.S. interests. These include export control systems for defense articles and services and dual-use items, the Foreign Military Sales program, anti-tamper policies, and reviews of transactions that could result in control of a U.S. business by a foreign person. These programs are administered by multiple federal agencies with various interests, including DOD and the Departments of Commerce, Homeland Security, Justice, State, and the Treasury. As GAO previously reported, each program has had its own set of challenges, which are largely attributable to poor coordination within complex interagency processes, inefficiencies in program operations, and a lack of systematic evaluations of program effectiveness. GAO designated this area as high risk in 2007 because these programs, established decades ago, were ill-equipped to address the evolving 21st century challenge of balancing national security concerns and economic interests. GAO believes that a strategic re-examination of existing programs is needed to identify changes that will ensure the advancement of U.S. interests.

What GAO Found

Since GAO first designated the effective protection of critical technologies as a high-risk area, agencies have taken steps to improve their individual programs. For example, DOD implemented guidance to ensure that weapons sold through the Foreign Military Sales program are protected as required. Also, in 2012, the Department of the Treasury adopted a new electronic licensing system to share license information on U.S. exports to Iran with other agencies, including U.S. Customs and Border Protection.

While these are positive steps, GAO has identified areas in which further action is needed to improve specific programs. For example, although DOD took steps to address previously identified weaknesses in updating and maintaining the Militarily Critical Technologies List (MCTL), the list is not being used to inform export control decisions—its original purpose. Further, the list remains outdated; in 2011, DOD ceased updating the MCTL because of funding constraints. DOD needs to ensure that a technical reference—MCTL or an alternative—is available for consistently identifying militarily critical technologies. Actions also are needed in other programs:

- Enforcement agencies need to improve data sharing with the intelligence community to monitor illicit transshipments of export-controlled items.

- The Departments of State and Commerce, in consultation with the Departments of Homeland Security and Justice, and other agencies as appropriate, need to improve the time frames for processing license determination requests. This process confirms whether an item is controlled and requires a license, and thereby helps officials determine whether an export control violation has occurred.

- DOD and the Department of State need to eliminate gaps and inconsistencies in implementing their respective end-use monitoring efforts.

The administration continues to move forward with its export control reform efforts that began in 2010, which have the potential to improve the efficiency and effectiveness of the export control process. As part of the reform efforts, the Department of Homeland Security was tasked with establishing the Export Enforcement Coordination Center, which opened in March 2012, to help improve agency coordination on export control enforcement investigations. Agencies are taking initial steps to address enforcement challenges identified by GAO, such as developing a more robust performance measurement system; however, enforcement agencies have yet to develop standard operating procedures to enhance coordination through the center. The administration also has taken steps to clarify which items will be controlled under the U.S. Munitions List versus the Commerce Control List, in part, to help companies seeking to export defense articles and services and dual-use items to more easily determine whether items are regulated by State or Commerce. This review is taking longer than originally anticipated and concerns exist that the removal of items controlled under the U.S. Munitions List could result in a decreased visibility of exports and an increased need for resources to perform compliance activities.

Multiple agencies, with different authorities, missions, and interests, administer or play a role in the programs that are responsible for identifying and protecting these critical technologies. GAO has expressed concern, however, that the programs do not work collectively as a system. To date, the administration has not taken steps to re-examine the portfolio of programs to address their collective effectiveness. Recent agency actions have been primarily limited to addressing challenges in individual programs and do not provide insight into whether the programs are collectively effective. Also, none of the agencies has taken or been assigned responsibility for addressing the challenges GAO has identified. However, in a recent meeting with senior administration officials across the agencies and the Office of Management and Budget, officials agreed to consider whether to assign a leadership role for this area and if it should be with an existing committee of representatives from each of the agencies. Senior DOD officials noted that in addition to its involvement in export control reform, DOD has initiatives underway to review multiple programs and processes designed to protect critical technologies. Because these initiatives are internal to DOD, other agencies with responsibilities for the various critical technology programs are not involved; however, these initiatives present an opportunity for the agencies to work together to re-examine the portfolio and address GAO's concerns.

What Remains to Be Done

GAO has made a number of recommendations in this area aimed at improving coordination among the programs that are intended to protect technologies critical to U.S. national security and has called for a re-examination of the entire portfolio. GAO's body of work underscores longstanding problems and shows that challenges persist within and across the programs designed to protect technologies critical to U.S. national security interests. To address these challenges, action is needed at three levels.

- First, individual agencies need to continue to implement GAO recommendations to address weaknesses in their respective programs—some of which remain unaddressed several years after GAO reported these weaknesses. For example, DOD, the Department of Homeland Security, and the Department of State have yet to address a 2009 GAO recommendation to improve interagency practices to facilitate reliable shipment verification of military items transferred through the Foreign Military Sales program. In addition, State and DOD have not yet made changes to clarify the use of export exemptions in support of defense activities.

- Second, as the administration continues its export control reform efforts, it should ensure that previously identified weaknesses in the system are addressed, such as the need for better coordination among enforcement agencies. Export control agencies, particularly the Departments of State and Commerce, should assess and report on the potential impact, including the benefits and risks of proposed export control list reforms, on the resource needs of their compliance activities.

- Finally, GAO has previously reported that the executive branch and Congress should consider re-evaluating the wider portfolio of critical technology-related programs. Ongoing export control reform efforts and other internal DOD reform initiatives present an opportunity to assess prospects for achieving full harmonization across separate but related programs designed to protect critical technologies. Key to demonstrating continued progress will be assigning leadership either to an agency or coordinating body to (1) assess the underlying causes of problems in individual programs and the resulting effect on the broader portfolio, (2) develop and implement effective solutions, and (3) monitor the effectiveness of corrective actions taken.

GAO Contact

For additional information about this high-risk area, contact Belva M. Martin at (202) 512-4841 or martinb@gao.gov.

Related GAO Products

Protecting Defense Technologies: DOD Assessment Needed to Determine Requirement for Critical Technologies List. GAO-13-157. Washington, D.C.: January 23, 2013.

Nonproliferation: Agencies Could Improve Information Sharing and End-Use Monitoring on Unmanned Aerial Vehicle Exports. GAO-12-536. Washington, D.C.: July 30, 2012.

Export Controls: U.S. Agencies Need to Assess Control List Reform's Impact on Compliance Activities. GAO-12-613. Washington, D.C.: April 23, 2012.

Export Controls: Proposed Reforms Create Opportunities to Address Enforcement Challenges. GAO-12-246. Washington, D.C.: March 27, 2012.

Persian Gulf: Implementation Gaps Limit the Effectiveness of End-Use Monitoring and Human Rights Vetting for U.S. Military Equipment. GAO-12-89. Washington, D.C.: November 17, 2011.

Revamping Federal Oversight of Food Safety

Why Area Is High Risk

The fragmented federal oversight of food safety has caused inconsistent oversight, ineffective coordination, and inefficient use of resources. The 2010 nationwide recall of more than 500 million eggs because of *Salmonella* contamination highlights this fragmentation. Several agencies have different roles and responsibilities in the egg production system, including the Food and Drug Administration (FDA) and the U.S. Department of Agriculture's (USDA) Food Safety Inspection Service (FSIS), USDA's Agricultural Marketing Service, and USDA's Animal and Plant Health Inspection Service. Three major trends also create food safety challenges: (1) a substantial and increasing portion of the U.S. food supply is imported, (2) consumers are eating more raw and minimally processed foods, and (3) growing segments of the population are increasingly susceptible to foodborne illnesses.

New food safety legislation, the FDA Food Safety Modernization Act (FSMA), which was signed into law in January 2011, strengthens a major part of the food safety system. It shifts the focus of FDA regulators from responding to contamination to preventing it, according to FDA, and expands FDA's oversight authority. While FSMA has several provisions that require interagency collaboration on food safety oversight, it does not apply to the federal food safety system as a whole or address USDA's authorities, which remain separate and distinct from FDA's. What's more, because FSMA is not yet fully implemented and a number of the regulations required under the law are still under development or review, it is too early to understand in depth the impact of the law on federal oversight of food safety.[1]

What GAO Found

GAO recommended that one of the actions to help reduce fragmentation was for the President to reconvene the Council on Food Safety. The President demonstrated strong commitment and top leadership support by establishing the Food Safety Working Group in 2009 to coordinate federal efforts and develop goals to make food safe. The working group is co-chaired by the Secretaries of Health and Human Services and Agriculture and includes officials from many federal agencies, including FDA and USDA. Through the working group, federal agencies have taken

---

[1]FDA has developed two draft rules—one on produce safety and the other on preventive controls for human food—which were issued in January 2013 and at the time of GAO's report were available for public comment. Other FSMA-related rules are still under development.

steps designed to increase collaboration in some areas that cross regulatory jurisdictions—in particular, improving produce safety, reducing *Salmonella* contamination, and developing food safety performance measures. In the case of *Salmonella*, for example, USDA officials told us that staff from USDA and FDA communicated on a regular basis to coordinate efforts to develop their respective agencies' goals, as they are closely intertwined. Both agencies set goals to reduce illness from *Salmonella* within their own areas of egg safety jurisdiction by the end of 2011. According to the USDA officials, USDA and FDA coordinated on ensuring that the goals complemented one another, utilized the same datasets, and covered the same time period so that the agencies measure their progress consistently. What's more, because FDA has not yet fully implemented the regulations required by FSMA, it is too early to understand in depth the impact of the law on federal oversight of food safety.

While such actions are encouraging, they are first steps. The agencies have not developed a government-wide performance plan for food safety that includes results-oriented goals and performance measures and information about resources. Such a plan is particularly important in an era, such as the present, of tight federal budgets. When GAO added food safety to the High Risk List in 2007, it said that what remains to be done is to develop a government-wide performance plan that is mission-based, has a results orientation, and provides a cross-agency perspective. Such a plan could be used to guide corrective actions for addressing fragmentation and monitoring progress by the 15 federal agencies that collectively administer at least 30 food-related laws. Without a government-wide plan, decision makers do not have a comprehensive picture of the federal government's performance on food safety.

Food safety oversight remains fragmented in several areas. The primary food safety agencies are FSIS, which is responsible for ensuring the safety of meat, poultry, and processed egg products, and FDA, which is responsible for ensuring the safety of virtually all other food.

GAO has also reported that food safety oversight is fragmented in the following areas:

- As GAO reported in August 2011, there is no centralized coordination to monitor the federal government's overall progress in implementing the nation's food and agriculture defense policy, established in Homeland Security Presidential Directive-9 (HSPD-9). HSPD-9 assigns more than nine federal agencies various responsibilities to enhance the nation's preparedness for food and agriculture emergencies. Without centralized oversight, however, the federal government cannot ensure that these nine agencies' efforts are coordinated to overcome fragmentation, efficiently use scarce funds, and promote the overall effectiveness of the federal government. GAO recommended that the Homeland Security Council direct the National Security Staff to establish an interagency process that would oversee agencies' implementation of HSPD-9 and that the Department of Homeland Security resume its efforts to coordinate agencies' overall HSPD-9 implementation efforts. The Department of Homeland Security (DHS) generally agreed with GAO's recommendation, and the National Security Staff stated that it agreed that a review of HSPD-9 is appropriate and that they would look for an opportunity to do so. DHS and NSS officials told us that they have taken some steps to address these recommendations; however, the recommendations have not yet been fully implemented.

- Fragmentation occurs in coordinating messages about recalls of food products during multistate outbreaks of foodborne illnesses. In these cases, many agencies, including FDA, USDA, DHS, the Centers for Disease Control and Prevention, and state and local governments, play a role in responding to these events. In July 2012, GAO reported that FDA had not implemented recommendations previously made by other entities, such as the Institute of Medicine, to help address challenges in advising the public about food recalls and food borne illness outbreaks. GAO recommended that FDA implement these recommendations, which included (1) developing a coordinated plan for crisis communications with other federal agencies and (2) consulting with USDA on lessons learned in advising consumers about recalls to determine whether any of USDA's practices may be feasible at FDA, as consistent with applicable law. The Department of Health and Human Services, FDA's parent agency, neither agreed nor disagreed with the recommendations in the report but stated that it and FDA will explore each recommendation as they consider how to implement the recall provisions of FSMA. The Department of Health and Human Services also indicated that FDA is working with DHS's National Incident Management System to improve interagency efforts during incidents and that FDA will continue to work with USDA to gain insight and determine whether any of USDA's current practices may be feasible at FDA. These actions, if appropriately implemented, could help address GAO's recommendations.

- Provisions of the Food, Conservation, and Energy Act of 2008 (Farm Bill) that assigned FSIS responsibility for issuing final regulations to carry out a catfish examination and inspection program would result in duplication of federal programs and cost taxpayers millions of dollars annually without enhancing the safety of catfish intended for human consumption. Specifically, FDA has traditionally overseen the safety of all seafood, including catfish, but the Farm Bill assigned regulatory responsibility for catfish inspection to USDA once USDA issues final regulations for a mandatory catfish examination and inspection program. Under its proposed program, FSIS would conduct continuous inspections of domestic catfish processing. As GAO reported in May 2012, if FSIS were to implement its proposed catfish inspection program, responsibility for overseeing seafood safety would be further divided and would duplicate existing federal programs at an additional cost. First, the FSIS program would require implementation of hazard analysis plans that are essentially the same as FDA's hazard analysis requirements for seafood. (FDA would still inspect all other types of seafood). Second, as many as three agencies—FDA, FSIS, and the National Marine Fisheries Service—could inspect facilities that process both catfish and other types of seafood. Both FDA and the National Marine Fisheries Service officials stated that continuous inspection will not improve catfish safety and is counter to the use of FDA's hazard analysis requirements, in which systems are most efficiently monitored periodically rather than daily. Third, under FSMA, FDA has an opportunity to enhance the safety of all imported seafood—including catfish—and avoid the duplication of effort and cost that would result from FSIS's implementation of its proposed program. To enhance the effectiveness of the food safety system for catfish and avoid duplication of effort and cost, GAO suggested that Congress consider repealing provisions of the Farm Bill that assigned USDA responsibility for examining and inspecting catfish and for creating a catfish inspection program. Congress has not taken such action.

GAO is monitoring the agencies' progress by following up on all these recommendations.

What Remains to Be Done

The executive branch should develop a government-wide performance plan that includes results-oriented goals and performance measures and a discussion of strategies and resources in order to guide corrective actions and monitor progress. The Working Group should continue to facilitate coordination between the food safety agencies. While FSMA expands FDA's oversight authority in many areas, it does not apply to the entire federal food safety system. Congress should continue to monitor the success of the Working Group and of FSMA. If, over the next several years, the Working Group does not provide sustained leadership, and if FSMA's prevention-based approach does not successfully address weaknesses in the food safety system, Congress may wish to assess the need for comprehensive, uniform, risk-based food safety legislation or amend FDA's and USDA's existing authorities—recognizing that tight budgets may constrain far-reaching actions for the foreseeable future. Congress should also consider commissioning a detailed analysis of alternative organizational structures for food safety. Finally, Congress should consider repealing provisions of the Farm Bill that assigned USDA responsibility for examining and inspecting catfish and for creating a catfish inspection program.

GAO Contact

For additional information about this high-risk area, contact J. Alfredo Gomez at (202) 512-3841 or gomezj@gao.gov.

Related GAO Products

Food Safety: FDA Can Better Oversee Food Imports by Assessing and Leveraging Other Countries' Oversight Resources. GAO-12-933. Washington, D.C.: September 28, 2012.

Food Safety: FDA's Food Advisory and Recall Process Needs Strengthening. GAO-12-589. Washington, D.C.: July 26, 2012.

Food Safety: Responsibility for Inspecting Catfish Should Not Be Assigned to USDA. GAO-12-411. Washington, D.C.: May 10, 2012.

Food Safety: Pre-Slaughter Interventions Could Reduce E.coli in Cattle. GAO-12-257. Washington, D.C.: March 9, 2012.

Antibiotic Resistance: Agencies Have Made Limited Progress Addressing Antibiotic Use in Animals. GAO-11-801. Washington, D.C.: September 7, 2011.

Homeland Security: Actions Needed to Improve Response to Potential Terrorist Attacks and Natural Disasters Affecting Food and Agriculture. GAO-11-652. Washington, D.C: August 19, 2011.

Federal Food Safety Oversight: Food Safety Working Group Is a Positive First Step but Governmentwide Planning Is Needed to Address Fragmentation. GAO-11-289. Washington, D.C.: March 18, 2011.

Food Safety: FDA Needs to Reassess Its Approach to Reducing an Illness Caused by Eating Raw Oysters. GAO-11-607. Washington, D.C.: September 8, 2011.

Food Labeling: FDA Needs to Reassess Its Approach to Protecting Consumers from False or Misleading Claims. GAO-11-102. Washington, D.C.: January 14, 2011.

Food and Drug Administration: Overseas Offices Have Taken Steps to Help Ensure Import Safety, but More Long-Term Planning Is Needed. GAO-10-960. Washington, D.C.: September 30, 2010.

Food Safety: FDA Could Strengthen Oversight of Imported Food by Improving Enforcement. GAO-10-699T. Washington, D.C.: May 6, 2010.

Food Safety: FDA Has Begun to Take Action to Address Weaknesses in Food Safety Research, but Gaps Remain. GAO-10-182R. Washington, D.C.: April 23, 2010.

Food Irradiation: FDA Could Improve Its Documentation and Communication of Key Decisions on Food Irradiation Petitions. GAO-10-309R, Washington, D.C.: February 16, 2010

Food Safety: Agencies Need to Address Gaps in Enforcement and Collaboration to Enhance Safety of Imported Food. GAO-09-873. Washington, D.C.: September 15, 2009.

Protecting Public Health through Enhanced Oversight of Medical Products

Why Area Is High Risk

Millions of medical products are used by Americans on a daily basis at home, in the hospital, and in other health care settings. The Food and Drug Administration (FDA) has the vital mission of protecting the public health by overseeing the safety and effectiveness of these products—drugs, biologics, and medical devices—marketed in the United States. The agency's responsibilities begin long before a product is brought to market and continue after a product's approval, regardless of whether it is manufactured here or abroad. The importance of FDA's role in ensuring our citizens' well-being cannot be overstated. In recent years, FDA has been confronted with multiple challenges. Rapid changes in science and technology, globalization, unpredictable public health crises, an increasing workload, and the continuing need to monitor the safety of thousands of marketed medical products have strained the agency's resources. The oversight of medical products was added to GAO's High Risk List in 2009 because FDA was facing a variety of difficulties that threatened to compromise its ability to protect the public health. While progress has been made, GAO has found considerable challenges remain.

What GAO Found

In recent years, GAO has identified a variety of weaknesses in FDA's oversight of medical products. It is important to note that FDA has made positive strides in certain areas. Also, the Food and Drug Administration Safety and Innovation Act, enacted in July 2012, contains provisions that should further help the agency protect public health. However, GAO continues to believe that FDA needs to enhance its oversight of medical products. FDA needs to address persistent and previously identified shortcomings as well as problematic issues that have more recently emerged. Key issues that GAO has focused attention on include:

- *Drug availability.* In recent years, hospitals and health care professionals have increasingly reported nationwide shortages of drugs, including those that are life-saving and life-sustaining. These shortages directly threaten public health by preventing patients from accessing essential medications. During shortages, physicians may have to ration their supplies, delay treatments, or use alternative medications that may be less effective or pose unwanted side effects. The number of drug shortages has grown substantially and increased each year from 2006 through 2010, with a record number reported in 2010. GAO found that FDA's ability to respond to drug shortages is constrained by a variety of management challenges. For example, FDA does not systematically maintain and track data on drug shortages, and therefore cannot monitor trends. It also lacks a set of results-oriented performance metrics and has not identified drug shortages as an area of strategic importance for the agency. As a result, FDA cannot ensure that it coordinates efficiently with officials across the agency as well as manufacturers regarding prevention or mitigation strategies.

While drug shortages remain a public health concern, positive steps have been taken. GAO recognized that FDA has increasingly prevented potential drug shortages from occurring when informed of a potential shortage in advance. However, GAO also noted that the agency's approach to managing shortages has been predominately reactive as it lacked authority to require manufacturers to take certain actions to prevent, alleviate, or resolve shortages, such as notifying the agency of an impending or potential shortage. In 2011, GAO suggested that Congress consider establishing a requirement for manufacturers to report to FDA any changes that could affect the supply of their drugs. The recently enacted Food and Drug Administration Safety and Innovation Act requires manufacturers of drugs that are life-supporting, life-sustaining, or used to prevent or treat debilitating diseases or conditions to notify FDA at least 6 months in advance if they either plan to discontinue manufacturing the drug or anticipate an interruption in manufacturing that is likely to lead to a meaningful disruption in the drug's supply. In addition, FDA has begun to devote more staff and resources to its Drug Shortage Program.

- *Medical device recalls.* Millions of medical devices are used daily to diagnose, treat, or prevent illness. These devices range from simple tools like bandages and surgical clamps to more complicated devices such as pacemakers and artificial heart valves. If one proves to be defective or unsafe once it is in widespread use, the ramifications can be severe, potentially resulting in permanent injuries or death to patients or providers using the device. From 2005 through 2009, firms initiated 3,510 medical device recalls, an average of just over 700 per year. Just over 40 percent of the recalls involved cardiovascular, radiological, or orthopedic devices. Recalls are an important tool to mitigate the risk of serious health consequences associated with defective or unsafe medical devices. Typically, a recall is voluntarily initiated by the firm that manufactured the device and FDA oversees implementation of the recall. However, FDA has not routinely analyzed recall data to determine whether there are systemic problems underlying trends in device recalls, thus missing an opportunity to proactively identify and address the risks presented by unsafe devices.

In addition, FDA's procedures for overseeing recalls are unclear. As a result, FDA officials examining similar situations sometimes reached opposite conclusions on whether recalls were conducted and completed effectively. FDA had also not established criteria, based on the nature or type of devices, for assessing whether firms corrected or removed a sufficient number of recalled devices. This is particularly important because, for many high-risk recalls—that is those FDA classified as having a reasonable probability of causing serious adverse health consequences or death—recalling firms faced challenges locating specific devices or users, and thus could not correct or remove all devices. Additionally, FDA's decisions to terminate completed recalls—that is, assess whether firms had taken sufficient actions to prevent a recurrence of the problems that led to the recalls—were frequently not made within its prescribed time frames. Finally, FDA did not document its justification for terminating recalls. Without such documentation, GAO was unable to assess the extent to which FDA's termination process appropriately evaluated recalling firms' corrective actions. FDA agreed with GAO's recommendations to address its findings and the Food and Drug Administration Safety and Innovation Act, enacted in 2012, requires the agency to take action consistent with them.

- *The Safe Medical Devices Act of 1990.* Of considerable importance is FDA's progress in implementing the Safe Medical Devices Act of 1990. The act requires FDA to determine the appropriate process for reviewing certain high-risk devices—either reclassifying certain high-risk medical device types to a less-risky class or establishing a schedule for such devices to be reviewed through its most stringent premarket approval process. While FDA determined that more than 100 device types were subject to this provision, the agency never established a timetable for its reclassification or re-review process. Although more than 20 years have elapsed, a significant number of high-risk devices—including device types that FDA has identified as implantable; life sustaining; or posing a significant risk to the health, safety, or welfare of a patient—still enter the market through FDA's less stringent premarket review process. FDA has agreed that implementing this act is important and has taken the step of requiring the submission of safety and effectiveness data for the remaining 26 device types. However, progress has been slow and the agency still must issue final rules for 19 of the 26 device types and develop a realistic timetable for completing the implementation of the act.

- *Globalization.* Globalization has fundamentally altered the medical product manufacturing landscape. It has significantly increased reliance on medical products manufactured overseas, thus complicating FDA's efforts to ensure that these products are of high quality. The sheer volume of medical products manufactured overseas poses significant challenges for FDA. There are thousands of foreign drug and medical device establishments registered to market their products in the United States. According to FDA, 80 percent of the active pharmaceutical ingredients in our medications come from other countries, as do 40 percent of finished dosage drugs. Imports of pharmaceutical and biological products have more than doubled since 2002 and half of all medical devices are also manufactured elsewhere. Globalization has also resulted in an increase in supply chain complexity—networks of handlers, suppliers, and middlemen—making it difficult to trace an ingredient back to its source. Although FDA inspects foreign manufacturing establishments and has increased the number of foreign establishments it inspects in recent years, it still conducts relatively few foreign establishment inspections, compared to those conducted domestically. Moreover, some foreign establishments may have never received an FDA inspection. In addition to more routine quality problems, there is growing concern with the deliberate substitution or addition of harmful ingredients to our medical products. This practice, known as economic adulteration, may be done to either increase the apparent value of products or to reduce their production costs. FDA recognizes that imported products may be particularly vulnerable to economic adulteration and has engaged many FDA offices and centers in the agency's efforts to address this problem. However, these components have not always communicated or coordinated effectively to combat adulteration. FDA has not issued specific written guidance on how its components should approach or address their various economic adulteration efforts.

It is important to recognize that FDA is taking action on a variety of fronts to meet the challenge of globalization. In 2011, FDA formed a new office—the Office of Global Regulatory Operations and Policy—comprised of its Office of Regulatory Affairs and its Office of International Programs. This reorganization was executed to emphasize the agency's commitment to confronting the challenges of globalization and to help prepare the agency to move from being a regulator of domestic products to one overseeing a worldwide market. FDA has also expanded its presence overseas and now has offices in Africa, Asia, Europe, Latin America, and the Middle East. FDA completed a formal strategic plan to guide the activities of its foreign offices in March 2011. Through its overseas offices, FDA is working to increase its knowledge base about the standards used by foreign regulators in countries that produce medical products destined for the U.S. market. It is also providing assistance to help certain countries improve their regulatory capacities. Among other things, FDA is enhancing collaboration with its regulatory counterparts around the world to harmonize standards, leverage resources, and conduct joint inspections of foreign manufacturing establishments. FDA also implemented GAO's 2011 recommendation to adopt a working definition of economic adulteration. Finally, recently enacted legislation should also help enhance FDA's ability to oversee the growing number of drugs coming into the U.S. market from overseas. The Food and Drug Administration Safety and Innovation Act, enacted in 2012, directed FDA to take a risk-based approach to inspecting both foreign and domestic drug manufacturing establishments, consistent with a 2008 GAO recommendation.

- *Timeliness of medical products application reviews.* Reviewing applications to market new medical products in the United States is one of FDA's major premarket responsibilities. FDA's evaluation is needed to ensure that new products are safe and effective. To help ensure that making such products available to patients in a timely manner is a priority, FDA has established performance goals that include time frames for reviewing and acting on these applications. Although FDA is meeting most of its goals, reviews of medical device applications are taking longer. Industry and consumer groups have also raised issues related to the review process, citing matters such as insufficient communication between FDA and stakeholders, a perceived lack of predictability and consistency in reviews, and inadequate assurances regarding the safety and effectiveness of new products. FDA is engaged in activities to address many of these issues and improve the review process for both drugs and devices. It is important for FDA to continue monitoring these efforts in order to increase the efficiency and effectiveness of the review process and thereby help ensure that safe and effective products are reaching the market in a timely manner.

- *Tracking medical products applications for children.* The physiological differences between adults and children, challenges with recruiting pediatric participants for clinical trials, and limited economic incentives make the development of medical products for the pediatric population challenging. It is therefore imperative that FDA's reviews of applications to market such products are closely tracked. Without available pediatric products, children may not receive treatment or may be exposed to incorrect dosing and ineffective or harmful care. Despite this, applications to market new products for children are not tracked by the agency. For example, GAO found that FDA lacks an important internal control process to ensure that the requirements contained in the Pediatric Research Equity Act are met. FDA does not track and aggregate data about applications for drugs or biologics subject to this law until near the end of the application review process. Because the law's requirements and FDA's goals focus on timely review and because some of the products studied may already be on the market for adult use, it is imperative that FDA have this information available to it not just at the end, but throughout the review process. FDA's inability to track how long it has had an application or whether an application contains pediatric study results until late in the process could delay the dissemination of important information. Similarly, GAO found that FDA lacks reliable and timely information regarding devices that have been approved for use in pediatric patients. FDA therefore cannot provide policymakers, innovators, and physicians with an understanding of the extent to which medical devices are available for children and the need for future development.

What Remains to Be Done

The oversight of medical products remains on GAO's High Risk List because more needs to be done to resolve both previously identified and new concerns. GAO believes that while FDA leaders are committed to addressing these weaknesses, the agency must effectively implement the necessary improvements before the high-risk designation can be removed. Specifically, FDA needs to:

- strengthen its Drug Shortage Program by assessing program resources, systematically tracking data on shortages, considering the availability of medically necessary drugs as a strategic priority, and developing relevant results-oriented performance metrics to gauge the agency's response to shortages;

- improve oversight of medical device recalls by routinely assessing information on device recalls, clarifying procedures for conducting recalls, developing criteria for evaluating the effectiveness of recalls, and documenting the agency's basis for terminating individual recalls;

- implement the Safe Medical Devices Act of 1990;

- conduct more inspections of foreign establishments manufacturing medical products for the U.S. market and utilize new authority to take a risk-based approach in selecting foreign drug establishments to ensure that they are inspected at a frequency comparable to domestic establishments with similar characteristics;

- emphasize the importance of timely medical product reviews, particularly for medical devices; and

- track applications to market medical products for children.

GAO Contact

For additional information about this high-risk area, contact Marcia Crosse at (202) 512-7114 or crossem@gao.gov.

Related GAO Products

Prescription Drugs: FDA Has Met Most Performance Goals for Reviewing Applications. GAO-12-500. Washington, D.C.: March 30, 2012.

Medical Devices: FDA Has Met Most Performance Goals but Device Reviews Are Taking Longer. GAO-12-418. Washington, D.C.: February 29, 2012.

Pediatric Medical Devices: Provisions Support Development, but Better Data Needed for Required Reporting. GAO-12-225. Washington, D.C.: December 20, 2011.

Drug Shortages: FDA's Ability to Respond Should Be Strengthened. GAO-12-116. Washington, D.C.: November 21, 2011.

Food and Drug Administration: Better Coordination Could Enhance Efforts to Address Economic Adulteration and Protect the Public Health. GAO-12-46. Washington, D.C.: October 24, 2011.

Drug Safety: FDA Faces Challenges Overseeing the Foreign Drug Manufacturing Supply Chain. GAO-11-936T. Washington, D.C.: September 14, 2011.

Medical Devices: FDA Should Enhance Its Oversight of Recalls. GAO-11-468, Washington, D.C.: June 14, 2011.

Pediatric Research: Products Studied under Two Related Laws, but Improved Tracking Needed by FDA. GAO-11-457. Washington, D.C.: May 31, 2011.

Transforming EPA's Processes for Assessing and Controlling Toxic Chemicals

Why Area Is High Risk	The Environmental Protection Agency's (EPA) ability to effectively implement its mission of protecting public health and the environment is critically dependent on credible and timely assessments of the risks posed by chemicals. Such assessments are the cornerstone of scientifically sound environmental decisions, policies, and regulations under a variety of statutes, such as the Safe Drinking Water Act, the Toxic Substances Control Act (TSCA), and the Clean Air Act. EPA conducts assessments of chemicals under its Integrated Risk Information System (IRIS) Program and is authorized under TSCA to obtain information on the risks of chemicals and to control those it determines pose an unreasonable risk. Because EPA had not developed sufficient chemical assessment information under these programs to limit exposure to many chemicals that may pose substantial health risks, GAO added this issue to the High Risk List in 2009.
What GAO Found	**IRIS.** EPA's IRIS database is intended to provide the basic information the agency needs to determine whether it should establish controls to, for example, protect the public from exposure to toxic chemicals in the air, in water, and at hazardous waste sites. In March 2008, GAO reported that the viability of the IRIS program was at risk because EPA had been unable to keep its existing assessments current, decrease its ongoing assessments workload to a manageable level, or complete assessments of the most important chemicals of concern. For example, of the 70 assessments that were in progress as of December 1, 2007, 48 had been in progress for more than 5 years, and 12 of those for more than 9 years. A factor that contributed to EPA's inability to complete IRIS assessments in a timely manner was a new interagency review process that limited EPA's control over the IRIS assessment process. In response to GAO's 2008 report and 2009 high-risk designation, EPA revised its IRIS assessment process in May 2009. In December 2011, GAO reported that EPA's May 2009 revisions to the IRIS process restored EPA's control of the process, increased transparency, and established a 23-month time frame for its less challenging assessments. Notably, EPA has addressed concerns GAO raised in its March 2008 report and now makes the determination of when to move an assessment to external peer review and issuance—decisions that were made by the Office of Management and Budget (OMB) under the prior IRIS process. In addition, EPA has increased the transparency of the IRIS process by making comments provided by other federal agencies during the interagency science consultation and discussion steps of the IRIS process available to the public.

Progress in other areas, however, has been limited. EPA's initial gains in productivity under the May 2009 process have not been sustained. After completing 16 assessments within the first year and a half of implementing the revised process, EPA completed 4 assessments in fiscal year 2011, and 4 in fiscal year 2012. Further, the increase in productivity does not appear to be entirely attributable to the revised IRIS assessment process and instead came largely from (1) clearing the backlog of IRIS assessments that had undergone work under the previous IRIS process and (2) issuing assessments that were less challenging to complete. In addition, EPA faces both long-standing and new challenges in implementing the IRIS program. First, EPA has not fully addressed recurring issues concerning the clarity and transparency of its development and presentation of draft IRIS assessments. In addition, EPA has not addressed other long-standing issues regarding the availability and accuracy of current information to users of IRIS information, such as EPA program offices, on the status of IRIS assessments, including when an assessment will be started, which assessments are ongoing and when an assessment is projected to be completed. GAO is currently reviewing EPA's efforts to evaluate demand for IRIS toxicity assessments and its approach for addressing any unmet users' needs.

TSCA. EPA has found it difficult to regulate chemicals under TSCA. For example, EPA has found it difficult to obtain adequate information on toxicity—that is, the degree to which the chemical is harmful or deadly—and exposure levels—that is, the frequency and duration of contact with the chemical. Without this information, it is difficult for EPA to determine whether a chemical poses an unreasonable risk to human health or the environment and then take any action necessary to regulate such chemicals. In contrast to the approach taken by the European Union—which generally places the burden on companies to provide data on the chemicals they produce on the risks they pose to human health and the environment—TSCA generally places the burden on EPA to obtain such information. For example, before EPA can require companies to test chemicals and provide EPA with the resulting toxicity and exposure information, TSCA requires EPA to demonstrate that certain health or environmental risks are likely. Consequently, EPA's reviews of approximately 1,000 new chemicals annually provide limited assurance that health and environmental risks are identified before they are introduced into commerce. Concerning the 80,000 chemicals previously introduced into commerce, EPA has not routinely assessed the risks of these chemicals and does not know how many are still in commerce. Even when EPA has toxicity and exposure information and determines that chemicals pose an unreasonable risk, the agency has had difficulty banning or placing limits on the production or use of chemicals due to a legal threshold that EPA has found difficult to meet. Consequently, EPA has used its authority to limit or ban the use of only five chemicals since TSCA was enacted in 1976.

The EPA Administrator has expressed support for TSCA reforms and developed principles for addressing them. In parallel with the announcement of these principles, in 2009 EPA also initiated a new approach to managing chemicals within the limits of existing authorities. Under this approach, according to agency documents, EPA will use more proactive action-oriented approach obtaining toxicity and exposure data and ensuring chemical safety. GAO is currently reviewing EPA's effort and the agency's progress.

What Remains to Be Done

With regard to EPA's IRIS program, the agency must demonstrate the ability to routinely complete timely, credible IRIS assessments. This will involve developing and achieving, over a sustained period of time, productivity goals for addressing its current backlog of assessments, routinely starting new assessments, and updating existing assessments. EPA must also fully address issues concerning the clarity and transparency of its development and presentation of draft IRIS assessments as well as issues regarding the availability and accuracy of current information to users of IRIS information on the status of IRIS assessments.

With regard to TSCA, EPA must demonstrate progress toward fully utilizing its existing authorities under the act to obtain the toxicity and exposure information, including information available from foreign governments, and take the necessary actions to regulate chemicals that pose an unreasonable risk to human health or the environment. In addition, EPA must identify and work with Congress to facilitate legislative changes needed to provide the agency with sufficient authority to effectively assess and control toxic chemicals, including the specific authorities and program requirements necessary for EPA to overcome limitations in it existing TSCA authorities.

GAO Contact

For additional information about this high-risk area, contact Alfredo Gomez at (202) 512-3841 or gomezj@gao.gov.

Related GAO Products

Chemical Assessments: Challenges Remain with EPA's Integrated Risk Information System Program. GAO-12-42. Washington, D.C.: December 9, 2011.

High-Risk Series: An Update. GAO-11-278. Washington, D.C.: February 2011.

Chemical Regulation: Observations on Improving the Toxic Substances Control Act. GAO-10-292T. Washington, D.C.: December 2, 2009.

EPA Chemical Assessments: Process Reforms Offer the Potential to Address Key Problems. GAO-09-774T. Washington, D.C.: June 11, 2009.

Chemical Regulation: Options for Enhancing the Effectiveness of the Toxic Substances Control Act. GAO-09-428T. Washington, D.C.: February 26, 2009.

High-Risk Series: An Update. GAO-09-271. Washington, D.C.: January 2009.

Toxic Chemicals: EPA's New Assessment Process Will Increase Challenges EPA Faces in Evaluating and Regulating Chemicals. GAO-08-743T. Washington, D.C.: April 29, 2008.

Chemical Assessments: Low Productivity and New Interagency Review Process Limit the Usefulness and Credibility of EPA's Integrated Risk Information System. GAO-08-440. Washington, D.C.: March 7, 2008.

DOD Contract Management

Why Area Is High Risk

The Department of Defense (DOD) obligated approximately $360 billion on contracts for goods and services in fiscal year 2012. Contracts were used for basic goods and services, such as office supplies and base maintenance, and for more complex goods and services, such as information technology systems and weapon systems maintenance. Contracts also included those in support of contingency operations, such as Operation Enduring Freedom in Afghanistan. At times, the lack of an adequate number of trained acquisition and contract oversight personnel, the use of ill-suited contracting arrangements, and the absence of a strategic approach for acquiring services placed DOD at risk of not getting needed goods and services in a timely manner or potentially paying more than necessary. This area was added to GAO's High Risk List in 1992.

What GAO Found

The ability to properly manage the acquisition of goods and services depends upon having a workforce with the right skills and capabilities. In recent years, DOD has made progress in building the capacity of the acquisition workforce by adding about 17,500 civilians from fiscal year 2009 to December 2011. DOD has identified the Defense Acquisition Workforce Development Fund (the Fund) as a key tool to address acquisition workforce gaps through additional hiring and training initiatives. However, GAO reported in June 2012 that DOD's ability to effectively execute hiring and other initiatives using the Fund has been hindered by delays in the funding and allocation processes and the absence of clear guidance on the Fund's availability and use. DOD also has completed competency assessments that identify the current skills and capabilities of the workforce and help identify areas needing further management attention. However, DOD has delayed its planned issuance of an updated strategic workforce plan for the acquisition workforce, in part because of future budget uncertainties. As GAO has previously reported, workforce planning provides agencies with the information they need to ensure that their annual budget requests include adequate funds to implement human capital strategies. Until DOD determines its future workforce needs, it will be difficult to determine what funding levels will be necessary to achieve the department's planned acquisition workforce growth and implement associated training initiatives.

DOD has continued its efforts to improve competition in the procurement of goods and services and to change its business practices to address previously identified weaknesses with contracting arrangements. In GAO's 2011 high risk update, GAO noted that DOD needed to assess the effectiveness of efforts to improve competition and address prior weaknesses with specific contracting arrangements. Doing so should involve developing an effective action plan that provides baseline data, goals, milestones, and metrics for assessing the effectiveness of these efforts. However, DOD continues to lack such a plan. As a result, DOD is not well positioned to determine whether its policies are having the intended effects, readily identify when policies are not being appropriately implemented, or take corrective actions. For example, through its 2010 Better Buying Power initiative, DOD has put particular emphasis on increasing "effective competition"—receiving more than one offer or bid under a competitive solicitation—and has issued guidance for situations when competitive procedures are used but only one offer or bid is received. Implementation of these policies, however, has been incomplete. As noted in an October 2012 DOD Inspector General's report, contracting officers did not follow applicable single-bid guidance when awarding more than $656 million in contracts and monitoring of implementation was not adequate. As a result, the military departments did not realize potential cost savings associated with increased competition.

DOD has made numerous changes to its approach for managing the acquisition of services, which accounted for more than 50 percent of DOD's contract obligations in fiscal year 2012. These services were acquired, in part, to augment DOD's workforce in critical areas, including its acquisition workforce. These changes include designating a senior manager for services acquisitions in each DOD component and adopting a standard approach for categorizing spending on services. DOD acknowledged in 2010 the need for a cohesive, integrated strategy for acquiring services but continues to lack such a strategy, as well as reliable data to inform decision making. For example, in September 2012, GAO reported that DOD had not made a sufficient commitment to identifying and taking advantage of opportunities to aggregate purchases and had not established goals and performance metrics for managing its spending, thereby missing opportunities to achieve cost savings. Further, DOD is statutorily required to prepare an annual inventory of contracted services. The inventory and the associated review can help DOD manage its acquisitions of services; make more strategic decisions about the right workforce mix of military, civilian, and contractor personnel; and better align resource needs through the budget process to achieve that mix. GAO concluded in April 2012 that although DOD has made incremental improvements to its inventory-related processes, as a whole DOD has much further to go in addressing the requirements for compiling and reviewing the inventory of contracted services.

In light of longstanding and recurring issues GAO identified in DOD's use of contractors to support contingency operations, such as those in Iraq and Afghanistan, in June 2010, GAO called for DOD to emphasize operational contract support throughout all aspects of the department's responsibilities, including planning, training, and personnel requirements. In January 2011, the Secretary of Defense issued a memorandum in which he expressed concern about the risks introduced by DOD's level of dependency on contractors and the need to better plan for operational contract support in the future. DOD also issued regulations in 2011 establishing policy, assigning responsibilities, and providing procedures for operational contract support and also began revising core guidance to further integrate operational contract support into planning military efforts. However, as GAO concluded in September 2012, sustained DOD leadership is needed in three areas to achieve meaningful change and effectively prepare for the next contingency. These areas pertain to (1) planning for the use of operational contract support, including ensuring through professional military education that commanders are cognizant of the roles contractors have in supporting DOD and DOD's role in overseeing contractors; (2) ensuring that DOD possesses the workforce needed to effectively manage and oversee contracts and contractors; and (3) improving DOD's ability to account for contracts and contractors.

What Remains to Be Done

DOD has generally agreed with GAO's prior recommendations pertaining to contract management and has efforts underway to implement them. DOD has also demonstrated sustained leadership to address contract management issues through, for example, the Better Buying Power initiative and the issuance of memorandums aimed at improving operational contract support. To further improve outcomes on the billions of dollars spent annually on goods and services, DOD needs to

- continue efforts, including strategic planning and alignment of funding, to increase the department's capacity to manage and oversee contracts by ensuring that its acquisition workforce is appropriately sized and trained to meet the department's needs;

- develop and implement an action plan to assess the effectiveness of efforts to improve competition and address prior weaknesses with specific contracting arrangements;

- strategically manage its acquisitions of services by defining desired outcomes, establishing goals and measures, and obtaining the data needed to monitor progress;

- determine the appropriate mix of military, civilian, and contractor personnel; and

- sustain efforts throughout the department to integrate operational contract support through policy, planning, and training for both current and future contingency operations.

GAO Contact

For additional information about this high-risk area, contact Timothy J. DiNapoli at (202) 512-4841 or dinapolit@gao.gov.

Related GAO Products

Strategic Sourcing: Improved and Expanded Use Could Save Billions in Annual Procurement Costs. GAO-12-919. Washington, D.C.: September 20, 2012.

Operational Contract Support: Sustained DOD Leadership Needed to Better Prepare for Future Contingencies. GAO-12-1026T. Washington, D.C.: September 12, 2012.

Defense Acquisition Workforce: Improved Processes, Guidance, and Planning Needed to Enhance Use of Workforce Funds. GAO-12-747R. Washington, D.C.: June 20, 2012.

Defense Acquisitions: Further Action Needed to Improve DOD's Insight and Management of Long-term Maintenance Contracts. GAO-12-558. Washington, D.C.: May 31, 2012.

Defense Acquisitions: Further Actions Needed to Improve Accountability for DOD's Inventory of Contracted Services. GAO-12-357. Washington, D.C.: April 6, 2012.

Operational Contract Support: Management and Oversight Improvements Needed in Afghanistan. GAO-12-290. Washington, D.C.: March 29, 2012.

Defense Contracting: Competition for Services and Recent Initiatives to Increase Competitive Procurements. GAO-12-384. Washington, D.C.: March 15, 2012.

Acquisition Workforce: DOD's Efforts to Rebuild Capacity Have Shown Some Progress. GAO-12-232T. Washington, D.C.: November 16, 2011.

Defense Contract Management Agency: Amid Ongoing Efforts to Rebuild Capacity, Several Factors Present Challenges in Meeting Its Missions. GAO-12-83. Washington, D.C.: November 3, 2011.

Afghanistan: U.S. Efforts to Vet Non-U.S. Vendors Need Improvement. GAO-11-355. Washington, D.C.: June 8, 2011.

DOE's Contract Management for the National Nuclear Security Administration and Office of Environmental Management

Why Area Is High Risk

The Department of Energy (DOE), the largest civilian contracting agency in the federal government, relies primarily on contractors to carry out its diverse missions and operate its laboratories and other facilities. Approximately 90 percent of DOE's budget is spent on contracts and large capital asset projects. GAO designated contract management—which includes both contract administration and project management—as a high-risk area in 1990 because DOE's record of inadequate management and oversight of contractors has left the department vulnerable to fraud, waste, abuse, and mismanagement. In January 2009, to recognize progress made at the Office of Science, GAO narrowed the focus of its high-risk designation to two DOE program elements—the National Nuclear Security Administration (NNSA) and Office of Environmental Management (EM). Together, these two programs accounted for almost 65 percent of DOE's fiscal year 2012 discretionary funding of more than $26 billion. This year, GAO is further narrowing the focus of its high-risk designation to major contracts and projects, those with values of at least $750 million, to acknowledge progress made in managing smaller value efforts.

What GAO Found

DOE has continued to take many steps to address contract and project management weaknesses, including (1) demonstrating strong commitment and top leadership support, (2) developing a corrective action plan that identifies effective solutions, and (3) demonstrating progress toward implementing corrective measures. These are three of the five criteria for removal from GAO's High Risk List. Since GAO's February 2011 high risk update, GAO has focused on evaluating the extent to which DOE has met the two remaining criteria for removal: (1) having the capacity (people and resources) to resolve the problems and (2) monitoring and independently validating the effectiveness and sustainability of corrective measures. In this regard, GAO has found that DOE has made progress toward implementing corrective measures for projects considered "nonmajor," those projects with values less than $750 million. While work remains to ensure that further improvements are made and all improvements are sustained, to recognize progress GAO is further narrowing its focus of this high-risk designation to major projects and contracts, those with values of $750 million or greater. These contracts include those for capital asset projects as well as management and operating contracts for national laboratories and nuclear production plants that are government owned and contractor operated.

DOE continues to demonstrate strong commitment and top leadership support for improving contract and project management in EM and NNSA,

DOE's Contract Management for the National
Nuclear Security Administration and Office of
Environmental Management

building on its corrective action plan developed in 2008. In December 2010, the Deputy Secretary convened a DOE Contract and Project Management Summit to discuss strategies for additional improvement in contract and project management. The participants identified six barriers to improved performance and reported in April 2012 on the status of initiatives to address these barriers. In addition, DOE has continued to release guides for implementing its revised order for Program and Project Management for the Acquisition of Capital Assets (DOE O 413.3B), such as for cost estimating, using earned value management, and for forming project teams. Further, DOE has taken steps to enhance project management and oversight by requiring peer reviews and independent cost estimates for projects with values of more than $100 million and by improving the accuracy and consistency of data in DOE's central repository for project data.

The steps DOE has taken are very important but have not yet consistently improved contract and project management of major projects in NNSA and EM. GAO's recent work on major projects and DOE's own reporting on the status of these projects show continued need for improvement. As of August 2012, NNSA was managing three major projects with estimated costs totaling as much as $17.2 billion. EM was managing seven major projects with estimated costs totaling as much as $48.5 billion. As part of this high risk update, GAO examined these 10 projects but was only able to analyze changes in schedule estimates for 5 projects and cost estimates for 7 projects because of limitations in the data. For those projects, GAO determined that DOE has added as much as 38.5 years to their initial schedules and $16.5 billion to original cost estimates with further delays and cost increases anticipated. For example, since GAO reported in February 2011 that NNSA's project to design and construct a new Uranium Processing Facility at the Y-12 National Security Complex had experienced nearly seven-fold cost growth from its 2004 estimate to the current estimate of between $4.2 billion and $6.5 billion, comments from the Defense Nuclear Facilities Safety Board at a public meeting in October 2012 indicate that the facility will be redesigned to correct issues concerning processing equipment with the potential for significant additional cost and schedule delay. Further, GAO reported in March 2012, that NNSA's project to design and construct a new plutonium facility at Los Alamos National Laboratory had experienced a nearly six-fold increase to between $3.7 billion and $5.8 billion before being deferred for at least 5 years. In addition, GAO is currently conducting work on NNSA's project to construct its Mixed Oxide Fuel Fabrication Facility at the Savannah River Site, to which NNSA recently added $2 billion to the project's cost estimate even as the facility nears completion.

DOE's Contract Management for the National
Nuclear Security Administration and Office of
Environmental Management

In December 2012, GAO also reported that the estimated cost to
construct the Waste Treatment and Immobilization Plant (WTP) at the
Hanford Site in Hanford, Washington, has tripled to $13.4 billion since its
inception in 2000, and the scheduled completion date has slipped by
nearly a decade to 2019. Significant additional cost increases and
schedule delays are likely to occur because DOE has not fully resolved
the technical challenges faced by the project. Further, In May 2011, GAO
reported that the Department of Defense and NNSA had experienced
difficulty in scoping the study of the planned refurbishment of the B61
nuclear bomb that was initially estimated to cost about $4 billion. A July
2012 Department of Defense estimate suggested the cost of this
refurbishment will be about $10 billion.

In addition to its focus on individual cleanup and construction projects,
GAO has increased its oversight attention on high value management
and operating (M&O) contracts. One of the six barriers DOE identified in
its Contract and Project Management Summit was that the department
needed to improve its ability to hold both federal employees and
contractors accountable for project and contract performance and to
award fees to contractors consistent with project performance and/or
operational targets. In addition, DOE reported that the department needs
to improve its process for documenting contractor performance.
Consistent with DOE's assessment, GAO has found weaknesses
particularly in the quality of the information contractors provide to DOE to
manage programs and to make cost- and risk-informed decisions. For
example, building on 2010 findings that NNSA could not accurately
identify the total cost to operate and maintain its nuclear weapons
facilities, in July 2012, GAO further found that NNSA does not thoroughly
review contractor-provided budget estimates before it incorporates them
into its proposed annual budget. According to NNSA officials, the
agency's trust in its contractors minimizes the need for formal review of its
budget estimates. Moreover, to address concerns about the proportion of
NNSA weapons laboratories' funds used for indirect costs, such as
general and administrative costs that indirectly support a program, GAO
is currently reviewing and will be reporting in mid-2013 on the extent of
NNSA's steps to assess the accuracy, reliability, and reasonableness of
its contractors' indirect costs.

In its corrective action plan, DOE recognized that having sufficient people
and other resources to resolve its contract and project management
problems was one of the top 10 issues facing the department.
Specifically, the plan said that the department lacked an adequate
number of federal contracting and project personnel with the appropriate

DOE's Contract Management for the National
Nuclear Security Administration and Office of
Environmental Management

skills (such as cost estimating, risk management, and technical expertise) to plan, direct, and oversee project execution. In April 2012, GAO reported on issues related to NNSA's workforce planning efforts. Specifically, GAO reported that NNSA and its site contractors face shortages in qualified critically skilled candidates and an aging workforce. NNSA and its site contractors told us that they are engaged in workforce planning to avoid potential critical skill gaps, but NNSA did not expect to complete NNSA-wide workforce plans until 2013. In December 2012, GAO reported that EM's workforce plans do not consistently identify mission-critical occupations and skills and current and future shortfalls in these areas for its federal workforce. In addition, many EM workforce plans indicate that EM may soon face shortfalls in a number of important areas, including project and contract management. EM officials said that they recognize these issues and have taken a number of steps to address them, including conducting a skills assessment to identify key occupational series to target for succession planning. GAO recommended, among other things, that EM clearly identify critical occupations and skills in its workforce plans.

DOE has made progress in managing nonmajor projects, and, in recognition of this progress, GAO is narrowing the focus of its high-risk designation to major contracts and projects. In GAO's February 2011 high risk update, GAO reported that DOE had been restructuring its portfolio of projects to break large projects into smaller, more manageable components where possible. As such, over the last 2 years, GAO has conducted oversight of nonmajor projects to determine the extent to which corrective actions have been implemented and whether project performance has improved. GAO found that in large part these nonmajor projects were being completed, but that project management guidance and documentation could continue to be strengthened. Specifically,

- GAO reported in its October 2012 report on EM's cleanup projects funded by the American Recovery and Reinvestment Act that at the time of its analysis 78 of 112 projects had been completed. Of those completed projects, 92 percent met the performance standard of completing project work scope without exceeding the cost target by more than 10 percent, according to EM data. GAO made four recommendations to DOE in this report aimed at improving how EM manages and documents projects, particularly with respect to establishing key performance parameters such as project scope targets and baselines for cost and schedule. DOE concurred with all of GAO's recommendations, recognizing that improvements could be made and that lessons learned from these projects can be applied to EM's broader portfolio of projects and activities.

DOE's Contract Management for the National
Nuclear Security Administration and Office of
Environmental Management

- GAO's December 2012 report on NNSA and EM nonmajor projects found that, of the 71 EM and NNSA nonmajor projects reviewed, GAO was able to determine performance for 44 projects. Among these 44 projects, 21 met or are expected to meet all three of their performance targets for (1) scope of work delivered, (2) cost, and (3) completion date; of the remaining 23 projects, 13 met or are expected to meet two of these three targets, and only 1 project did not meet any of its targets. For the remaining 27 projects, many lacked sufficiently documented performance targets for scope, cost, or completion date, which prevented GAO from determining whether they met their performance targets. GAO's December 2012 report included recommendations to DOE to clearly define, document, and track the scope, cost, and completion date targets for each of its projects, as required by DOE's project management order. DOE agreed with these recommendations.

In recognition of these results coupled with DOE's continued efforts and commitment by top leadership to address contract and project management weaknesses, GAO will be focusing more on major contracts and projects. However, GAO will continue to monitor nonmajor projects to ensure that progress in this area continues and is sustained through related work and follow-up on GAO's report recommendations. With additional and sustained attention to adequately setting and documenting performance baselines and further demonstration that these actions result in improved performance, nonmajor project performance issues will have been sufficiently addressed.

What Remains to Be Done

DOE's removal from the High Risk List requires meeting all five of GAO's long-established criteria. DOE has already demonstrated and must continue to sustain leadership commitment and progress implementing corrective measures and also ensure the successful implementation of its corrective action pan. Additional actions are needed to meet the remaining two criteria. DOE needs to commit sufficient people and resources to resolve its contract management problems. Furthermore, DOE must monitor and independently validate the effectiveness and sustainability of its corrective measures, particularly for major projects, but also for nonmajor projects. Specifically, DOE must ensure that the corrective measures it is taking result in sustained improvements to the achievement of cost, schedule, and scope targets and that federal managers are receiving and validating accurate and reliable information from contractors that can be used to make decisions and to hold them and the department accountable for performance.

DOE's Contract Management for the National
Nuclear Security Administration and Office of
Environmental Management

GAO Contact

For additional information about this high-risk area, contact David Trimble at 202-512-3841 or trimbled@gao.gov.

Related GAO Products

Department of Energy: Better Information Needed to Determine if Nonmajor Projects Meet Performance Targets. GAO-13-129. Washington, D.C.: December 19, 2012.

Hanford Waste Treatment Plant: DOE Needs to Take Action to Resolve Technical and Management Challenges. GAO-13-38. Washington, D.C.: December 19, 2012.

Recovery Act: Most DOE Projects Are Complete, but Project Management Guidance Could Be Strengthened. GAO-13-23. Washington, D.C.: October 15, 2012.

Modernizing the Nuclear Security Enterprise: Observations on the National Nuclear Security Administration's Oversight of Safety, Security, and Project Management. GAO-12-912T. Washington, D.C.: September 12, 2012.

Modernizing the Nuclear Security Enterprise: NNSA's Reviews of Budget Estimates and Decisions on Resource Trade-offs Need Strengthening. GAO-12-806. Washington, D.C.: July 31, 2012

Modernizing the Nuclear Security Enterprise: Strategies and Challenges in Sustaining Critical Skills in Federal and Contractor Workforces. GAO-12-468. Washington, D.C.: April 26, 2012.

Modernizing the Nuclear Security Enterprise: New Plutonium Facility at Los Alamos May Not Meet All Mission Needs. GAO-12-337. Washington, D.C.: March 26, 2012.

National Nuclear Security Administration: Observations on NNSA's Management and Oversight of the Nuclear Security Enterprise. GAO-12-473T. Washington, D.C.: February 16, 2012.

Modernizing the Nuclear Security Enterprise: The National Nuclear Security Administration's Proposed Acquisition Strategy Needs Further Clarification and Assessment. GAO-11-848. Washington, D.C.: September 20, 2011.

DOE's Contract Management for the National
Nuclear Security Administration and Office of
Environmental Management

*Nuclear Weapons: DOD and NNSA Need to Better Manage Scope of
Future Refurbishments and Risks to Maintaining U.S. Commitment to
NATO.* GAO-11-387. Washington, D.C.: May 2, 2011.

*Nuclear Weapons: National Nuclear Security Administration's Plans for Its
Uranium Processing Facility Should Better Reflect Funding Estimates and
Technology Readiness.* GAO-11-103. Washington, D.C.: November 19,
2010.

NASA Acquisition Management

Why Area Is High Risk	The National Aeronautics and Space Administration (NASA) plans to invest billions of dollars in the coming years to explore space, understand Earth's environment, and conduct aeronautics research. GAO has designated NASA's acquisition management as high risk in view of NASA's history of persistent cost growth and schedule slippage in the majority of its major projects. GAO's work has identified a number of causal factors, including antiquated financial management systems, poor cost estimating, and underestimating risks associated with the development of its major systems. This area was added to GAO's High Risk List in 1990.
What GAO Found	NASA has taken steps to address issues with its acquisition management function, which, as GAO has reported, have helped the agency to make progress in improving overall acquisition outcomes. For example, NASA has revised and implemented new policies, such as enhanced cost estimating, that have increased oversight of its projects both internally and externally. NASA leadership has also been focused on continuous monitoring and reporting of progress for its major projects. As a result of these efforts and others, NASA has been able to demonstrate progress in meeting its cost and schedule goals for some of its more recent projects. For example, in 2011, two of NASA's spacecraft projects—Juno and the Gravity Recovery and Interior Laboratory—launched within their cost and schedule baselines. In addition, GAO reported in 2012 that many of the newer projects in the portfolio have not reported significant cost and schedule growth from established baselines.

Continued schedule and cost growth on other projects, however, indicates that it may take several years before it is apparent whether initiatives NASA has undertaken to improve its acquisition performance will be sustained and ultimately effective. For example, GAO reported that cost and schedule growth on one of NASA's most expensive and complex science projects, the James Webb Space Telescope (JWST), has had a significant impact on NASA's overall performance. JWST was rebaselined in 2011 with a $3.7 billion increase in lifecycle costs and a 52 month launch delay. Such a significant increase impacted NASA's ability to fund other important missions going forward. Even after acknowledging this large cost and schedule growth through rebaselining the project, GAO reported in December 2012 that the reliability of the JWST project's rebaselined cost estimate could have been strengthened. Also, GAO found that the JWST's schedule lacked reserve flexibility in the latter, complex phases of the project which could challenge NASA's ability to complete the JWST project on schedule. Significant effort to ensure that other large, complex and expensive projects—such as the Space Launch System and Orion Multi-Purpose Crew Vehicle, which are in early stages of development—are planned and executed appropriately will be key to ensuring continued agency progress in meeting cost and schedule goals as issues with large projects often can have reverberating effects across the portfolio of projects.

NASA has taken steps to improve its acquisition management and continues to work to address systemic weaknesses by adopting practices that focus on closing gaps in knowledge about requirements, technology, design, funding, time, and other resources before commitments are made to a new project. Based upon findings of several GAO reports over the last 2 years, however, NASA needs to take additional steps to continue to refine its practices to better ensure that improvements are implemented effectively as an important part of managing and overseeing major project development. For example, since 2009, NASA has enhanced its cost-estimating methodologies to ensure that independent analyses are used to provide decision makers with an objective representation of likely project cost and schedule results. Specifically, NASA began using an estimation tool to calculate a particular Joint Cost and Schedule Confidence Level (JCL) for development cost and schedule estimates.[1] NASA has adopted a policy to budget its projects at a 70 percent JCL, unless approved otherwise. NASA's budget documentation shows that for the most part, projects are reporting JCL's in line with this policy. However, in March 2012, GAO reported that there was a lack of uniformity in the methodology used to create the JCL. For example, some projects excluded or did not consider relevant risks, such as launch vehicle costs. In addition, in December 2012, GAO reported that the schedule used by the JWST project to conduct its JCL could impact its overall reliability. GAO reported in March 2012 that NASA has not yet launched a project that used a JCL to inform its budget and schedule baselines; therefore, NASA officials stated it will take several years to evaluate the impact of the JCL in improving cost and schedule estimating for its major projects.

---

[1]The JCL is a probabilistic analysis that includes among other things, all cost and schedule elements, incorporates and quantifies potential risks, assesses the impacts of cost and schedule to date, and addresses available annual resources to arrive at development cost and schedule estimates associated with various confidence levels.

NASA has implemented additional changes to its policies governing acquisition to enable managers to more effectively monitor a project's performance related to cost, schedule, and cross-cutting technical and nontechnical issues. Cultural, resource, and other issues, however, have led to less than optimal implementation of these efforts. For example, NASA has undertaken several initiatives aimed at improving the agency's use of Earned Value Management (EVM)—a tool designed to help project managers' monitor risks. Specifically, NASA recently strengthened its spaceflight management policy to reflect the industry EVM standard and has developed the processes and tools for projects to meet these standards through its new EVM system. While these are positive steps, GAO reported in November 2012 that EVM has not been fully and consistently implemented by NASA's major projects and as a result many projects lack reliable data for monitoring contractor performance. GAO reported that cultural influences resulted in a devaluing of cost and schedule data as a way to help manage projects, because traditionally project officials have focused more on addressing science and engineering challenges. Another challenge cited by NASA EVM experts, headquarters officials, and project and program representatives include a lack of staff with the skill set needed to analyze EVM data. GAO reported that these factors are impediments to the effective use of EVM at the agency. Reliable EVM data is one mechanism that NASA can use as a means to support identification of measurable project progress toward meeting cost and schedule goals.

GAO reported in 2011 that NASA lacked a common set of measurable and proven criteria, such as the percentage of engineering drawings employed at a key point in the development lifecycle, to provide evidence and insight to decision-makers that the requisite knowledge has been attained to allow the project to proceed. GAO recommended that NASA develop such criteria to provide NASA management with the information necessary to assess the performance of individual projects against the overall portfolio of projects. NASA's newer projects have come closer to meeting GAO's best practices metric for assessing design stability and increasing their design knowledge at critical design reviews. NASA, however, continues to lack its own proven, consistent metric for assessing design stability. In 2012, NASA took steps to address this issue and modified its systems engineering policy to improve its ability to monitor project progress throughout a project's development. Specifically, the new policy requires projects to monitor three technical indicators during the design process. While GAO agrees that this is a positive step to bring more focus to a project's design progress, there is a lack of data from NASA's projects to support the agency's metrics as indicators of design stability. Additional time will be required to monitor their effectiveness.

What Remains to Be Done

GAO has previously reported that NASA implemented a plan for improvement for how it manages its acquisitions, which included points of accountability and metrics to assess progress. The ultimate test of whether the plan is successful and improvements NASA has made over the past several years are effective is whether the agency can demonstrate sustained positive outcomes in controlling cost and schedule growth across its portfolio of major projects. Key to doing so is ensuring that improvements to its acquisition policies and practices are effectively implemented and refined as needed. This includes, for example, the JCL approach, strengthened EVM requirements, and metrics to consistently and effectively assess design stability. Successful implementation of such improvements will gain even more importance in an increasingly constrained fiscal environment when there may be limited, if any, additional resources available for projects that overrun on cost and schedule without major impacts to the mission. GAO will monitor NASA's efforts in this regard to determine whether it can sustain and expand the progress made thus far.

GAO Contact

For additional information about this high-risk area, contact Cristina T. Chaplain at (202) 512-4841 or chaplainc@gao.gov.

Related GAO Products

James Webb Space Telescope: Actions Needed to Improve Cost Estimate and Oversight of Test and Integration. GAO-13-4. Washington, D.C.: December 3, 2012.

NASA: Earned Value Management Implementation across Major Spaceflight Projects is Uneven. GAO-13-22. Washington, D.C.: November 19, 2012.

NASA: Assessments of Selected Large-Scale Projects. GAO-12-207SP. Washington, D.C.: March 1, 2012.

NASA: Assessments of Selected Large-Scale Projects. GAO-11-239SP. Washington, D.C.: March 3, 2011.

Additional Cost Transparency and Design Criteria Needed for National Aeronautics and Space Administration (NASA) Projects. GAO-11-364R. Washington, D.C.: March 3, 2011

NASA: Issues Implementing the NASA Authorization Act of 2010. GAO-11-216T. Washington, D.C.: December 1, 2010.

NASA: Key Management and Program Challenges. GAO-10-387T. Washington, D.C.: February 3, 2010.

Enforcement of Tax Laws

Why Area Is High Risk

The Internal Revenue Service (IRS) recently estimated that the gross tax gap—the difference between taxes owed and taxes paid on time—was $450 billion for tax year 2006. For a portion of the gap, IRS is able to identify the responsible taxpayers. IRS estimated that it would collect $65 billion from these taxpayers through enforcement actions and late payments, leaving a net tax gap of $385 billion. The tax gap has been a persistent problem in spite of a myriad of congressional and IRS efforts to reduce it, as the rate at which taxpayers voluntarily comply with U.S. tax laws has changed little over the past three decades. Given that the tax gap has been persistent and dispersed across different types of taxes and taxpayers, coupled with tax code complexity and a globalizing economy, reducing the tax gap will require applying multiple strategies over a sustained period of time.

IRS enforcement of the tax laws is vital for financing the U.S. government. Through enforcement, IRS collects revenue from noncompliant taxpayers and, perhaps more importantly, promotes voluntary compliance by giving taxpayers confidence that others are paying their fair share. GAO designated the enforcement of tax laws as a high-risk area in 1990.

What GAO Found

IRS and Congress have shown a commitment to addressing the tax gap. Importantly, IRS continues to research the extent and causes of taxpayer noncompliance and is using the results to revise its examination programs. While still in the early planning stages, IRS has met with key stakeholders to develop options for expanding compliance checks before issuing refunds to taxpayers. IRS is also extending a program to encourage taxpayers to voluntarily report their previously undisclosed foreign accounts and assets, which has resulted in billions of dollars in collections. IRS, as well as Congress, has taken other innovative actions aimed at further improving tax compliance, often directly based on GAO's work, including the following:

- Since 2012, brokers have been required to report their clients' basis for securities sales.

- Since 2011, banks and other third parties have been required to report businesses' credit card and similar receipts.

- Starting in 2014, U.S. financial institutions and other entities are required to withhold a portion of certain payments made to foreign financial institutions that have not entered into an agreement with IRS to report details on U.S. account holders to IRS.

- Starting with tax year 2010, IRS is requiring businesses to report on their tax returns uncertain tax positions—those for which a business reported a reserve amount in its financial statements to account for the possibility that IRS does not sustain the position upon examination or that the position may be litigated.

- IRS is continuing its multiyear effort to replace the systems it uses to process individual tax returns and receive electronically filed tax returns.

The impact of these initiatives on taxpayer compliance and the tax gap may not be known for years and will depend, in part, on how IRS implements them. Using the new information from financial institutions could require IRS to develop new business processes and uses of information technology. Implementation will also be influenced by IRS's ability to provide quality taxpayer services, such as telephone, correspondence, and online assistance. GAO found that some services have experienced performance declines in recent years and IRS's website could offer additional interactivity for taxpayers.

Another initiative IRS undertook in 2010 was to begin implementing new requirements for paid tax return preparers, such as competency testing, with the goals of leveraging relationships with paid preparers and improving the accuracy of the tax returns they prepare. Given that they prepare approximately 60 percent of all tax returns filed, paid preparers have an enormous impact on IRS's ability to administer tax laws effectively. In January 2013, the U.S. District Court for the District of Columbia enjoined IRS from enforcing the new requirements for paid preparers. IRS has filed a motion to suspend the injunction and intends to appeal the District Court's decision.

Further refining of direct revenue return-on-investment measures of its enforcement programs could improve how IRS allocates resources across its programs. Better use of such measures, subject to other considerations of tax administration, such as minimizing compliance costs and ensuring equitable treatment across different groups of taxpayers, could help maximize income tax collections. Resource allocation will become increasingly important as IRS is tasked with broader responsibilities, such as those in the Patient Protection and Affordable Care Act, in a time of tight budgets.

Additionally, targeted legislative action may be needed to address some compliance issues. IRS has statutory authority—called math error authority—to correct certain errors, such as calculation mistakes or omitted or inconsistent entries, during tax return processing. Expanding such math error authority could help IRS correct additional errors before interest is owed by taxpayers and avoid burdensome audits.

Additional types of information reporting could also help improve compliance. Taxpayers are much more likely to report their income accurately when the income is also reported to IRS by a third party. By matching information received from third-party payers with what payees report on their tax returns, IRS can detect income underreporting, including the failure to file a tax return. Currently, businesses must report to IRS payments for services they make to unincorporated persons or businesses, but payments to corporations generally do not have to be reported. Taxpayers who rent out real estate are required to report to IRS expense payments for certain services, such as payments for property repairs, only if their rental activity is considered a trade or business. Expanding information reporting in these areas could increase payee reporting compliance. In 2010, the Joint Committee on Taxation estimated revenue increases for a 10-year period from third-party reporting of (1) rental real estate service payments to be $2.5 billion and (2) service payments to corporations to be $3.4 billion.

A broader opportunity to address the tax gap involves simplifying the Internal Revenue Code, as complexity can cause taxpayer confusion and provide opportunities to hide willful noncompliance. Fundamental tax reform could result in a smaller tax gap if the new system has fewer tax preferences or complex tax code provisions, reducing IRS's enforcement challenges and increasing public confidence in the fairness of the tax system. Short of fundamental reform, targeted simplification opportunities exist. For example, changing tax laws to include more consistent definitions across tax provisions, such as which higher education expenses qualify for some of the savings and tax credit provisions in the tax code, could help taxpayers more easily understand and comply with their obligations.

What Remains to Be Done

For IRS to improve its enforcement of tax laws it must continue to

- perform compliance research on a regular basis and use the results to identify areas of noncompliance;

- seek ways to leverage paid preparers to improve tax compliance;

- implement new (1) requirements for sources of taxpayer information and (2) technologies to enhance the effectiveness and timeliness of service and enforcement corrective measures; and

- develop return on investment measures to better allocate resources and maximize income tax collection.

In that regard, IRS should implement GAO's open recommendations, such as those on developing measures of direct revenue return on investment.

To assist IRS in reducing the tax gap, Congress should consider expanding IRS's math error authority to correct taxpayer calculation mistakes or omitted or inconsistent entries during tax return processing before issuing refunds. Congress should also consider requiring payers to report service payments to corporations and making rental real estate owners subject to the same payment reporting requirements regardless of whether they engaged in a trade or business under current law. In the event that IRS cannot implement its new requirements without additional statutory authority, Congress should consider whether tax compliance could be improved by regulating paid preparers. The ongoing debate about tax reform also provides opportunities to consider the effect of tax simplification on taxpayer compliance and the tax gap.

GAO Contact

For additional information about this high-risk area, contact James White at (202) 512-9110 or whitej@gao.gov.

Related GAO Products

Tax Gap: IRS Could Increase Revenues by Better Targeting Enforcement Resources. GAO-13-151. Washington, D.C.: December 5, 2012.

IRS 2013 Budget: Continuing to Improve Information on Program Costs and Results Could Aid in Resource Decision Making. GAO-12-603. Washington, D.C.: June 8, 2012.

Tax Gap: Sources of Noncompliance and Strategies to Reduce It. GAO-12-651T. Washington, D.C.: April 19, 2012.

Foreign Account Reporting Requirements: IRS Needs to Further Develop Risk, Compliance, and Cost Plans. GAO-12-484. Washington, D.C.: April 16, 2012.

Financial Derivatives: Disparate Tax Treatment and Information Gaps Create Uncertainty and Potential Abuse. GAO-11-750. Washington, D.C.: September 20, 2011

Tax Gap: Complexity and Taxpayer Compliance. GAO-11-747T. Washington, D.C.: June 28, 2011.

Information Reporting: IRS Could Improve Cost Basis and Transaction Settlement Reporting Information. GAO-11-557. Washington, D.C.: May 19, 2011.

Tax Preparer Regulation: IRS Needs a Documented Framework to Achieve Goal of Improving Taxpayer Compliance. GAO-11-336. Washington, D.C.: March 31, 2011.

2011 Tax Filing: IRS Dealt with Challenges to Date but Needs Additional Authority to Verify Compliance. GAO-11-481. Washington, D.C.: March 29, 2011.

Improving and Modernizing Federal Disability Programs

<table>
<tr><td>

Why Area Is High Risk

</td><td>

Federal disability programs remain in need of modernization. Numerous federal programs provide a range of services and supports for people with disabilities—including 45 employment-related programs—that together represent a patchwork of policies and programs without a unified strategy or set of national goals. Further, three of the largest federal disability programs—managed by the Social Security Administration (SSA) and Department of Veterans Affairs (VA)—rely on out-of-date criteria to a great extent in making disability benefit decisions. While SSA and VA have taken concrete steps toward updating their criteria, these disability programs emphasize medical conditions in assessing an individual's work incapacity without adequate consideration of the work opportunities afforded by advances in medicine, technology, and job demands. Finally, federal disability benefit programs are experiencing growing disability claim workloads as the demand for benefits has increased under a difficult job market. Thus, challenges are likely to persist, despite concerted efforts to process more claims annually. GAO designated improving and modernizing federal disability programs as high risk in 2003.

</td></tr>
<tr><td>

What GAO Found

</td><td>

GAO recently identified 45 programs under nine agencies that helped people with disabilities obtain or retain employment, reflecting a fragmented system of services and supports. Many of these programs overlapped in whom they served and the types of services they provided. Such fragmentation and overlap may frustrate and confuse program beneficiaries and limit the overall effectiveness of the federal effort. Having extensive coordination and overarching goals can help address program fragmentation. Although GAO identified promising coordination efforts among some programs, most reported not coordinating with each other, and some officials told us they lacked funding and staff time to pursue coordination. Coordination efforts can be enhanced when programs work toward a common goal; however, the number and type of outcome measures used by the 45 programs varied greatly. To improve coordination, efficiency, and effectiveness, GAO suggested that the Office of Management and Budget (OMB)—the focal point for management in the executive branch—consider establishing government-wide goals for employment of people with disabilities. Consistent with this suggestion, OMB officials stated that the Domestic Policy Council began an internal review intended to improve the effectiveness of some disability programs through better coordination and alignment. According to OMB officials, this review included six agencies and, to date, has resulted in the U.S. Departments of Education and Labor coordinating their spending plans related to disability technical assistance and research. Further, OMB

</td></tr>
</table>

officials reported that Education is coordinating with three other federal agencies to implement a pilot that supports positive education and employment outcomes for youth receiving Social Security's Supplemental Security Income benefits. The administration also issued an executive order that reaffirmed goals for hiring people with disabilities in the federal government and has reported making progress toward those goals. However, hiring goals do not extend to hiring sectors other than the federal government.

Since the 2011 high risk update, SSA and VA have taken important and concrete steps toward updating and modernizing their eligibility criteria used to determine disability benefits, but varied challenges may impede their progress. SSA and VA have developed plans and committed resources toward comprehensively updating the medical and labor market information that underlie their respective disability criteria. However, GAO recently found that both agencies face challenges in ensuring timely updates. For example, resource constraints have impeded SSA's efforts to ensure timely updates to its medical criteria, while VA lacks sufficient capacity to produce timely research on veterans' average earnings loss associated with service-connected disabilities. Further, SSA lacks a complete, reliable, and transparent cost estimate and schedule for replacing its outdated occupational information system, and risks schedule and performance shortfalls. VA lacks complete planning in key areas that could jeopardize project outcomes and, in the end, could result in outdated disability criteria whereby some individuals may be overcompensated while others may be unfairly denied benefits or undercompensated. GAO recommended actions the agencies could take to address these issues, and SSA and VA agreed with GAO's recommendations.

Finally, although both agencies have taken steps toward greater consideration of an individual's ability to function with a disability—consistent with modern views of disability—the agencies still do not take into consideration the full range of assistive devices—such as a device to assist with vision impairment—or, in the case of SSA, workplace accommodations available today. SSA has disagreed with GAO's recommendation to conduct limited, focused studies on how to more fully consider such factors in its disability determinations, stating that such studies would be inconsistent with Congress' intentions. However, GAO noted that Congress has not explicitly prohibited SSA from considering these factors and believes that conducting these studies would put SSA in a better position to thoughtfully weigh the costs and benefits of these various policy options before deciding on a course of action.

Agencies have made real progress in managing growing workloads related to processing claims for disability benefits; however, workload challenges persist due in part to unprecedented demand for benefits. Over the last several years and through fiscal year 2012, SSA and VA have steadily and significantly increased the number of disability claims processed—at the initial decision level for both agencies and the appellate level for SSA. Thus, for initial claims, SSA has reported drops in claims pending since fiscal year 2010 and improvements in processing times, while for hearings workloads, SSA reported improved processing times for and reductions in the number of aged cases—the oldest and often the most complex cases—through 2011. Likewise, VA has increased case completion since 2009 by 6 percent. Finally, VA's and the Department of Defense's (DOD) Integrated Disability Evaluation System (IDES) has shown promise for expediting the delivery of VA and DOD benefits for wounded, injured, and ill servicemembers leaving military service. However, with a challenging job market, a fiscally strained environment, and hundreds of thousands of military servicemembers returning to civilian life, these agencies still face challenges associated with managing significant and persistent workload increases.

- While SSA is processing more initial claims annually, and has reduced initial claims pending since fiscal year 2010, incoming claims are growing, such that SSA's 759,000 initial claims pending in fiscal year 2011 were 36 percent higher than fiscal year 2008 levels. Further, many claims denied at the initial level often result in a request for a hearing. As a result, SSA experienced sizeable new hearings workloads and a substantial number of pending hearings (about 850,000) in 2012. SSA's mitigation plans to address these challenges include leveraging technology and identifying ways to simplify its claims process.

- The number of claims that VA received grew 29 percent from fiscal year 2009 to fiscal year 2011. As a result, as of August 2012, VA had more than 856,092 claims pending, of which 66 percent were considered backlogged. The overall time VA takes to decide veterans' claims has also increased: average days pending more than doubled from 2009 to August 2012, and timeliness for processing appeals also worsened. VA is taking steps to redesign the claims process but is not yet fully positioned to evaluate its effectiveness.

- Although still faster than the legacy process, IDES case processing timeliness has worsened, as the program has expanded from a pilot with smaller caseloads to 139 locations with larger caseloads worldwide. Specifically, GAO found that annual average processing times increased by more than 100 days between fiscal years 2008 and 2011. DOD subsequently reported improved overall processing times compared to fiscal year 2011 levels, but still above agency goals. Extended time in the disability determination process has, in turn, negatively affected servicemembers' ability to plan for their future as well as lengthened the period for which the military must care for and house these servicemembers. VA and DOD are undertaking a business process review to understand and address the complex factors influencing timeliness, but the completion date and efficacy of that review are not yet known.

What Remains to Be Done

Actions taken by OMB and the Domestic Policy Council to study and consider options for better coordinating and improving the effectiveness of federal disability programs represent an important step forward. However, sustained attention is needed in this area to assure enduring progress. Specifically, OMB needs to maintain and expand its role in improving coordination across programs—such as the 45 GAO identified—that support employment for those with disabilities, and ultimately work with all relevant agencies to develop measurable government-wide goals to spur further coordination and improved outcomes for those who are seeking to find and maintain employment.

With respect to updating and modernizing disability criteria, SSA and VA have demonstrated a strong commitment, but still need to take additional actions to manage this process more strategically, particularly around the agencies' planning and research efforts. Specifically, GAO recently recommended that SSA explicitly identify resources needed to update its medical listings and that VA develop a written strategy for seamlessly implementing revisions to its criteria. Further, GAO recommended that SSA complete plans to replace its occupational information system in line with best practices for developing a cost estimate, schedule, and risk assessment, and that VA develop a more complete plan to conduct earnings loss and validation studies. In terms of research, GAO recommended that SSA conduct focused studies on how to more fully consider assistive devices and workplace accommodations in its disability determinations. GAO also recommended that VA increase its research capacity to determine the impact of impairments on veterans' earnings in a timely manner, ensuring that decisions about compensation benefits are informed by current information.

To address growing claims workloads, SSA, VA, and DOD leadership have demonstrated a strong commitment and invested additional resources. However, in the face of persistent disability claims workloads and constrained resources, SSA will require continued management attention to initiatives articulated in its strategic plan to sustain progress toward meeting key goals. As GAO has noted in recent work, VA needs to ensure the development of a robust backlog reduction plan that includes performance goals incorporating the impact of improvement initiatives on processing timeliness. Finally, VA and DOD need to develop frames for the ongoing IDES business process review as well as for implementing any resulting recommendations.

GAO Contact

For additional information about this high-risk area, contact Daniel Bertoni at (202) 512-7215 or bertonid@gao.gov.

Related GAO Products

Veterans' Disability Benefits: Timely Processing Remains a Daunting Challenge. GAO-13-89. Washington, D.C.: December 21, 2012.

SSA Disability Programs: Progress and Challenges Related to Modernizing. GAO-12-891T. Washington, D.C.: September 14, 2012.

VA Disability Compensation: Actions Needed to Address Hurdles Facing Program Modernization. GAO-12-846. Washington, D.C.: September 10, 2012.

Military Disability System: Improved Monitoring Needed to Better Track and Manage Performance. GAO-12-676. Washington, D.C.: August 28, 2012.

Employment for People with Disabilities: Little Is Known about the Effectiveness of Fragmented and Overlapping Programs. GAO-12-677. Washington, D.C.: June 29, 2012.

Modernizing SSA Disability Programs: Progress Made, but Key Efforts Warrant More Management Focus. GAO-12-420. Washington, D.C.: June 19, 2012.

Military Disability System: Preliminary Observations on Efforts to Improve Performance. GAO-12-718T. Washington, D.C.: May 23, 2012.

Modernizing SSA Disability Programs: Preliminary Observations on Updates of Medical and Occupational Criteria. GAO-12-511T. Washington, D.C.: March 20, 2012.

2012 Annual Report: Opportunities to Reduce Duplication, Overlap and Fragmentation, Achieve Savings, and Enhance Revenue. GAO-12-342SP. February 28, 2012.

Military and Veterans Disability System: Worldwide Deployment of Integrated System Warrants Careful Monitoring. GAO-11-633T. Washington, D.C.: May 4, 2011.

Pension Benefit Guaranty Corporation Insurance Programs

Why Area Is High Risk

The Pension Benefit Guaranty Corporation (PBGC) insures the pension benefits of 43 million American workers and retirees participating in nearly 26,000 private sector defined benefit plans through its single-employer and multiemployer insurance programs. PBGC's financial portfolio is one of the largest of any federal government corporation, with more than $80 billion in assets. Yet, because of long-term challenges related to PBGC's governance and funding structure, PBGC's financial future is uncertain. At the end of fiscal year 2012, PBGC's net accumulated financial deficit was $34 billion—an increase of over $23 billion from the end of fiscal year 2008, and significantly worse than in 2000, when PBGC reported a $10 billion surplus (see figure 6). PBGC estimates that its financial risk for potential termination of underfunded plans sponsored by financially weak firms is about $295 billion, an amount that has continued to worsen since the economic downturn in 2008. The Pension Protection Act of 2006 (PPA)[1] strengthened some aspects of funding rules, but in response to the recession, subsequent legislation has softened these provisions— initially by phasing in PPA's changes,[2] and more recently, through changes in how minimum contributions are calculated.[3] Thus, while Congress has enacted various provisions to strengthen PBGC's governance and PBGC has implemented various measures to improve its operations, weaknesses in the structure of its board and its revenue streams continue to undermine the agency's long-term financial stability. GAO designated the single-employer program as high risk in July 2003, and added the multiemployer program in January 2009.

---

[1]Pub. L. No. 109-280, tits. I and II, 120 Stat. 780, 784-919.

[2]Worker, Retiree, and Employer Recovery Act of 2008, Pub. L. No. 110-458, §§ 101, 102, 121 and 122, 122 Stat. 5092, 5093-5103, 5113-14.

[3]Preservation of Access to Care for Medicare Beneficiaries and Pension Relief Act of 2010, Pub. L. No. 111-192, tit. II, 124 Stat.1280, 1283-1306.

Figure 6: PBGC's Net Financial Position, Single-Employer and Multiemployer Programs Combined

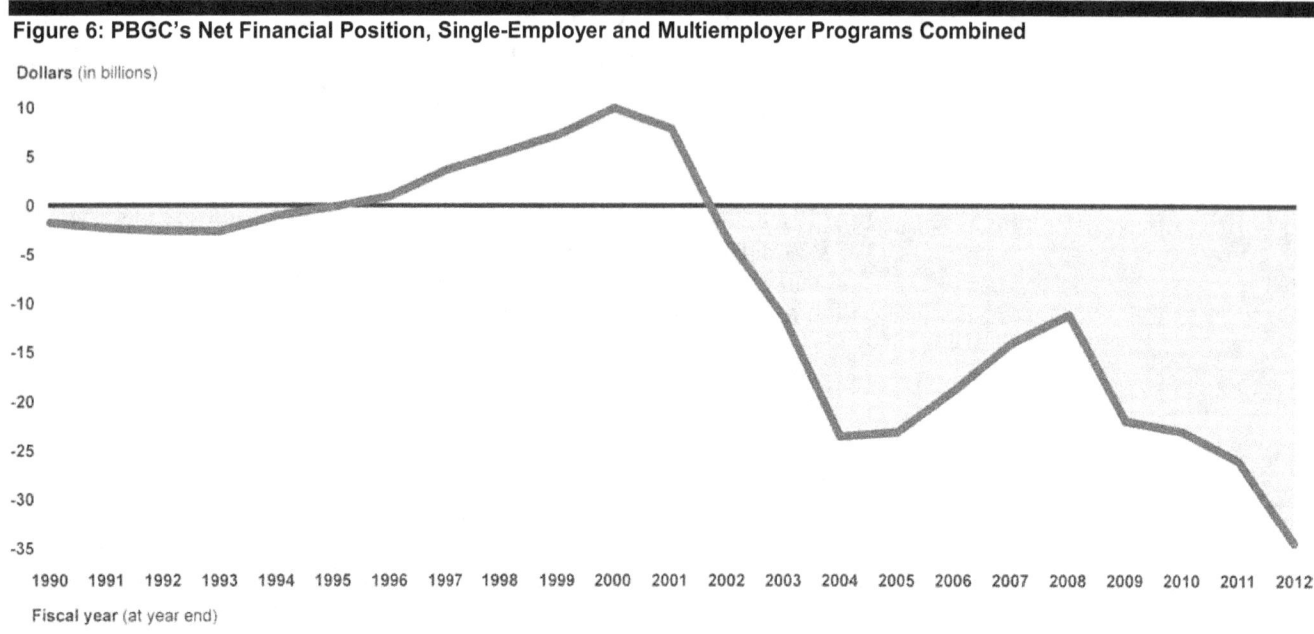

Source: PBGC

What GAO Found

Congress has recently taken action to strengthen PBGC's overall management and governance structure, addressing many of the concerns GAO has raised over the years. In July 2012, the Moving Ahead for Progress in the 21st Century Act (MAP-21) became law, with several provisions pertaining to PBGC, including measures to stabilize pension contribution requirements, adjust premium rates, and improve PBGC's governance[4]—all areas that GAO has targeted in its previous recommendations for strengthening PBGC. The provisions intended to improve PBGC's governance include such things as detailing the working relationships between PBGC's Board of Directors and PBGC's Inspector General, General Counsel, and Advisory Committee; creating new positions for a Risk Management Officer and a Participant and Plan Sponsor Advocate; requiring an independent peer review of PBGC's insurance modeling systems, to be conducted annually; and providing for the National Academy of Public Administration to conduct a study and, within a year, make recommendations to Congress regarding PBGC's governance structure. GAO has long recommended that the composition

---

[4]Pub. L. No.112-141, 126 Stat. 405, 846-864.

of PBGC's board—currently made up of the Secretaries of the Treasury, Commerce, and Labor—be expanded to include additional members with diverse backgrounds who possess knowledge and expertise useful to PBGC's mission.

PBGC has also taken steps to address several areas of weakness noted in previous GAO reports. For example, in response to concerns about the agency's management of its assets and to ensure a more disciplined and long-term approach to investment, PBGC issued a new investment policy statement in May 2011. The new statement is more comprehensive than in the past, providing clear organizational accountability, well-defined goals, and risk management parameters. In addition, with proper oversight from the Chief Financial Officer (CFO), PBGC has subsequently aligned its portfolio with these new objectives and has the CFO provide regular reports to the Board of Directors at each board meeting regarding financial and investment-related activities and results. PBGC officials also reported that, consistent with the new requirements under MAP-21, the agency implemented a practice of holding board meetings more regularly, four times a year. Due to improved market conditions since PBGC adopted a new investment policy in May 2011, the agency's investment income has rebounded from its sharp decline in 2008.

Another area of weakness noted in past GAO reports is the structure of PBGC's premium rates, which are set by law. Currently, the level of plan underfunding is the only risk factor considered in determining a sponsor's premium rate. To strengthen PBGC's finances and encourage companies to preserve sound pensions, in 2011 the Administration proposed legislative reforms calling for the consideration of additional risk factors in how rates are calculated. Such risk factors might include a plan's investment strategies, benefit structure and benefit level, demographic profile, or the plan sponsor's financial strength. PBGC has made efforts to enhance understanding of the proposed reforms by analyzing the limitations of the current system, and by modeling various premium options that factor in consideration of a sponsor's financial health as well as plan underfunding. GAO agrees that incorporation of additional risk factors into a redesign of PBGC's premium structure could better align rates with a sponsor's risk of terminating an underfunded plan and placing a future claim on PBGC. However, no action has been taken as yet in response to these proposed reforms.

In light of PBGC's heavy reliance on contractors, the agency's contract management practices have long been another area of concern highlighted in several previous reports from GAO and from PBGC's

Inspector General. However, GAO's recent work in this area found that PBGC has taken several steps to strengthen accountability of its contract management in response to the recommendations in these reports. For example, PBGC has implemented new practices requiring that service contracts more than $100,000 include documentation of the decision to use contractors instead of federal employees, that contract files be reviewed annually, and that staff assigned contract monitoring duties have their performance of these duties reflected in their performance evaluations.

What Remains to Be Done

Both Congress and PBGC's insurance programs have taken significant steps to address many of GAO's concerns with PBGC's overall management and governance structure, reflecting increased top-level attention to the challenges facing this agency. Once fully implemented, the changes enacted under MAP-21 and improvements made by PBGC should allow the agency to improve its management and better protect the retirement incomes of workers with private-sector defined benefit pension plans. However, despite these actions, certain challenges related to PBGC's governance and funding structure remain. PBGC continues to face the ongoing threat of losses from the termination of underfunded plans, while grappling with a steady decline in the defined benefit pension system (with fewer plans participating in the single-employer program with each passing year) and inadequate sources of revenue to finance future claims. As a result, PBGC's financial future remains uncertain.

To improve the financial stability of PBGC's insurance programs, Congress should consider taking the following actions:

- adopting further changes to PBGC's governance structure—in particular, expanding the composition of its Board of Directors;

- authorizing a redesign of PBGC's premium structure to better align rates with sponsor risk;

- strengthening funding requirements for plan sponsors as the economy improves; and

- working with PBGC to develop a strategy for funding PBGC claims over the long term as the defined benefit sector continues to decline.

GAO Contact

For additional information about this high-risk area, contact Charles A. Jeszeck at (202) 512-7215 or jeszeckc@gao.gov.

Related GAO Products

Pension Benefit Guaranty Corporation: Redesigned Premium Structure Could Better Align Rates with risk from Plan Sponsors. GAO-13-58. Washington, D.C.: November 7, 2012.

Pension Benefit Guaranty Corporation: Asset Management Needs Better Stewardship. GAO-11-271. Washington, D.C.: June 30, 2011.

Pension Benefit Guaranty Corporation: More Strategic Approach to Contracting Still Needed. GAO-11-588. Washington, D.C.: June 29, 2011.

Pension Benefit Guaranty Corporation: Improvements Needed to Strengthen Governance Structure and Strategic Management. GAO-11-182T. Washington, D.C.: December 1, 2010.

Private Pensions: Changes Needed to Better Protect Multiemployer Pension Benefits. GAO-11-79. Washington, D.C.: October 18, 2010.

Private Pensions: Long-standing Challenges Remain for Multiemployer Pension Plans. GAO-10-708T. Washington, D.C.: May 27, 2010.

Pension Benefit Guaranty Corporation: More Strategic Approach Needed for Processing Complex Plans Prone to Delays and Overpayments. GAO-09-716. Washington, D.C.: August 17, 2009.

Pension Benefit Guaranty Corporation: Financial Challenges Highlight Need for Improved Governance and Management. GAO-09-702T. Washington, D.C.: May 20, 2009.

Defined Benefit Plans: Proposed Plan Buyouts by Financial Firms Pose Potential Risks and Benefits. GAO-09-207. Washington, D.C.: March 2009.

Pension Benefit Guaranty Corporation: Some Steps Have Been Taken to Improve Contracting, but a More Strategic Approach Is Needed. GAO-08-871. Washington, D.C.: August 18, 2008.

Medicare Program

Why Area Is High Risk	In 2012, the Medicare program covered more than 49 million elderly and disabled beneficiaries at an estimated cost of $555 billion, and reported improper payments estimated to be more than $44 billion. The Centers for Medicare & Medicaid Services (CMS), which administers Medicare for the Department of Health and Human Services (HHS), is responsible for implementing payment methods that encourage efficient service delivery, managing Medicare to provide efficient and cost-effective services to beneficiaries, safeguarding the program from loss, and overseeing patient safety and care. Like health care spending in general, Medicare spending has grown faster than growth in the economy for many years. In the coming years, continued growth in the number of Medicare beneficiaries and program spending will create increasing challenges for the federal government.
What GAO Found	GAO designated Medicare as a high-risk area in 1990 because its complexity and susceptibility to improper payments, added to its size, have led to serious management challenges. Medicare spending must be held much more firmly in check to sustain the program over the long term, while continuing to ensure that beneficiaries have access to appropriate health care. To help do so, GAO has identified opportunities to make Medicare payment methods more efficient and cost-effective. In addition, the size of the program makes it important for CMS to manage program functions more effectively and better oversee the program's integrity and quality of patient care. The following areas delineate where GAO has identified opportunities for improvements.

- *Reforming and refining payments.* CMS has implemented broad-based reforms to payment systems in the traditional Medicare fee-for-service (FFS) program as well as Medicare Advantage (MA) plans, where about a quarter of Medicare beneficiaries receive their care. Many reforms introduce financial incentives into payment structures to explicitly reward quality and efficiency. Important initiatives include steps toward transitioning Medicare's FFS physician payment system from one that rewards volume of services to one in which value—as measured by quality and cost of care—is used to determine payment. For example, CMS has begun to provide feedback to physicians about their resource use—an important step in encouraging efficiency—and this information, along with indicators of the quality of care delivered, will be used as part of calculating the value-based payment. GAO's work on the Physician Feedback Program found that CMS was experiencing both methodological and implementation challenges. As CMS progresses to full implementation of its value-based payment system, it will be important for the agency to use reliable quality and cost measures and methodological approaches that maximize the number of physicians for whom value can be determined.

GAO's work identified opportunities for CMS to introduce additional payment method refinements and controls in Medicare FFS to encourage appropriate use of services. For example, self referral, where a provider refers patients to entities in which the provider or the provider's family has a financial interest, continues to be a problem for advanced imaging services. GAO's analysis showed that providers' referrals of advanced imaging services substantially increased once they start to self-refer. GAO estimated that such additional referrals cost more than $100 million in 1 year. However, CMS does not obtain information to identify which advanced imaging services are self-referred and monitor their use. Further, Medicare pays the same amount for self-referred services, even though certain efficiencies may be gained when the same provider orders, performs, and interprets an advanced imaging service. In addition, Medicare prices for certain services may be too high. For example, Medicare added drugs used to treat complications of end-stage renal disease (ESRD) to its bundled payment for ESRD care services starting on January 1, 2011, but based the payment on 2007 care patterns. However, utilization of these drugs to treat ESRD patients has declined since 2007. GAO estimates that Medicare expenditures would have been $650 million to $880 million lower in 2011 if the bundled payment rate was rebased to reflect 2011 utilization of ESRD drugs. Similarly, although Medicare's payment system gives hospitals an incentive to seek the best price for implantable medical devices (IMD), GAO determined that hospitals may vary in their ability to do so. The lack of price transparency and variation in amounts hospitals pay for some IMDs—and may pass on to the Medicare program—raise questions about whether hospitals are achieving the best prices possible.

For the Medicare Advantage (MA) program, CMS has made progress implementing required adjustments to plan payments to align them more closely with the cost of care in the traditional Medicare program. However, in a January 2012 report, GAO indicated that CMS could still improve the accuracy of payments to MA plans. The report found that an adjustment CMS makes to MA plan payments to improve accuracy to account for differences in beneficiary diagnostic coding between MA plans and Medicare FFS is inadequate, resulting in excess payments to MA plans estimated to be at least $3 billion from 2010 to 2012. While federal law requires an increase in the minimum adjustment CMS must make, CMS will still need to modify its methodology to ensure the accuracy of adjustments in future years. In another report, GAO found that instead of implementing the MA quality bonus payment provisions in the Patient Protection and Affordable Care Act (PPACA), as amended, CMS established a demonstration to test an alternative bonus payment structure. This demonstration is estimated to cost more than $8.3 billion over 10 years and offsets a significant portion of the act's MA payment reductions during its 3-year time frame. GAO identified significant shortcomings in the demonstration's design that preclude a credible evaluation of the effect of incentives on plans' quality improvement. For this reason, GAO recommended that the Secretary of HHS cancel the demonstration and implement the quality bonus payments provided for under PPACA. GAO also raised concerns about whether the demonstration meets the requirements of the statute under which it is being conducted and therefore, falls within CMS's authority.

- *Improving program management.* CMS has overcome some challenges in managing Medicare as it implemented some recent program improvements. For example, GAO had previously reported that Medicare sometimes overpaid for durable medical equipment (DME) items relative to other payers. To achieve Medicare savings, in 2009 CMS began implementing a DME competitive bidding program. In this program, CMS contracts with select suppliers to provide DME to beneficiaries and pays them at competitively determined prices based on the bids. GAO found that beneficiary access and satisfaction appeared stable in early assessments, and the competitive bidding program has led to savings. Similarly, in the past, CMS was sometimes hampered in identifying situations when Medicare should be the secondary payer, and the Medicare, Medicaid, and State Children's Health Insurance Program Extension Act of 2007 mandated reporting of such situations. Since CMS's implementation of the mandatory reporting for nongroup health plans, program savings increased by $124 million from 2008 through 2011. However, GAO found that the increase in contractors' workload to comply with increased mandatory reporting led to problems processing the cases promptly and that CMS's guidance and communications with non-group health plans could be improved. GAO also reported that Medicare is implementing two new programs to provide incentive payments to eligible providers that adopt and use health information technology, but the programs have some inconsistent requirements and have separate reporting requirements, which could increase the burden on providers trying to access the incentives.

CMS has improved its overall guidance and oversight of contracts, an area where GAO found pervasive internal control weaknesses in 2009 that put billions of taxpayers' dollars at risk. Improvements include adding internal controls and testing the agency's review of contract payments, adding new checklists and policies to document compliance with federal acquisition requirements, and enhancing its policies and procedures for tracking, investigating, and resolving contract audit and evaluation findings.

- *Enhancing program integrity.* The administration and CMS have made reducing improper payments one of their priority initiatives. CMS has made progress in error rate measurement and in 2011 was able to report the error rate for all Medicare components for the first time, including the prescription drug benefit (Part D). CMS's performance plan has set targets for percentages of improper payments, with the targets slightly lower in each year. As reported in 2012, the rate of improper payments in Part D (3.1 percent) was lower than the target CMS set (3.2 percent)—however, the rate of improper payments in FFS and Part C—at 8.5 percent and 11.4 percent respectively—exceeded CMS's target rates of 5.4 percent and 10.4 percent. Thus, additional efforts will be needed to further reduce improper payments in FFS and Part C. If CMS reaches its targets for improper payments, it will take several more years to assess whether CMS can sustain progress in reducing improper payments. The estimation methodology for Parts C and D are relatively new, with few assessments made to develop a trend. Further, refinements to the methodology used to determine the final 2009 and 2010 FFS improper payment rates make them not comparable to estimates for earlier years.

CMS has also taken steps to try to strengthen Medicare program integrity and reduce vulnerabilities to improper payment, but some problems have yet to be fully addressed. For example, GAO's previous work found persistent weaknesses in Medicare's enrollment standards and procedures that increased the risk of providing billing privileges to entities intent on defrauding the program. CMS has implemented provisions in PPACA designed to strengthen provider enrollment procedures in several ways, such as designating risk levels for categories of providers and applying different screening procedures for providers at each level. In addition, CMS contracted with two new entities at the end of 2011 to assume centralized responsibility for automated screening of provider and supplier enrollment and for conducting site visits of providers. However, CMS has not completed other actions required by this legislation, including (1) determining which providers will be required to post surety bonds to help ensure the recovery of payments made for fraudulent billing, (2) contracting for fingerprint screening services for high-risk providers, (3) issuing a final regulation to require providers to disclose additional information, and (4) establishing core elements for provider compliance programs.

Sound and sufficient prepayment controls and post-payment analytic capability to examine the appropriateness of paid claims are critical for proper payment. CMS has incorporated prepayment controls designed to automatically deny claims that do not meet Medicare's requirements, but GAO found that not all of these controls were working as intended. Further, the processes to identify the need for the controls and implement them had weaknesses that can lead to overpayments. For example, CMS has improved its corrective action process, including developing written guidance on its operation. However, the guidance still lacks procedures to specify time frames for taking corrective actions, methods for assessing the effects of corrective actions, and procedures to ensure that CMS considers instituting prepayment controls whenever possible to prevent making improper payments.

CMS also has implemented the Fraud Prevention System (FPS), which uses analytic methods to examine claims before payment to help identify and prioritize investigations of potential fraud. Specifically, FPS analyzes Medicare claims data using models of potentially fraudulent behavior, which results in automatic alerts on specific claims and providers, which are then prioritized for program integrity analysts to review and investigate as appropriate. According to program integrity officials, FPS is intended to help facilitate the agency's shift from focusing on recovering fraudulent payments after they have been made, to taking actions more quickly when aberrant billing patterns are identified. However, the system is not fully integrated with CMS's existing information technology systems, and CMS has not defined and measured quantifiable benefits and performance goals for it. For CMS's existing information technology for detecting improper or fraudulent claims after payment has been made, GAO reported in 2011 that CMS had not incorporated all the data into its Integrated Data Repository, as planned, which limited the repository's use for identifying potentially fraudulent claims. In 2011 CMS also had not taken all steps needed to ensure wide usage of its One Program Integrity information technology portal, a tool to help identify patterns of fraud, waste, or abuse. Nor was CMS in a position to identify, measure, and track benefits from these two information technology efforts. Since 2011, CMS has added data to its Integrated Data Repository and increased training to encourage the use of One Program Integrity.

- *Overseeing patient care and safety.* Although preventive care may reduce expenditures and improve health outcomes, GAO found in January 2012 that the use of preventive services by Medicare beneficiaries—those in FFS Medicare as well as those in MA plans—does not always align with the U.S. Preventive Services Task Force's clinical recommendations. Better alignment of preventive service use with Task Force recommendations depends on appropriate Medicare coverage and cost sharing policies to encourage greater use of high-valued preventive services recommended by the Task Force and discourage use of low-value services for which clinical evidence suggests that the risks generally outweigh the benefits.

For some of the most vulnerable beneficiaries—those in nursing homes—weaknesses remain in oversight of the quality of care, although CMS has taken steps to improve it. For example, CMS contracts with state survey agencies to investigate complaints about nursing homes and helps ensure the adequacy of complaint processes by issuing guidance, monitoring data that state survey agencies enter into CMS's database, and annually assessing state agencies' performance against specific standards, but the agency found that states had difficulties meeting some of its standards for their complaint processes. CMS has taken steps to address GAO's recommendations to improve nursing home oversight, such as strengthening enforcement against nursing homes that have provided poor quality care, by increasing the number of facilities that will be subject to more intensive oversight and sanctions for failure to show improved care quality.

To provide information to consumers and improve provider quality, in 2008, CMS implemented the Five-Star Quality Rating System, which assigns each nursing home an overall rating and three component ratings—health inspections, staffing, and quality measures—based on the extent to which the nursing home meets CMS's quality standards and other measures. CMS has several efforts planned to improve the usability of the Five-Star System and provide additional information and quality measures. However, the agency lacks GAO-identified leading strategic planning practices—the use of milestones and timelines to guide and gauge progress toward desired results and the alignment of activities, resources, and goals—that could help it more efficiently and effectively improve the Five-Star System.

What Remains to Be Done

As discussed, CMS has demonstrated high-level management commitment to measuring its payment error rate, as demonstrated by its development of a payment error rate for each part of the program. It has taken steps to reduce improper payments, such as by implementing some of the new provider enrollment requirements in PPACA and implementing certain payment controls. Further, CMS has introduced other initiatives to address its management challenges, such as implementing a competitive bidding program for DME and making serious efforts to better oversee nursing quality care and management of contracts. However, CMS has not met GAO's criteria to have the Medicare program removed from the

High Risk List—for example, although CMS has made progress in measuring and reducing improper payment rates in different parts of the program, it has yet to demonstrate sustained progress in lowering the rates. Because the size of Medicare relative to other programs leads to aggregate improper payments that are extremely large, continuing to reduce improper payments in this program should remain a priority for CMS. Further, CMS should complete some actions required by PPACA that were designed to improve the integrity of the program, such as determining which providers must post surety bonds to help in recovering payments for fraudulent billing, using fingerprint screening for high-risk providers, issuing a final regulation that requires providers to disclose additional information, and establishing core elements for provider compliance programs.

CMS has implemented certain GAO recommendations—for example, for nursing home and contract oversight—but further action is needed on other recommendations. To refine Medicare payment methods to encourage efficient provision of services, CMS should

- ensure the implementation of an effective physician profiling system, to help support use of value-based modifiers;

- develop and implement approaches to identify self-referred claims, reduce payments to recognize efficiencies achieved when the same provider refers and provides the service, and take steps to ensure the appropriateness of service provision;

- cancel the current MA Quality Bonus Demonstration and implement the quality bonus payment provisions in PPACA, as amended; and

- improve the accuracy of the adjustment of payments to MA plans for diagnostic coding differences, such as by using more current data in determining the amount of the adjustment.

To improve program management, CMS should

- improve the cost-effectiveness of recovery of payments made improperly because Medicare was the secondary payer in situations involving non-group health plans, and decrease the reporting burden for non-group health plans while improving communication with plans' stakeholders.

To enhance program integrity, CMS should

- improve the structure and processes related to use of prepayment controls and assess the feasibility of increasing contractors' incentives for their use, and

- develop or finalize schedules and plans for its information technology efforts related to improper payments and fraud; define quantifiable benefits, measurable performance targets, and goals for these efforts; and use the targets and goals to determine their effectiveness.

To improve oversight of patient care and safety, CMS should

- provide coverage for preventive services recommended by the Preventive Services Task Force, as appropriate, considering cost-effectiveness and other criteria;

- strengthen oversight of nursing home complaint investigations by improving the reliability of its complaints database and clarifying guidance for its state performance standards; and

- use strategic planning to guide and gauge the progress of its planned efforts to meet the goals of the Five-Star Quality Rating System for nursing homes.

In addition, Congress should consider requiring the Secretary of HHS to rebase the ESRD bundled payment rate as soon as possible and on a periodic basis thereafter, using the most current available data, and requiring beneficiaries to share the cost of those preventive services that the Preventive Services Task Force has recommended against.

GAO Contact

For additional information about this high-risk area, contact James Cosgrove at (202) 512-7114 or cosgrovej@gao.gov, or Kathleen King at (202) 512-7114 or kingk@gao.gov.

Related GAO Products

End-Stage Renal Disease: Reduction in Drug Utilization Suggests Bundled Payment Is Too High. GAO-13-190R. Washington, D.C.: December 7, 2012.

Medicare Program Integrity: Greater Prepayment Control Efforts Could Increase Savings and Better Ensure Proper Payment. GAO-13-102. Washington, D.C.: November 13, 2012.

Medicare Fraud Prevention: CMS Has Implemented a Predictive Analysis System, but Needs to Define Measures to Determine Its Effectiveness. GAO-13-104. Washington, D.C.: October 15, 2012.

Medicare: Higher Use of Advanced Imaging Services by Providers Who Self Refer Costing Medicare Millions. GAO-12-966. Washington, D.C.: September 28, 2012.

Medicare Advantage: Quality Bonus Payment Demonstration Has Design Flaws and Raises Legal Concerns. GAO-12-964T. Washington, D.C.: July 25, 2012.

Medicare: Progress Made to Deter Fraud, but More Could Be Done. GAO-12-801T. Washington, D.C.: June 8, 2012.

Nursing Homes: CMS Needs Milestones and Timelines to Ensure Goals for the Five-Star Quality Rating System Are Met. GAO-12-390. Washington, D.C.: March 23, 2012.

Medicare Secondary Payer: Additional Steps Are Needed to Improve Program Effectiveness for Non-Group Health Plans. GAO-12-333. Washington, D.C.: March 9, 2012.

Medicare: Use of Preventive Services Could Be Better Aligned with Clinical Recommendations. GAO-12-81. Washington, D.C.: January 18, 2012.

Nursing Homes: More Reliable Data and Consistent Guidance Would Improve CMS Oversight of State Complaint Investigations. GAO-11-280. Washington, D.C.: April 7, 2011.

Medicaid Program

Why Area Is High Risk

GAO designated Medicaid as a high-risk program due to its size, growth, diversity of programs, and concerns about the adequacy of fiscal oversight, which is necessary to prevent inappropriate program spending. This federal and state program covered acute health care, long-term care, and other services for about 70 million low-income people in fiscal year 2011; it is one of the largest sources of funding for medical and health-related services for America's most vulnerable populations. Medicaid consists of more than 50 distinct state-based programs. The federal government matches state expenditures for most Medicaid services using the Federal Medical Assistance Percentage, a statutory formula based in part on each state's per capita income. Medicaid is a significant expenditure for the federal government and the states, with total expenditures of $436 billion in 2011. The Centers for Medicare & Medicaid Services (CMS) in the Department of Health and Human Services (HHS) is responsible for overseeing the program at the federal level, while states administer their respective programs' day-to-day operations.

What GAO Found

Both Congress and the administration have demonstrated commitment and leadership to making Medicaid fiscal and program integrity a priority. In 2012, committees in Congress held hearings on reducing Medicaid improper payments and on improving oversight of the program. HHS continues to review and report on the rate of Medicaid improper payments, and continues to train and provide technical assistance to states on approaches to prevent improper payments. Among other actions, CMS issued guidance to states on removing providers from their Medicaid programs who have been terminated for committing fraud in other states' Medicaid programs or in Medicare, and required improved reporting and independent audits of states' Medicaid supplemental payments made to certain providers known as disproportionate share hospitals. However, stronger federal oversight of Medicaid is warranted as the program continues to grow in size and spending. For example, potential Medicaid expansions under the Patient Protection and Affordable Care Act (PPACA) are estimated to result in the enrollment of about 7 million additional individuals in 2014, growing to 11 million in 2022. The federal government is responsible for paying more than 90 percent of the increased costs associated with this expansion. CMS will need new tools and resources as the law is implemented, including more reliable data for assessing expenditures, measuring performance, and preventing improper payments. Medicaid remains high risk due to concerns about the adequacy of fiscal oversight of this large, diverse, and growing program. Areas where program oversight has been insufficient include the following:

- *Improper payments to Medicaid providers serving program beneficiaries.* Improper payments to providers who submit inappropriate claims can result in substantial financial losses to states and the federal government. Medicaid payments can be improper for various reasons, such as if payments are made for people not eligible for Medicaid or made for services not provided. Effective program integrity processes at the state and federal level are critical to preventing improper payments. In its 2012 financial report, HHS estimated—on the basis of individual state error rates from a sample of 17 states reviewed on an annual rotating basis—a national improper payment rate for Medicaid of 7.1 percent (with the federal share estimated at $19.2 billion). While states have the first-line responsibility in preventing improper payments, CMS has an important role through its Medicaid Integrity Group in overseeing and supporting state efforts, including conducting various types of federal audits of states' claims data (known as the national Medicaid audit program), and providing training and technical assistance to states.

  Positive steps toward improving the transparency and reducing improper payments have been taken in recent years. In May 2011, CMS issued guidance to states on processes to remove providers from their program when they have been terminated from another state's Medicaid program or terminated from Medicare as required by PPACA. In addition, CMS has committed to (1) redesigning its national Medicaid audit program, which relied on data that were incomplete, not reliable, and not timely, and, as a result cost significantly more than the potential overpayments it identified, and (2) using its comprehensive reviews of state integrity program activities to better target audits toward states with significant weaknesses in their ability to detect overpayments. Separate from this initiative, CMS is also testing the cost-effectiveness and feasibility of establishing a fraud prevention system (prepayment edits) for Medicaid by April 1, 2015. Key challenges remain, including improving key data systems so that they provide reliable and complete data needed to implement effective programs to identify and prevent improper payments; eliminating duplication between CMS and state program integrity efforts; and refocusing national audit efforts on approaches that are cost-effective. While CMS actions are under way to address these and other issues, it is too soon to assess their effectiveness on reducing improper payments.

- *Financing methods that are inappropriate, and large supplemental payments that are not always transparent.* Some states have established varied financing arrangements involving Medicaid supplemental payments that inappropriately increase federal Medicaid matching payments. Subject to certain requirements, states may make supplemental payments to Medicaid providers that are separate from and in addition to regular state Medicaid payments for services. The total amount of supplemental payments has increased in recent years. In fiscal year 2011, states reported spending at least $43 billion, up from $32 billion in fiscal year 2010 and $23 billion in fiscal year 2006. GAO and others have reported concerns with states' Medicaid supplemental payments over the last decade, including the use of supplemental payment arrangements to increase federal funding without a commensurate increase in state funding, and concerns that the payments were not used for Medicaid purposes. Large increases in reported supplemental payments have been identified as a major factor that contributed to increased Medicaid spending on hospital services in 2010.

A variety of federal legislative, regulatory, and CMS actions have helped curb inappropriate arrangements, but gaps remain. In 2003, CMS began an initiative to closely review state supplemental payments and required states to end those it found inappropriate; however, in 2008, GAO reported that CMS had not reviewed all supplemental payment arrangements to ensure payments were appropriate and for Medicaid purposes. Starting in 2010, CMS implemented new transparency and accountability requirements for certain Medicaid supplemental payments, known as Disproportionate Share Hospital (DSH) payments, including new reporting and auditing requirements for these payments. In 2012, GAO found that the new requirements improve CMS's ability to oversee DSH payments by better assuring states comply with federal requirements, including accurate calculation of payment amounts to ensure payments are not excessive. However, similar standards for calculating, reporting, and auditing of other types of Medicaid supplemental payments—referred to here as non-DSH supplemental payments—have not been established even though these payments have increased significantly in recent years and exceeded DSH supplemental payments in total amounts. In its 2012 report, GAO found that establishing transparency and accountability requirements similar to those in place for DSH payments could improve CMS's ability to oversee non-DSH supplemental payments. Using the limited available information from the new DSH reports, GAO found in 39 states a total of 505 hospitals received regular and non-DSH supplemental Medicaid payments in excess of their costs of providing services to Medicaid beneficiaries, by a total of about $2.7 billion. Although Medicaid payments are not limited to the costs of delivering Medicaid services, Medicaid payments that greatly exceed Medicaid costs raise questions about the purpose of the payments, how payments relate to Medicaid services, whether payments are consistent with economy and efficiency, and whether payments contribute to beneficiaries' access to quality care.

- *Managed care rate setting and quality of data used to set such rates has not been consistently reviewed by CMS.* Requirements for Medicaid managed care rates to be actuarially sound are key safeguards in efforts to ensure that federal spending is appropriate. In 2010, GAO reported that CMS had been inconsistent in ensuring that states are complying with the actuarial soundness requirements. Further, GAO found that CMS efforts were not sufficient to ensure the quality of the data used by states to set managed care rates. With limited information on data quality, CMS cannot ensure that states' managed care rates are appropriate, which places billions of dollars at risk for misspending. GAO recommended that CMS implement a mechanism to track state compliance with actuarial soundness requirements, clarify federal guidance on rate-setting reviews, and make use of information on data quality in overseeing states' rate setting. HHS agreed with the recommendations. As of December 2012, CMS was working on enhancing data systems to improve the oversight of managed care rate-setting.

- *Demonstrations that inappropriately increase federal costs.* HHS has the authority to waive certain statutory provisions to allow states to implement demonstrations that test ideas for achieving program objectives. By policy, demonstrations should not increase federal costs. However, GAO reported in 2008 that HHS had approved two state demonstrations that could substantially increase the federal financial liability. At the time of GAO's work in 2007, HHS disagreed with GAO's recommendation to improve the demonstration review process through steps such as clarifying the criteria for reviewing and approving states' proposed spending limits, and ensuring that valid methods were used to demonstrate budget neutrality. Consequently, GAO elevated this recommendation to Congress for consideration. HHS subsequently reported taking steps, such as monitoring the spending under ongoing approved demonstrations, to improve its oversight; however, as of December 2012, HHS had not planned any changes in the criteria and methods used to determine budget neutrality of demonstrations prior to approving them. Such actions are needed in order to ensure that only those proposed demonstrations that do not increase the federal financial liability are approved.

What Remains to Be Done

Congress, HHS, and CMS have taken steps to improve the fiscal integrity of Medicaid, and CMS has implemented certain GAO recommendations, such as improving the information collected on certain supplemental payments and issuing guidance to states to better prevent payment of improper claims. However, more federal oversight of Medicaid's fiscal and program integrity is needed. For example, CMS oversight of program integrity has been challenged by data systems that do not provide reliable, complete, and timely data. States also have key roles in reducing improper payments to providers in developing, implementing, and evaluating the effectiveness of corrective plans to reduce improper payments.

CMS should also continue taking steps to improve oversight of Medicaid managed care payment rate-setting and Medicaid supplemental payments. In November 2012, GAO suggested that Congress require CMS to take certain steps to improve the transparency of and accountability for Medicaid non-DSH supplemental payments, including requiring improved reporting and independent audits of these payments. In addition, GAO's suggestion that Congress require HHS to improve the criteria and methods used to ensure the budget neutrality of Medicaid demonstrations remains valid.

GAO Contact

For additional information about this high-risk area, contact Katherine Iritani at (202) 512-7114 or iritanik@gao.gov, or Carolyn L. Yocom at (202) 512-7114 or yocomc@gao.gov.

Related GAO Products

Medicaid: More Transparency of and Accountability for Supplemental Payments Are Needed. GAO-13-48. Washington, D.C.: November 26, 2012.

Medicaid Integrity Program: CMS Should Take Steps to Eliminate Duplication and Improve Efficiency. GAO-13-50. Washington, D.C.: November 13, 2012.

Medicaid: States Made Multiple Program Changes and Beneficiaries Generally Reported Access Comparable to Private Insurance. GAO-13-55. Washington, D.C.: November 15, 2012.

Medicaid: Data Sets Provide Inconsistent Picture of Expenditures. GAO-13-47. Washington, D.C.: October 29, 2012.

Health Care Fraud: Types of Providers Involved in Medicare, Medicaid, and the Children's Health Insurance Program Case. GAO-12-820. Washington, D.C.: September 7, 2012.

Medicaid: States Reported Billions More in Supplemental Payments in Recent Years. GAO-12-694. Washington, D.C.: July 20, 2012.

National Medicaid Audit Program: CMS Should Improve Reporting and Focus on Collaboration with States. GAO-12-627. Washington, D.C.: June 14, 2012.

Medicaid: Federal Oversight of Payments and Program Integrity Needs Improvement. GAO-12-674T. Washington, D.C.: April 25, 2012.

Medicaid Program Integrity: Expanded Federal Role Presents Challenges to and Opportunities for Assisting States. GAO-12-288T. Washington, D.C.: December 7, 2011.

Fraud Detection Systems: Centers for Medicare and Medicaid Services Needs to Expand Efforts to Support Program Integrity Initiatives. GAO-12-292T. Washington, D.C.: December 7, 2011.

National Flood Insurance Program

Why Area is High Risk

The National Flood Insurance Program (NFIP) is a key component of the federal government's efforts to limit the damage and financial impact of floods; however, it likely will not generate sufficient revenues to repay the billions of dollars borrowed from the Treasury to cover claims from the 2005 hurricanes or future catastrophic losses. This lack of sufficient revenues highlights what have been structural weaknesses in how the program is funded. The Biggert-Waters Flood Insurance Reform Act of 2012 (the act) addresses a number of these weaknesses, but the extent to which the changes included in the act will reduce the financial exposure created by the program is not yet clear. Weaknesses in NFIP management and operations, including financial reporting processes and internal controls, and oversight of contractors have also placed the program at risk. The Federal Emergency Management Agency (FEMA), within the Department of Homeland Security, is responsible for managing NFIP. While FEMA has taken some steps to address these issues, it continues to face complex challenges. In October 2012, Superstorm Sandy caused extensive damages in several states on the eastern coast of United States, raising the prospect that NFIP would not be able to pay all the resulting claims without borrowing additional funds from the Treasury. In January 2013, Congress, passed legislation to temporarily increase NFIP's borrowing authority by $9.7 billion, from $20.7 billion to $30.4 billion to address these claims.

What GAO Found

The potential losses generated by NFIP have created substantial financial exposure for the federal government and U.S. taxpayers. While Congress and FEMA intended that NFIP be funded with premiums collected from policyholders and not with tax dollars, the program was, by design, not actuarially sound. As of November 2012, FEMA owes the Treasury approximately $20 billion, up from $17.8 billion pre-Sandy, and had not repaid any principal on the loan since 2010. GAO added NFIP to the High Risk List in 2006. The act addresses some structural challenges that have contributed to the program's financial instability. It excludes subsidized premium rates for new flood insurance policies and phases them out for many other properties, including those that have sustained repeated, severe losses and second homes. In addition, it requires FEMA to establish a reserve fund to be available for meeting the expected future obligations of NFIP, including the payment of claims and the repayment of all amounts outstanding. While these changes may help increase NFIP's long-term financial stability, the program still faces several challenges and the ultimate effect of the changes is not yet known. For example, in order to repay the program's existing debt and build up a reserve fund, FEMA will need to increase premium rates significantly. In a 2009 report, GAO noted that building a loss fund, even if NFIP's debt was forgiven, might increase annual subsidized premium rates anywhere from 150 to 325 percent. Such rate increases could have negative effects on participation in NFIP, particularly among lower income property owners. In addition, catastrophic losses can occur before the targeted total for a reserve fund is reached, which would require the program to borrow funds to pay losses.

Weaknesses in the management and operations of NFIP also create a risk that funds allocated to NFIP and premiums paid by policyholders are not being used efficiently or effectively. As noted in GAO's June 2011 report, FEMA faces significant management challenges in areas that affect NFIP, including strategic and human capital planning; collaboration among offices; and records, financial, and acquisition management. For example, because FEMA has not developed goals, objectives, or performance measures for NFIP, it needs a strategic focus for ensuring program effectiveness. FEMA has begun to address some of these challenges, but the results of its efforts remain to be seen. GAO also found that FEMA faces challenges modernizing NFIP's insurance policy and claims management system. After 7 years and $40 million, FEMA ultimately canceled its latest effort (NextGen) in November 2009 because the system did not meet user expectations. As a result, the agency continues to rely on an ineffective and inefficient 30-year old system. While FEMA has begun implementing some changes to its acquisition management practices, it remains to be seen if they will help FEMA avoid some of the problems that led to NextGen's failure. In GAO's December 2010 report, GAO also noted that while FEMA has taken a number of actions to increase the accuracy of flood maps—which are used in determining NFIP premium rates—challenges remain. For example, while FEMA has adopted a risk-based method to prioritize mapping projects, and implemented mapping standards and guidance, the standards and FEMA's quality control process for ensuring the accuracy of flood maps could be improved.[1] Unless these management issues are addressed, FEMA risks ongoing challenges in effectively and efficiently managing NFIP, including its management and use of information, data, and technology.

---

[1]For more information about FEMA's challenges related to flood maps, see GAO, *FEMA Flood Maps: Some Standards and Processes in Place to Promote Map Accuracy and Outreach, but Opportunities Exist to Address Implementation Challenges,* GAO-11-17 (Washington, D.C.: Dec. 2, 2010).

Similarly, in June 2011, GAO noted that external factors continue to complicate the administration of NFIP and affect its financial stability. Specifically, FEMA historically has not been authorized to account for long-term erosion—which results from climate change and rising sea levels—when updating flood maps used to set premium rates for NFIP. The purpose of flood maps are supposed to accurately estimate the likelihood of flooding in specific areas given certain characteristics including elevation and topography, but they can quickly become inaccurate because of changes from long-term erosion, particularly in coastal areas. Not accurately reflecting the actual risk of flooding increases the likelihood that even full-risk premiums will not cover future losses and adds to concerns about NFIP's financial stability. Consequently, among a range of other recommendations, GAO in June 2011 suggested that Congress authorize NFIP to account for long-term flood erosion in its flood maps. The Biggert-Waters Flood Insurance Reform Act of 2012 requires FEMA to include, among other things, relevant information on topography, coastal erosion areas, changing lake levels, future changes in sea levels, and intensity of hurricanes.

What Remains to Be Done

The financial reforms included in the act could go a long way toward reducing the financial exposure created by the program, but they will be phased in over time and in order to be fully effective, FEMA will need to successfully implement them. For example, FEMA will need to determine and charge actuarially sound premium rates that account for the creation of a reserve fund as well as the phasing out of subsidized premium rates on certain properties. FEMA officials have taken some actions to improve NFIP operations, including many of GAO's recommendations, and must continue to demonstrate strong commitment and support for these actions. These actions should include, among other things, the completion of strategic planning efforts for NFIP and the implementation of a new insurance policy and claims management system using improved contactor oversight processes. Finally, the growing debt owed to Treasury continues to highlight the financial challenges associated with this program.

GAO Contact

For additional information about this high-risk area, contact Orice Williams Brown at (202) 512-8678 or williamso@gao.gov.

Related GAO Products

Flood Insurance: Participation of Indian Tribes in Federal and Private Programs. GAO-13-226. Washington, D.C.: January 4, 2013.

Flood Insurance: Public Policy Goals Provide a Framework for Reform. GAO-11-670T. Washington, D.C.: June 23, 2011.

FEMA: Action Needed to Improve Administration of the National Flood Insurance Program. GAO-11-297. Washington, D.C.: June 9, 2011.

FEMA Flood Maps: Some Standards and Process in Place to Promote Map Accuracy and Outreach, but Opportunities Exist to Address Implementation Challenges. GAO-11-17, Washington, D.C.: December 2, 2010.

National Flood Insurance Program: Continued Actions Needed to Address Financial and Operational Issues. GAO-10-1063T. Washington, D.C.: September 22, 2010.

Financial Management: Improvements Needed in National Flood Insurance Program's Financial Controls and Oversight. GAO-10-66. Washington, D.C.: December 22, 2009.

Flood Insurance: Opportunities Exist to Improve Oversight of the WYO Program. GAO-09-455. Washington, D.C.: August 21, 2009.

Information on Proposed Changes to the National Flood Insurance Program. GAO-09-420R. Washington, D.C.: February 27, 2009.

Flood Insurance: Options for Addressing the Financial Impact of Subsidized Premium Rates on the National Flood Insurance Program. GAO-09-20. Washington, D.C.: November 14, 2008.

Flood Insurance: FEMA's Rate-Setting Process Warrants Attention. GAO-09-12. Washington, D.C.: October 31, 2008.

National Flood Insurance Program: Financial Challenges Underscore Need for Improved Oversight of Mitigation Programs and Key Contracts GAO-08-437. Washington, D.C.: June 16, 2008.

National Flood Insurance Program: Greater Transparency and Oversight of Wind and Flood Damage Determinations Are Needed. GAO-08-28. Washington, D.C.: December 28, 2007.

Federal Emergency Management Agency: Ongoing Challenges Facing the National Flood Insurance Program. GAO-08-118T. Washington, D.C.: December 28, 2007.

National Flood Insurance Program: FEMA's Management and Oversight of Payments for Insurance Company Services Should Be Improved. GAO-07-1078. Washington, D.C.: September 5, 2007.

National Flood Insurance Program: Preliminary Views on FEMA's Ability to Ensure Accurate Payments on Hurricane-Damaged Properties. GAO-07-991T. Washington, D.C.: June 12, 2007.

National Flood Insurance Program: New Processes Aided Hurricane Katrina Claims Handling, but FEMA's Oversight Should Be Improved. GAO-07-169. Washington, D.C.: December 15, 2006.

Federal Emergency Management Agency: Challenges for the National Flood Insurance Program. GAO-06-335T. Washington, D.C.: January 25, 2006.

Federal Emergency Management Agency: Improvements Needed to Enhance Oversight and Management of the National Flood Insurance Program. GAO-06-119. Washington, D.C.: October 18, 2005.

Flood Map Modernization: Federal Emergency Management Agency's Implementation of a National Strategy. GAO-05-894T. Washington, D.C.: July 12, 2005.

Appendix I: High Risk Program History

In 1990, we began a program to report on government operations that we identified as "high risk." Since then, generally coinciding with the start of each new Congress, we have reported on the status of progress to address high-risk areas and updated the High Risk List. Our most recent high risk update was in February 2011, which identified 30 high-risk areas.[1]

Overall, our high risk program has served to identify and help resolve serious weaknesses in areas that involve substantial resources and provide critical services to the public. Since our program began, the government has taken high-risk problems seriously and has made long-needed progress toward correcting them. In a number of cases, progress has been sufficient for us to remove the high-risk designation. A summary of changes to our High Risk List over the past 23 years is shown in table 8. Areas removed from the High Risk List over that same period are shown in table 9. The areas on our 2013 High Risk List, and the year each was designated as high risk, are shown in table 10.

Table 8: Changes to High Risk List, 1990-2013

	Number of areas
Original high risk list in 1990	14
High-risk areas added since 1990	41
High-risk areas removed since 1990	23
High-risk areas consolidated since 1990	2
High risk list in 2013	30

Source: GAO.

---

[1]GAO, *High-Risk Series: An Update*, GAO-11-278 (Washington, D.C.: February 2011).

Table 9: Areas Removed from High Risk List, 1990-2013

Area	Year removed	Year designated high risk
1. Federal Transit Administration Grant Management	1995	1990
2. Pension Benefit Guaranty Corporation	1995	1990
3. Resolution Trust Corporation	1995	1990
4. State Department Management of Overseas Real Property	1995	1990
5. Bank Insurance Fund	1995	1991
6. Customs Service Financial Management	1999	1991
7. Farm Loan Programs	2001	1990
8. Superfund Programs	2001	1990
9. National Weather Service Modernization	2001	1995
10. The 2000 Census	2001	1997
11. The Year 2000 Computing Challenge	2001	1997
12. Asset Forfeiture Programs	2003	1990
13. Supplemental Security Income	2003	1997
14. Student Financial Aid Programs	2005	1990
15. Federal Aviation Administration Financial Management	2005	1999
16. Forest Service Financial Management	2005	1999
17. HUD Single-Family Mortgage Insurance and Rental Housing Assistance Programs	2007	1994
18. U.S. Postal Service's Transformation Efforts and Long-Term Outlook	2007	2001
19. FAA's Air Traffic Control Modernization	2009	1995
20. 2010 Census	2011	2008
21. DOD Personnel Security Clearance Program	2011	2005
22. Management of Interagency Contracting	2013	2005
23. IRS Business Systems Modernization	2013	1995

Source: GAO.

Table 10: Year That Area's on GAO's 2013 High Risk List Were Designated High Risk

Area		Year designated high risk
1.	Medicare Program	1990
2.	DOD Supply Chain Management	1990
3.	DOD Weapon Systems Acquisition	1990
4.	DOE's Contract Management for the National Nuclear Security Administration and Office of Environmental Management	1990
5.	NASA Acquisition Management	1990
6.	Enforcement of Tax Laws	1990
7.	DOD Contract Management	1992
8.	DOD Financial Management	1995
9.	DOD Business Systems Modernization	1995
10.	Protecting the Federal Government's Information Systems and the Nation's Cyber Critical Infrastructures	1997
11.	DOD Support Infrastructure Management	1997
12.	Strategic Human Capital Management	2001
13.	Medicaid Program	2003
14.	Managing Federal Real Property	2003
15.	Improving and Modernizing Federal Disability Programs	2003
16.	Strengthening Department of Homeland Security Management Functions	2003
17.	Pension Benefit Guaranty Corporation Insurance Programs	2003
18.	Establishing Effective Mechanisms for Sharing and Managing Terrorism-Related Information to Protect the Homeland	2005
19.	DOD Approach to Business Transformation	2005
20.	National Flood Insurance Program	2006
21.	Funding the Nation's Surface Transportation System	2007
22.	Ensuring the Effective Protection of Technologies Critical to U.S. National Security Interests	2007
23.	Revamping Federal Oversight of Food Safety	2007
24.	Modernizing the U.S. Financial Regulatory System and Federal Role in Housing Finance	2009
25.	Protecting Public Health through Enhanced Oversight of Medical Products	2009
26.	Transforming EPA's Processes for Assessing and Controlling Toxic Chemicals	2009
27.	Restructuring the U.S. Postal Service to Achieve Sustainable Financial Viability	2009
28.	Management of Federal Oil and Gas Resources	2011
29.	Limiting the Federal Government's Fiscal Exposure by Better Managing Climate Change Risks	2013
30.	Mitigating Gaps in Weather Satellite Data	2013

Source: GAO.